Building Sino-American Relations

The Washington Institute for Values in Public Policy

The Washington Institute sponsors research that helps provide the information and fresh insights necessary for formulating policy in a democratic society. Founded in 1982, the Institute is an independent, non-profit educational and research organization which examines current and upcoming issues with particular attention to ethical implications.

ADDITIONAL TITLES

Korean Challenges and American Policy
Edited by Ilpyong J. Kim (1991)

The Carter Years: Toward a New Global Order
By Richard C. Thornton (1991)

Reform and Transformation in Communist Systems: Comparative Perspectives
Edited by Ilpyong J. Kim and Jane Shapiro Zacek (1991)

Asian-Pacific Regional Security
Edited by June Teufel Dreyer (1990)

Confucianism and Economic Development: An Oriental Alternative
Edited by Hung-chao Tai (1989)

Vietnam: Strategy for a Stalemate
By F. Charles Parker (1989)

The East Wind Subsides: Chinese Foreign Policy and the Origins of the Cultural Revolution
By Andrew Hall Wedeman (1987)

Rebuilding a Nation: Philippine Challenges and American Policy
Edited by Carl H. Landé (1987)

Building Sino-American Relations

An Analysis for the 1990s

Edited by

William T. Tow

A Washington Institute Press Book

Paragon House ◆ New York

Published in the United States by
Paragon House Publishers
90 Fifth Avenue
New York, New York 10011

A Washington Institute Press Book

First printing: July 1991

Printed in the United States of America
Cover design by Larry Orman
Typesetting by Edington-Rand, Inc.

Library of Congress Cataloging-in-Publication Data

Building Sino-American relations: an analysis for the 1990s / edited by William T. Tow

p. cm.

"A Washington Institute Book."

Includes index.

ISBN: 0-88702-061-5: $18.95

1. United States — Foreign relations — China. 2. China — Foreign relations — United States. 3. United States — Foreign Relations — 1989– I. Tow, William T.

E183.8.C5B79 1991

327.73051 — dc20 91-792

CIP

Contents

Acknowledgments

A number of individuals contributed substantially to the production of this volume. Due to space limitations only a few of them can be cited here. In particular, the editor would like to thank Dr. Richard L. Rubenstein, president of the Washington Institute; Neil Salonen, the director of that institution, and his former deputy director, Robert O. Sullivan, Jr., for their organizational efforts leading to the conference from which this volume is derived. Special accolades also are due to Ms. Olivia Vieira, the Institute's administrative coordinator, for her logistical assistance and to Ms. Rebecca Salonen for her editorial support. Kathy Matthes, an administrative assistant at the University of Southern California's School of International Relations, provided critical typing support for the project. Finally, thanks to my wife Leslie and my daughter Shannon for their support and love during the long hours needed to see this project through to its completion.

— WTT

U.S.S.R.
Lake Balkhash
Karamay
Yining
Urumqi
MONGOLIA
Kashi
Xinjiang
AFG.
PAK.
Yumen
Golmud
Qinghai
Shiqunhe
Xizang
INDIA
Lhasa
NEPAL
BHUTAN
INDIA
BANGLADESH
BURMA
Bay of Bengal
THAILAND
China
National Capital
Xi'an
City
International Boundary
Provincial Boundary
Hunan
Province Name
Disputed Boundary
0
Miles
500

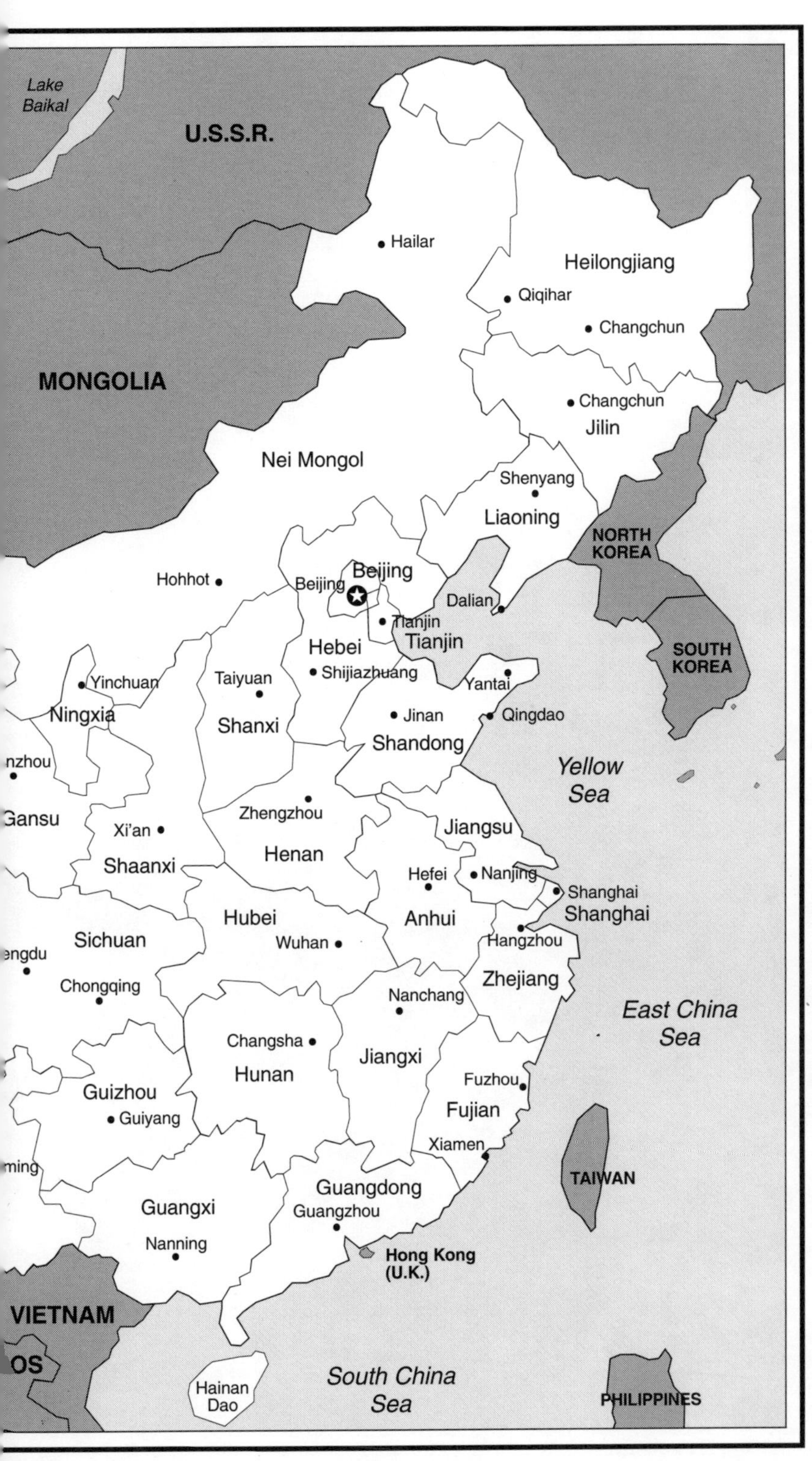
Lake Baikal
U.S.S.R.
MONGOLIA
Hailar
Heilongjiang
Qiqihar
Changchun
Changchun
Jilin
Nei Mongol
Shenyang
Liaoning
NORTH KOREA
SOUTH KOREA
Hohhot
Beijing
Beijing
Dalian
Tianjin
Tianjin
Hebei
Shijiazhuang
Yantai
Qingdao
Yinchuan
Ningxia
Taiyuan
Shanxi
Jinan
Shandong
Yellow Sea
Gansu
Zhengzhou
Xi'an
Shaanxi
Henan
Jiangsu
Hefei
Nanjing
Shanghai
Shanghai
Hubei
Anhui
Sichuan
Wuhan
Hangzhou
Chongqing
Zhejiang
Nanchang
East China Sea
Changsha
Hunan
Jiangxi
Fuzhou
Guizhou
Guiyang
Fujian
Xiamen
TAIWAN
Guangdong
Guangxi
Guangzhou
Nanning
Hong Kong (U.K.)
VIETNAM
Hainan Dao
South China Sea
PHILIPPINES

Introduction

William T. Tow

THE CHINESE GOVERNMENT's latest suppression of domestic political reform, symbolized most graphically by the use of force against pro-democracy demonstrations around Beijing's Tiananmen Square in early June 1989, deflated previous optimism shared by a broad cross-section of citizens and elites in America about the future of Sino-American relations. Yet, from a historical perspective, recent events culminating at Tiananmen constituted merely the latest episode in the Chinese people's struggle in coming to terms with their own national tradition and culture of authoritarian rule and with the forces of democratic change more integral to the West's industrially and technologically advanced states. Chinese leaders and people yearn for their state to take its place as one of the world's truly great powers; they differ to the point of violence on the means for their country to achieve such status.

From the American perspective, the means China adopts to pursue modernization and reform is the key criterion for judging how Washington's relations with the People's Republic of China (PRC) should evolve. To many in the United States, the current Chinese regime's behavior since mid-1989 cannot be justified either in terms of the PRC's national security or as exclusively an internal Chinese affair. It is instead to be viewed as a blatant disregard for fundamental human rights and political reform which cannot be ignored when considering future ties between the two countries. Despite the Bush administration's effort to disassociate American public revulsion over China's political system of state controls from "normal" state-to-state relations, American concern for the fate of China's democratic forces remains critical to future prospects for Sino-American cooperation.

The contributors to this volume were concerned with identifying and examining the developing context of relations between the United States and China following the suppression of China's pro-democracy movement. Three broad trends emerge as particularly significant from the chapters that follow: (1) the growing awareness in each country of the importance of the other's bureaucratic and legislative institutions, reflecting the unique social and cultural mores of the people they represent and serve; (2) the ability of Chinese and American commercial and diplomatic sectors to overcome strains generated by the two countries' political and social differences; and (3) the degree to which both the United States and China can adjust to the ongoing and rapid shift in the international balance of power from superpower-dominated bipolarity to a more complex multipolar international system.

The importance of these trends, along with the obvious and substantial shift in American perceptions about China following the PRC's reversion to greater political authoritarianism after June 1989, prompted the Washington Institute to commission a series of papers by respected Western experts on China assessing how the United States and the PRC have adjusted their relations in a number of key issue-areas and evaluating future directions in Sino-American relations. The intent of the conference, convened in mid-October 1990 for the presentation and review of these papers, was to derive at least some preliminary consensus among the experts involved on the viability of ties between the United States and the PRC and how probable would be China's reentry as a major player into the international marketing and diplomatic communities.

Sino-American Relations and Domestic Imperatives

If both Beijing's and Washington's policy behavior appear to lack the self-confidence and enthusiasm that underscored their relations during much of the late 1970s, and again in the mid- to late 1980s, it may be due to the dawning realization by both sides that they know far too little about one another's decisionmaking systems and processes to have confidence in their dealings with each other.[1] The critical importance of the United States and China understanding the workings of each other's political systems has become increasingly evident as both systems have come under increasing strain. The Bush administration confronted an international crisis in the Persian Gulf which tested its constitutional prerogatives and promised to undercut American fiscal stability even in the process. Deng Xiaoping's regime (or that which could soon be formed by a coalition of his immediate successors, perhaps including Yang Shankun, Li Peng, and Jiang Zemin) faces the prospect of continued challenges to its legitimacy by both regional leaders and a suppressed democratic movement. This is especially true if the PRC's efforts to strengthen its collective economic activities continue to languish, its military infrastructure remains divided, and the key elements of the Chinese Communist party (CCP) remain in their current state of disarray. Prospects are that both Washington and Beijing will have increasing difficulty in generating the needed capacity and resources to overcome their domestic challenges and face international problems in a systematic and consistent fashion.

Most of the contributors to this volume have addressed in some way the difficulties American and Chinese policy planners have experienced in coming to terms with each other's political and economic systems in the course of their efforts to implement more effective policy toward one another. Robert Ross and Robert Sutter address how the executive and legislative branches of the American government have approached the problem of balance between the need to sustain Sino-American relations in a time of historic global change and the equally compelling American policy requirement of encouraging political and economic reform in the PRC by pressuring it in the areas of human rights and economic fair play. Above all, both Ross and Sutter emphasize the need for the United States to stake out a clear and consistent set of China policies and to collaborate selectively with Beijing for enhancing prospects of regional stability in Asia and for strengthening global collective security. In this context, Washington's decision to rescind its arms sales commitments to China until a clearer picture of how China's hardline leaders view political relations with their more democratic Asian neighbors is more understandable, both in regard to the recent warming of Sino-

Soviet relations and to how China's military power has traditionally been feared by Asia's regional elites. Along more positive lines, China's general willingness to support — or at least not to resist — United Nations Security Council measures to deal with Iraq's invasion of Kuwait in August 1990 can only be regarded as a very positive sign by both the Bush administration and Congress in terms of global collective security cooperation.

David Zweig's chapter on human rights flows properly from Sutter's assessment of relations between China and the United States Congress. Both authors focus on American concerns that the Chinese government's repression of political dissent could undercut the rationale for the Bush administration to preserve Sino-American ties in the interest of fulfilling geopolitical imperatives. Both argue that President Bush and his advisers were slow to recognize that the intensity of concern in the United States about the Chinese government's behavior toward its populace could preempt the president's inclination to conduct foreign affairs as usual with China.

By the end of 1990, the PRC had retained its coveted most-favored-nation (MFN) trading status with the United States and had seen its foreign minister meet with President Bush in the White House to discuss the Persian Gulf crisis. China had earlier allowed its most famous dissident, Fang Lizhi, to leave the country and had released many of the student leaders of the pro-democracy movement. On balance, these developments should have neutralized much of the momentum in the United States for opposing the eventual restoration of fully normalized Sino-American relations. However, as the 1990 MFN debate showed, the Congress, and particularly the House of Representatives, refuses to accept "business as usual" as long as China's leaders continue to oppress the citizenry. At the same time, the Chinese government pressed ahead with its trials of dissidents in Beijing under cover of the Persian Gulf conflict, only reinforcing the potential for rekindling American interest in and hostility toward the human rights situation in China. These developments reinforced what Zweig asserts is a contemporary reality acknowledged by some leaders in Beijing: the world has become too interdependent for China to risk total isolation and the loss of the outside assistance necessary to achieve its aspirations to economic modernization and greater international influence. Like it or not, human rights has become at least as important a factor determining Sino-American relations as global or regional security.

Functional Collaboration

The prospect of Sino-American interaction based upon interdependence in cultural, economic, and politico-strategic areas is a key consideration for both Washington and Beijing to explore the strength of their relationship. In an uneasy era of *perestroika* and potential Soviet economic collapse, the days when Washington and Beijing could resort to "strategic triangularity" as the predominant rationale for Sino-American ties are clearly far in the past. As the contributors to the second part of this book all argue, however, serious barriers exist to the realization of more effective collaboration between the United States and the PRC in a number of sectors. There is a lingering Chinese reluctance to relinquish state controls to the extent needed to create incentives for domestic and foreign participation in China's development programs, and glaring inefficiencies are still inherent in the PRC's management, procurement, and distribution systems.

Dorothy Solinger provides useful insights into the attempts of China's political leaders and economic planners to reconcile their sense of "external threat" stemming from intensified contacts with Western capitalists with their desire to continue attracting foreign trade and investment. In late 1988, China's government opted to impose an economic austerity program for countering inflation and for controlling the rate of, and dependency upon, outside investment. Yet this strategy was undercut by the "international pariahhood" which China's leaders experienced in the aftermath of the Tiananmen incident. She links the significance of China's failure to realize greater mileage from its general economic approach and specific industrial projects with a complicated policy dilemma for the United States: if American firms are disinclined to become involved in what are almost surely short-term losing investments in China, they risk sacrificing long-term access to and competitiveness in a Chinese market which may someday be more lucrative, if simultaneously more prone to falling into the orbit of an East Asian economic hegemon (Japan).

John Frankenstein considers a similar dilemma: how to recon-

cile highly variant American and Chinese trade policies, with the former earmarked for promoting laissez faire approaches restrained by protectionist instincts and the latter adhering to the classical postwar Asian model of import substitution and export promotion as a means for attaining national prosperity. The difficulties wrought by these countervailing American and Chinese trade policies were compounded by the Chinese leadership's ultimate rejection, in late 1988, of Zhao Ziyang's earlier efforts to decontrol prices and stimulate China's domestic markets. Frankenstein outlines the diversity of trade issues, ranging from concerns over textile quotas and intellectual property rights at the macro-level to operational difficulties and impediments at the micro-level of the firm. These difficulties may not be easy to bridge, but if China's ultimate goal is to join GATT and participate fully in the world's trading system, accommodation will have to be made. The chapter concludes on a guardedly optimistic note by maintaining that a continued American orientation toward liberal trade policies might facilitate China's willingness to institute the necessary reforms.

An optimistic forecast is also provided by Richard Suttmeier in the realm of science and technology (S&T) relationships. He equates the rising volume of commerce and information flows in East Asia to an inevitable improvement in China's capabilities to assimilate, employ, and even export technology cost-efficiently. Suttmeier argues that Washington should adopt policies designed to incorporate China's technological strengths into the international community's S&T efforts related to arms control, environmental policy, communications, higher education, and other critical sectors. His arguments rest upon the assumption that the forces of technological and scientific collaboration will prevail over those which have previously spawned "techno-nationalism" and preoccupation with the satisfying of China's national security requirements. More fundamentally (and implicit in Suttmeier's speculations about a "Greater China"), the PRC still has a reputation for entering into bilateral and multilateral agreements for S&T collaboration and exchange merely to extract knowledge from the industrialized world it could not possibly otherwise obtain as rapidly and inexpensively. It will need to offer more compelling "quid pro quos" to future S&T collaborators than a cheap labor force or mere promises to respect increasingly fluid export control regulations.

Stanley Rosen presents data that reveal how the Chinese regime had lost the ideological and political support of its students even before the military crackdown in Tiananmen Square. He argues that the loss of regime authority over Chinese students combined with open skepticism over core values at the elite level to create a fertile environment for the introduction of Western values into China, primarily through the United States. The regime's problems were clearly exacerbated by the policy of sending students overseas — a tacit admission that China was unable to succeed without the help of the West. The June 4 crackdown further complicated the Sino-American relationship as the American government offered temporary sanctuary to the tens of thousands of Chinese students in the United States. Rosen concludes that the current efforts of the Chinese authorities to discredit the American policy toward China in the eyes of the students at home and abroad will inevitably fail, not least because the Chinese government must still rely on advanced Western technology and foreign investment to fuel its modernization.

Visible tensions undermined the People's Liberation Army (PLA) following the Tiananmen Square massacre, centering around the hardline civilian leadership's efforts to reverse the military's drive toward greater professionalization along Western lines and to reassert CCP control throughout the PLA. Under these conditions, past American calculations that the United States could use weapons sales and defense technology sales to China to extract leverage on geostrategic and commercial issues were rendered inoperative. June Dreyer traces the development of Sino-American military ties during the Bush administration and argues that American military sales to China have produced "no evidence whatsoever that . . . they . . . influenced the PRC leadership to side with the United States on geostrategic issues, or that it [the military sales relationship] has had positive spinoffs in terms of [China's] domestic liberalization." She notes that recent Chinese involvement in arms sales to Middle East clients, especially missile systems sales to Saudi Arabia, Iran, and Iraq, have greatly complicated American arms control efforts in what must be viewed as the world's most volatile region. She postulates that China will not have much difficulty in finding alternative sources to

Washington for satisfying its own arms requirements, with France and the Soviet Union topping the list of probable suppliers. What continued Chinese military modernization under more dogmatic Marxist guidance will mean for future Asian stability is a disturbing question to which American policy planners have derived few answers.

Sino-American Relations in the New International Order

Dreyer's observations about China's behavior in a revised international balance of power, in which regional security issues will become paramount to superpower competition, leads naturally into questions weighed by Thomas Bernstein, Harvey Feldman, Gerald Segal, and Douglas Stuart. All these chapters deal in some way with how traditional issues within the Sino-American relationship will affect ties between the United States and the PRC in an emerging — and very uncertain — post–cold war security order.

Bernstein examines Sino-Soviet relations from the aspect of the legitimacy crisis faced by both the Soviet and Chinese Marxist regimes and offers comparative analysis of the United States' response to both of them. He provides the reader with a comprehensive basis on which to judge American policy toward both communist powers at a time when the USSR's and PRC's domestic vulnerabilities have led both to become consumed with their own destinies and less prone to stake out central positions on the world stage. The United States has moved largely on its own to define and implement a new multipolar international order based on collective security — mostly with Soviet and Chinese acquiescence, if not absolute indifference. While Soviet generals and hardline Chinese Communist party cadres may dissent from this overall state of affairs, the hard-pressed Soviet government and a Chinese leadership riddled by factionalism are still too preoccupied with economic challenges and, in the Soviets' case, ethnic dissent to exploit the fruits of limited Sino-Soviet rapprochement in order to challenge Washington's current prescriptions for international security. The implications of Bernstein's chapter are clear: for the first time since the end of the short-lived Sino-Soviet alliance of the 1950s, both communist powers need the cooperation of the United States more than the Americans need either Moscow or Beijing to counterbalance the other as a threat to Western and global security.

Feldman's chapter on Taiwan as a factor in Sino-American ties asks the intriguing question of whether the United States and China must consider Taiwan as an independent entity due to the power of the Taiwanese economy, its military strength, and the accelerated pace of political democratization now under way on that island. Feldman argues that changes in Soviet-American relations are diminishing the PRC's weight as a global strategic actor and that, for America's business concerns, China's market has been disappointing compared to that of Taiwan, which is becoming the United States' fifth-largest trading partner. Consequently, the Bush administration and its successors may well be less prone to give credence to Beijing's views when structuring their policies toward Taiwan. Whether China is able to assimilate Hong Kong without destroying its financial viability will constitute a test case on how steadfastly Washington remains tied to its current policy of honoring the Shanghai Communiqué (there is only one China and it is the PRC), insisting that Taiwan's political status is a domestic matter to be negotiated exclusively by Beijing and Taipei.

Gerald Segal makes a case for viewing the "geometry" of Sino-Soviet-American relations as a legitimate measure of how they affect the international balance of power and that this geometry was misunderstood throughout much of the postwar era. He contends that the United States mistook Chinese intentions in allying with the Soviets in the early 1950s and thus precipitated a Sino-American military confrontation in the Korean peninsula; that the Soviet Union miscalculated the extent of Chinese alienation during Nikita Khrushchev's campaign to seek peaceful coexistence with the West; and that China forced a later Soviet-American detente as a result of its insistence that it was as qualified as Moscow to interpret and apply the true tenets of Marxist-Leninist revolutionary thought. Further miscalculations about the strategic triangle made by all three powers throughout the 1970s and 1980s are also reviewed. Segal concludes by observing that the triangle can be applied usefully to settle long-standing territorial and ideological disputes, particularly in Asia and perhaps even in the arms control arena, although China's attitudes towards arms control in general would need to be adjusted substantially. He also raises the very useful question about the interrelationship of the great power triangle with a "great economic triangle": the European Community, East Asia (spearheaded by Japan and that region's newly industrializing countries), and North America.

The arms control question as a component of Sino-American relations is treated in detail by Douglas Stuart. He links Chinese perceptions of nuclear doctrine and strategic arms control with recent structural changes in the international system, arguing that both Chinese and superpower threat perceptions will be increasingly formed by more diversified factors. Underlying many of this chapter's assumptions is the continued reality that China has relatively little to bargain with in terms of modern strategic weapons systems. Consequently, as Stuart notes in the latter part of his analysis, "Beijing's opportunities for manipulating the situation of superpower antagonism will be undermined by the politics of East-West reconciliation." Along with several other authors, he strongly implies that American policymakers feel less of a need to take Chinese interests into account than was previously the case. This is especially the case given Chinese leaders' preoccupation with heightened challenges to China's internal security brought about by its recent episodes of political dissent and violence. At best, China can pursue "more of the same" — taking modest steps to reduce tensions along the Sino-Soviet and Sino-Vietnamese borders, working with Moscow and Washington to reduce tensions between the Koreas, and reaching a modus vivendi with India.

Common Themes

What can this book contribute to the ongoing policy debate in the United States about how to relate to China at a time when that country is experiencing or is on the verge of monumental shifts in its social, economic, and political composition? While no group of experts may claim infallibility in their ability to predict the outcome of issues and trends as complex as those considered here, several themes are evident in the chapters that follow.

First, the United States and China are pursuing relations with each other along "dualistic" lines: a determination to preserve their state-to-state relations to the extent that collaboration is possible on issues where mutual security interests are involved, but simultaneously resisting important components of each other's cultural and ideological identity. Specifically, China has tacitly supported the Bush administration's efforts to forge viable collective security policies when the United States constructively reaffirms China's own long-term arguments about respecting the inviolability of national sovereignty. At the same time, China's present government resists Western influence among its own youth as corrupting of China's heritage and undermining of Marxist-Leninist revolutionary thought, pointing to events at Tiananmen Square as evidence for the validity of its concerns. The United States has applauded China's recent initiatives to affiliate itself in a qualified fashion with nuclear nonproliferation and arms control efforts (joining the International Atomic Energy Agency and extending commitments to refrain from transferring nuclear weapons-grade material or nuclear-capable delivery systems to Middle Eastern or South Asian belligerents). The Bush administration has experienced great difficulty encouraging tolerance of the Chinese regime's hard line on domestic ideological and human rights issues by the American Congress and the electorate-at-large. The emotional reaction by Western activists and institutions to China's suppression of its own people confounds the American government's efforts to pursue state-to-state relations with the PRC.

Along with the dilemmas of dualism, Sino-American relations will continue to be affected by trends and forces in the broader international system over which neither country really has control. One can surmise that both the Chinese and American leaderships might yearn at times for the simpler geometry of the cold war, where China was able to maneuver for policy gain according to a relatively simple calculus of superpower deterrence and containment politics. In turn, the United States then possessed a comparatively more formidable economic and strategic resource base than what it can now apply in a world where critical energy supplies are in the hands of bellicose or vulnerable third world regimes and where any number of underdeveloped and authoritarian regimes possess state-of-the-art weapons systems. The pace and complexity of global geostrategic change is rendering the old tenets of Maoist "three worlds theory" and of postwar American containment strategy inadequate to confront today's economic, technological, and diplomatic challenges.

If what follows stimulates new thinking and debate on how Sino-American relations fit into what must be a revised American policy framework for confronting those challenges, the book will have served its purpose. Collectively, the authors reflect the hopes of most Western analysts concerned with China: that the Chinese people will be successful in achieving political and economic reform and that China will work successfully with the United States to realize a more stable and equitable world.

NOTE

1. Two notable American efforts to overcome this perceptional gap are by Michael Oksenberg and Kenneth Lieberthal, *Policy Making in China: Leaders, Structures and Processes* (Princeton: Princeton University Press, 1988) and M. David Lampton, *Policy Implementation in Post-Mao China* (Berkeley: University of California Press, 1987). Also see Lampton and Lieberthal, eds., *Bureaucracy, Politics, and Decision Making in Post-Mao China* (Berkeley: University of California Press, forthcoming); and Michael D. Swain, "China Faces the 1990s: A System in Crisis," *Problems of Communism* 39, No. 3 (May–June 1990), pp. 20–35.

Part One

Sino-American Relations and Domestic Imperatives

ONE

The Bush Administration and China:

The Development of a Post–Cold War China Policy

Robert S. Ross

DURING HIS FIRST TWO YEARS IN OFFICE, President George Bush spent considerable time and energy seeking a China policy which both served his administration's foreign policy objectives of stable and cooperative Sino-American relations and satisfied the demands of Congress and the American people for a China policy reflecting their common outrage at the Chinese government's June 4, 1989, massacre of democracy activists and the ongoing repression of the Chinese pro-democracy movement. Indeed, most of the problems the administration has faced in dealing with Congress on China reflect its inability to reconcile these two objectives.

Yet, satisfaction of public opinion and stable bilateral relations are precisely the requirements of a successful American China policy in the post–cold war security environment. For the foreseeable future, Sino-American relations will continue to be characterized by more limited cooperation due to the combination of the post–cold war security environment and Chinese human rights policies. Simultaneously, the relationship will experience repeated challenges to stability. Chinese domestic instability and bilateral conflicts of interest suggest that American policymakers will repeatedly face the dilemma of protecting Washington's interests in Sino-American cooperation while pursuing a policy which attracts widespread domestic support.

Under such circumstances, American policy toward China must develop a new character reflecting the United States' reduced need for Sino-American strategic cooperation, Beijing's inability to reform its political system, the likelihood of recurring conflicts of interest, and American interest in maintaining domestic support for its China policy. At a minimum, this policy must have a high-profile human rights component. This will enable it to both express American interest in Chinese political reform and establish the domestic consensus necessary for pursuing, when necessary and possible, cooperative relations with the Chinese leadership.

China and the Reagan Administration

President Reagan left a complex and ambiguous legacy for his successor. On the one hand, the Reagan administration's accomplishments were important and numerous. At the same time, its management of Sino-American relations created a new set of problems for American policymakers.

The Reagan administration left to its successor a strategic environment that maximized Washington's negotiating leverage with China. The relative decline of Soviet global influence and the signs of the end of the cold war had reduced the significance of relations between the United States and the PRC and, thus, the Americans' imperative to conciliate to Chinese interests. This trend was apparent as early as 1983 when the Reagan administration adopted a less forthcoming China policy and also established stable Sino-American cooperation despite continued Chinese discontent with various aspects of Sino-American relations, including Washington's policy toward Taiwan and American human rights policy.

A vital element in the definition of more enduring Sino-American ties was the design of American diplomacy fashioned by Secretary of State George Shultz. He shaped a China policy which enabled the United States to place the burden on the Chinese leadership to initiate conflict and instability in Sino-American ties. Given Washington's strategic advantages, China predictably chose to avoid conflict. There were three elements to Shultz's diplomacy which combined to produce the American policy advantage. First, in 1983 Shultz announced that China no longer occupied center stage as a global power in American foreign policy. Rather, he stressed, China was an Asian power and second in importance to Japan from the American vantage point. Thus, Beijing was put on notice that it could not pressure the United States to acquiesce to Chinese interests in order to secure Chinese cooperation against the Soviet Union.

Second, during this same period of time Secretary Shultz insisted that he was not concerned over what conflict did exist in Sino-American relations. On the contrary, he expected continued conflict over a range of issues, not only over Taiwan, because of the differences between the American and Chinese political systems and societies. Such disagreements, Shultz argued, were normal and not cause for alarm. He reinforced his argument that China was of reduced strategic importance by suggesting that the United States would prefer not to compromise with China merely to try to eliminate inevitable sources of tension. Indeed, on a variety of issues, including human rights and Taiwan, the Reagan administration allowed China to challenge American policy with frequent protests and did not scramble to resolve the conflicts.

Finally, when there was disagreement, Shultz limited the United States' policy response to the immediate issue area. When there was conflict over human rights, Washington adopted a human rights policy, as in the cases of Chinese asylum seekers in the United States and American opposition to China's birth control policy. A similar approach was taken to differences over civil aviation issues and Taiwan. This strategy enabled the United States to accept the bilateral tension in its relations with China because no single issue could simultaneously undermine other American interests within that relationship. Moreover, it placed the responsibility on the Chinese for escalated tension and reduced diplomatic cooperation. In contemporary Chinese parlance, Shultz compelled Beijing to decide whether or not to "tie the knot" in Sino-American relations. Given the fairly high level of American strategic confidence by the mid-1980s and the Reagan administration's reluctance to compromise on major strategic issues, China ultimately chose to eschew conflict with Washington rather than disrupt what had become perhaps its most important bilateral relationship by that time.

During President Reagan's last years in office, with the post–cold war era emerging and the Soviet military withdrawal from Afghanistan imminent, and with the superpowers agreeing in principle to substantially reduce their nuclear arsenals, the United States demonstrated even greater flexibility in dealing with China.

The development of a possibly lasting Soviet-American detente on Washington's terms significantly reduced the strategic imperative previously underscoring Sino-American relations and further modified the necessity for the United States to placate Beijing. Thus, the ultimate strategic legacy of the Reagan administration was the end of the cold war and the corresponding American ability to weigh Sino-American relations largely in a bilateral rather than a triangular context.

Nonetheless, new policy challenges accompanied the changing dimensions of the Sino-American relationship. As the necessity for strategic cooperation with China diminished, the American consensus calling for closer ties between the United States and the PRC also eroded. In the era of the "strategic triangle," during the 1970s and 1980s, the all-encompassing threat of Soviet expansion had silenced American critics of both China and Sino-American relations (see Gerald Segal's chapter in this volume). Certainly there was much about China that Americans did not like, including its political and economic systems and its human rights practices, and many Americans were unhappy with Washington's apparent insensitivity to these issues. Yet most Americans, regardless of political persuasion, supported Washington's preoccupation with continued strategic cooperation between the United States and China as a necessary evil in an age of Soviet expansionism.

The end of the cold war, however, removed the immediate necessity for strategic collaboration between the two nations and, thus, the basis for American silence regarding the more disagreeable aspects of Chinese politics and Sino-American policy. This was readily apparent in 1988 when the United States Congress adopted a critical stance toward China's policy in Tibet and the editorial pages of numerous American newspapers and magazines called for greater White House attention to China's human rights policy. Pressures also intensified for a more balanced treatment of the Soviet Union and China on human rights in an era of diminished apprehension over the Soviet threat.[1]

Under such circumstances, it was incumbent on American policymakers to develop a China policy which could both meet the United States' foreign policy objectives and provide the basis for a new domestic consensus incorporating many of the demands now placed on Washington's China policy. It was in this area that the Reagan administration failed to provide the Bush administration with a policy legacy. In fact, at the time President Reagan completed his second term, his administration was still coping with new issues as they emerged and had not developed a coherent policy package for the post–cold war period.

The Reagan administration's ad hoc approach to post–cold war issues in Sino-American relations was most apparent in the administration's handling of Chinese human rights violations. When members of Congress spoke out against Beijing's violent suppression of independence demonstrations in Tibet, the State Department responded that criticism of China was inappropriate and counterproductive and that Americans should instead focus on the great strides China had made in reform of its economic and political systems. Rather than adjusting to the domestic post-cold war environment, the administration resisted it. This atavistic approach to Sino-American relations inevitably fueled domestic criticism, which quickly forced the administration to change direction and join the public condemnation of Chinese policy.[2]

Thus, at the end of 1988 the Reagan administration had created a mixed policy legacy for its successor. On the one hand, it left a diplomatic strategy which maximized American advantages in the United States' relations with China. On the other hand, it failed to develop a means for dealing with the new domestic and international context of policymaking. For the Bush administration, the challenge would be to develop a China policy which would allow the United States to maintain the advantageous diplomatic strategy of the Reagan administration while simultaneously establishing a domestic consensus encompassing the post-cold war demands imposed on the United States' China policy. But the Bush administration's ability to cope with this challenge was limited by the priority it placed on stable Sino-American ties (in contrast to the policy of the Reagan administration) and the profound and abrupt threat posed to relations by the 1989 Beijing massacre. These factors compelled President Bush to make "policy on the run," undercutting the cohesion of administration behavior toward the Chinese and complicating any chance of realizing success in its own policy approaches to the PRC.

Coping with the Beijing Massacre

Unlike the Reagan administration, the Bush administration emphasized China's great strategic significance. Nevertheless, its foreign policy focus was not the Soviet threat that had so motivated the China policy of the Nixon, Ford, and Carter administrations. President Bush and his advisers gradually recognized the significant developments in Soviet domestic politics and the implications of such trends for United States security. Consequently, the Soviet threat was no longer the primary foundation of Washington's policy toward China. However, as Deputy Secretary of State Lawrence Eagleburger noted, "While U.S.-Soviet tensions may be declining, the strategic value of our relationship with China is not."[3]

One reason the Bush administration emphasized China's importance in its own right was the career background of its three key policymakers. President Bush, National Security Adviser Brent Scowcroft, and Deputy Secretary of State Lawrence Eagleburger all developed their foreign policy expertise during the 1970s, when triangular diplomacy was an integral element of American strategic policy. The president, in particular, as chief of the United States Liaison Office in Beijing and director of the Central Intelligence Agency during the mid-1970s, developed a strong sense that Sino-American relations were a significant component of overall American foreign policy, even in the absence of heightened superpower tensions.[4]

In this context, although the administration readily agreed that China was a regional power and not a global power, it elevated regional issues to high priority. It argued that coping with instability on the Korean peninsula and in Indochina, achieving Chinese cooperation in preventing missile and nuclear weapons proliferation, and dealing with ongoing Soviet presence in Asia all required stable relations with Beijing. Moreover, future regional considerations necessitated giving attention to Sino-American relations. In particular, the rise of Japanese power and the uncertainties surrounding American and Soviet contributions to the evolving regional balance demanded a contemporary foundation of cooperation between China and the United States. The president insisted that there were "Asian reasons" to "stay engaged" with Chinese leaders.[5]

Thus, as the Bush administration entered office, it clearly possessed a fundamentally different perspective than its predecessor regarding the importance of relations with China. The perceptual shift alone would have had a major impact on the new administration's response to developments in China's human rights policy insofar as there would have been less tolerance by Washington for tension between the two countries. The White House's response to the Beijing massacre, however, was also shaped by its lack of preparation for dealing with various American domestic political factions in the post-cold war era. The Reagan administration did not create any policy guidelines in this regard, and the Bush administration had yet to formulate its own strategy, both to stress Sino-American cooperation and to develop the post-cold war domestic content of China policy, in which China's human rights performance assumed growing importance. When the administration was confronted with the events in Tiananmen Square, it was compelled to make policy on a daily basis with insufficient forethought and analytical guidance. It is no wonder that the Bush administration's China policy failed to serve its own interests and required immediate corrective action, which led to tortuous diplomacy and costly battles with the Democratic-controlled Congress.

In the immediate aftermath of the Beijing massacre, President Bush tried to cushion the impact on overall Sino-American relations of the Chinese government's brutality. Bush limited his rhetorical attacks on the Chinese leadership in an effort to maintain communication with the Chinese leadership and to avoid exacerbating the domestic difficulties of China's reformist politicians. Reflecting the role of the Chinese military in the Beijing massacre, the White House's initial diplomatic response was to cut off all military transfers to China and to suspend all diplomatic exchanges between American and Chinese military organizations.

The sanction against United States military relations with China attracted widespread support from the American electorate. Moreover, the president's policy both met his foreign policy objective of maintaining stable Sino-American relations and formed the basis for a revised domestic consensus on China policy. Yet as the Chinese government continued to make arrests and carried out executions, support for the president's policy eroded and the administration developed an ad hoc policy response. On

June 20, 1989, Secretary of State James Baker, during questioning at Senate hearings on Soviet-American relations, announced that he had advised President Bush to suspend all high-level diplomatic "exchanges" with China and that, should the president act on his suggestion, Secretary of Commerce Robert Mosbacher's upcoming visit to China would be delayed.[6]

This announcement was the turning point in the administration's China policy. Preoccupied with preserving cooperative Sino-American relations, the administration had in fact adopted a policy which had set them back. Now Chinese cooperation would be needed in order to lift the sanction on high-level exchanges and restore cooperative relations. During the next eighteen months United States negotiators pursued constructive Chinese behavior which would allow the Bush administration to stabilize diplomatic relations without destabilizing the American policy-making environment.

Over the short term, however, Washington's China policy actually caused the deterioration of this environment, creating further obstacles for restoring normal relations between the United States and the PRC. The secret Scowcroft missions to Beijing in July and December provided an opportunity for an American envoy to impress upon the Chinese leaders the gravity of the situation and the need for Chinese cooperation in order to salvage the relationship.[7] But White House diplomacy undermined its own policy objective because it did not integrate the domestic and international demands of China policy. In December, when the American public learned about the July secret mission, President Bush's vulnerability to congressional criticism increased. By apparently violating its own sanctions against high-level exchanges, despite its insistence that these were only "contacts," the administration fueled further domestic opposition to its China policy, encouraging the widespread belief among American voters that the president could not be trusted to incorporate human rights values in its China policy. The result was that in February 1990 the White House was forced to engage in a costly battle with Congress over legislation protecting Chinese students in the United States, despite the president's personal assurances that the White House would provide such protection.

After a rancorous debate, in which many House Republicans abandoned the president rather than risk the political repercussions of supporting his widely unpopular China policy, the president's veto of the Pelosi bill was sustained in the Senate by a mere four-vote margin (see David Zweig's chapter in this volume). Shortly thereafter, however, the administration began preparing for the congressional debate over maintaining most-favored-nation (MFN) status for Chinese exports to the United States. Wary of another battle with Congress, the White House signalled that it would not fight for MFN and that it was up to China and American business interests to prepare the groundwork for congressional acquiescence to the president's recommendation (see John Frankenstein's analysis of the MFN clarification problem later in this volume).[8] Ultimately, a combination of Chinese concessions (including the release of Fang Lizhi), American economic interests in trade with China, and the widespread domestic understanding of the importance to Sino-American interaction of continued MFN undermined the Democratic party's opposition.[9]

Thus, the Bush administration spent a year and a half following the Beijing massacre trying to create the circumstances which would allow it to restore normal Sino-American diplomatic relations, and it largely succeeded. In the first half of 1990 China ended martial law, released numerous political prisoners, resumed cooperation with the United States on the Fulbright and Peace Corps programs, eased its jamming of the Voice of America, and permitted the dissident Fang Lizhi to leave China. These developments, as well as the importance of trade with China for American commercial/industrial interests, facilitated the Bush administration's effort to sustain MFN treatment for China. Thus, by the end of 1990 the agenda was clear of immediate issues requiring negotiation between the United States and the PRC.

In the midst of these events, the administration began easing away from its prohibition on high-level exchanges. In July, Shanghai Mayor Zhu Rongji visited Washington and met with Scowcroft, Eagleburger, and other American officials. Shortly thereafter, former Chinese Ambassador to the United States Han Xu and current Ambassador Zhu Jizhen met with President Bush at the White House. Finally, in December, in the aftermath of China's disclosure that it would not veto the crucial UN Security Council resolution sanctioning use of force against Iraq, the United States invited Chinese Foreign Minister Qian Quchen to Washington to meet with President Bush and Secretary of State

Baker. Despite the administration's insistence that these were only diplomatic "contacts," it was clear that the White House was ending its sanction against high-level exchanges. Indeed, Foreign Minister Qian insisted, "I don't see what difference there is between contacts and exchanges."[10] Similarly, with American support, by the end of 1990 international financial institutions had restored their lending programs with China. Clearly, the price Beijing was paying for its violent suppression of the Chinese democracy movement — its isolation from Western economic and political interests — was being reduced.

Sino-American Cooperation and Conflict in the Post–Cold War Era

By December 1990, Washington had for all intents and purposes restored diplomatic relations with the PRC to the pre-Beijing crackdown level. Nevertheless, Sino-American relations will not return to the politics of strategic triangularity which highlighted collaboration between Washington and Beijing during the cold war era. Instead, Sino-American ties must be adjusted to the new realities of post–cold war international politics.

For the very reason that the Bush administration places such great importance on Sino-American relations, in the post–cold war era the United States will require a stable working relationship with China, though it will be qualitatively different from that of the 1970s and 1980s. Insofar as China has limited global strategic significance, earlier American attitudes that "the China factor" should be integral in every aspect of Western policies toward the Soviet Union and third world states are now obsolete. Rather, Washington and its allies in Europe and Asia will consider Chinese interests and will cooperate with China in discrete issue areas in which China exercises influence. When China matters, it will be consulted; but when China policy is not a factor, Washington will not invite it to the table.

Within these parameters, the United States can conduct a great deal of business with Chinese leaders. There are many issues on which China has a voice, and Washington will have to work with Chinese leaders to secure American interests. These issues include resolution of regional conflicts, including the war in Cambodia and the conflict between South Korea and North Korea. In each case China is a pivotal actor, and its cooperation is essential in resolving these conflicts. Indeed, in the case of the Koreas, China's interest in closer economic relations with South Korea has contributed to Pyongyang's gradual but definite moderation of its foreign policy. In Indochina, Chinese ties to the Khmer Rouge guarantee that there cannot be peace without Chinese cooperation. Most recently, Chinese influence has affected American policy toward Iraq. Although neither Chinese flexibility nor its influence in Persian Gulf matters is as great as in Indochina, Beijing can contribute to American interests relative to Iraq; and in this context American cooperation with China is important.

Various functional issues will also require Chinese cooperation. Beijing is a major arms exporter, and its participation is essential in limiting the proliferation of nuclear weapons and ballistic missiles. Chinese arms sales are a major source of foreign exchange and yield Beijing significant regional influence. Once again, the Middle East is a main concern. During the Iran-Iraq war China supplied both countries with significant amounts of weapons and it continued to supply Baghdad with weaponry until Iraq invaded Kuwait.[11] In the aftermath of the Kuwait crisis, future Middle East stability will depend in part on Chinese cooperation. Another functional issue requiring Chinese willingness is the global environment. China is the world's largest user of coal, and any attempt to reduce global pollution will require Beijing's participation.

But even in pursuing these important issues, human rights should not be ignored. Indeed, there is little likelihood that China's human rights policy will soon cease to be a problem in American politics. Even should Beijing restore the full reform program planned before June 1989, this would not be sufficient to win praise from American human rights activists. The fundamental changes in the Soviet Union and Eastern Europe in 1989 have raised American expectations of political reform in socialist countries. Chinese reform policies that earned lavish praise in the 1980s will be widely scorned as inadequate in the 1990s. Moreover, various groups in the United States will work to keep China's human rights violations on the public agenda. Activists, pleased with the expansion of democracy in Latin America, Eastern Europe, and the Soviet Union, have turned their professional focus toward China and will devote their energies to calling attention to Beijing's ongoing repression. Chinese students in this country will play a similar role.[12] Although the direct political clout of Chinese students in United States policymaking will likely be negligible, their criticism of Chinese government policy will receive widespread attention in the United States, ensuring that China's human rights abuses remain in the public view.

Moreover, continued attention to China's human rights policies will occur in the context of ongoing Chinese political instability. Although the international reaction to the Beijing massacre may caution Chinese leaders from taking similar action in the future, China's leaders may have concluded that the eighteen months of isolation from Western countries and international financial institutions was a small price to pay for what they perceived as restoring order; and, thus, they may not be deterred from using similar tactics should domestic instability recur in the context of intensified succession politics. Indeed, the Chinese decision to place two democracy activists on trial for "counterrevolutionary acts," a capital offense, just prior to Foreign Minister Qian's visit to Washington suggests that Chinese leaders have not been deterred from pursuing their repressive domestic agenda.[13] At the very minimum, there will continue to be instability at high levels in China, undermining the chances for renewed reform and thus sustaining international hostility toward Beijing and providing additional challenges to American policymakers.

Human rights will not be the only continuing issue in Sino-American relations. If Washington needs Chinese cooperation to deal with such problems as weapons proliferation and the war in Cambodia, that is because Chinese policy often interferes with American objectives. In the post–cold war era and in the context of widespread contempt for Beijing's human rights policies, such bilateral conflicts will likely attract greater attention and raise domestic American demands for retaliation. These stresses on Sino-American ties will continue to plague relations and could well become more troublesome.

Compared to the 1980s, therefore, the 1990s will be a period in which the stability of Sino-American relations will experience frequent challenges. But exacerbating the importance of sources of tension in these ties will be the attenuation of the sources of stability; the very factors which will create ongoing conflict will also undermine the institutions of cooperation that have been developing since the normalization of Sino-American relations in 1979.

The one area of cooperation that cannot be restored is American arms sales to China. Now that the cold war is over, the strategic value of this policy is gone while the human rights aspect of it has increased. The mere idea of sending weaponry to the murderers of Chinese students is politically untenable, no matter how pro-reform the Chinese military may be and no matter how reluctant the military may have been to fire on the democracy demonstrators. Indeed, China's decision to cancel its agreement with Grumman for upgrading the avionics of its F-8 fighter removed the most sophisticated and high-profile arms package from Sino-American military cooperation, easing the political dilemma faced by American policymakers. It is unlikely that in the near future Washington will restore the remaining arms sales programs, much less seek further arms sales agreements with Beijing.[14] (For further analysis, see June Teufel Dreyer's chapter in this volume.)

Nevertheless, other aspects of Sino-American military relations can be and are likely to be resumed. These include bilateral exchanges between Chinese and American officers and working sessions between American and Chinese military specialists on a wide range of issues. In important respects, such exchanges are far more valuable than arms sales relations. While less controversial, they contribute to greater understanding of each country's threat perception, capabilities, and strategic planning and help to promote a significant rapport between the two militaries.[15] During periods of tension, this relationship may prove helpful in minimizing misunderstandings and contributing to reliable communication.

Economic relations is another area in which Sino-American ties cannot return to levels before the Beijing crackdown. Prior to June 1989, the United States carried on a wide array of economic contacts with China. In addition to maintaining extensive trade, the United States was the largest source of direct private investment in China.[16] Although in the aftermath of the Beijing massacre American businesses focused on protecting their existing interests in China, China is now a much less attractive investment opportunity. Relatively risk-free trade relations may continue to develop, but the public relations cost of doing business with a universally condemned leadership and the prospect of continued political instability warns American and other foreign business concerns away from making new investments in China. Moreover, as American interest in trade with China diminishes, new economic issues will take on heightened importance. Of particular concern will be the United States trade deficit with China. American trade officials forecast that in 1991 only Japan will have a greater trade surplus with the United States than China. In the context of reduced American interest in investing in China, diminished Chinese imports from the United States, and China's dismal human rights record, domestic political pressures for trade retaliation will be more difficult to resist.[17]

Similarly, China's relations with international financial institutions are likely to remain somewhat attenuated in the 1990s. Prior to the Tiananmen incident, the World Bank, for example, lent China $2 billion each year. This was a very large share of the bank's total annual lending, reflecting the international community's support for China's extensive program of economic reform. Beijing's current status as an anachronistic communist regime undermines support for such extensive programs in the World Bank and other international financial organizations, such as the Asian Development Bank. Hence, although these institutions have already resumed their lending programs to China, the scale of their involvement in Chinese modernization will pale in contrast to that of the pre-June 1989 period.

Thus, one of the key sources of stability in Sino-American relations — China's economic relations with the United States and the international community — will have diminished influence for the foreseeable future, enabling sources of Sino-American discord to assume greater importance. Moreover, to the extent that China's reform leadership and the economic beneficiaries of reform derived domestic political advantage from the contribution to Chinese development offered by the international economic system, they will be correspondingly less influential. The interests of both the international community and the Chinese people will be hurt by this trend.

Diminished Sino-American economic relations will also affect China's relations with other countries. In particular, Japan will likely play an increasingly important role in Chinese economic development. Compared to the United States, Japan has greater interests in Asia, and partly for this reason it accords relatively less attention to human rights considerations in its China policy. Thus, as the United States reduces its economic relationship with China, Japan's stake in the Chinese economy will likely expand proportionately. Indeed, Japan has granted China its third yen loan, and Japanese business interests are apt to follow Tokyo's lead and expand their activities in China. Given China's ambivalence regarding Japanese economic capability and its political ramifications, Chinese reliance on Japan may create additional friction in Sino-Japanese relations with implications for the stability of Washington's interests in Asia.[18]

In the current international environment, Sino-American cultural relations are also liable to suffer. This will be primarily due to the reluctance of China's conservative leaders to expose their educated youth and the next generation of leaders to Western "bourgeois" societies. Thus, despite the Bush administration's successful efforts to restore the Fulbright and Peace Corps programs, Sino-American educational ties are apt to remain at a reduced level, undercutting Washington's ability to promote Chinese political and economic reform and cultural ties with significant elements of the Chinese elite. Although the United States should continue to press for expanded educational exchanges with the Chinese, it appears that this is yet another facet of the overall bilateral relationship destined to play a reduced role in promoting stable political relations between the United States and the PRC.

Finally, it is important to realize that no matter how much individual Chinese leaders may desire stable Sino-American relations, political developments in Beijing may undermine the Chinese leadership's ultimate ability to cooperate with its American counterpart. As China's succession politics intensify, if Western support for China's democracy movement is sustained, any policy suggesting accommodation with Washington's interests would evoke the opposition of China's still-powerful conservative ideologues and Communist party bureaucrats. Thus, while they may prefer to cultivate better relations with the United States over time, China's present leaders and foreign-policymakers may foist the responsibility of maintaining good Sino-American relations onto the Bush administration.

Conclusion

In the absence of a strategic imperative and in the context of Beijing's ongoing political reforms, the Sino-American relationship will be more limited and more subject to recurring challenges. Moreover, the future of this relationship will be primarily determined by developments in China. Should China return to the path of political stability and reform, there is little question that American politics will enable policy responses promoting closer Sino-American ties. But for the foreseeable future, the likely prospects are that China will continue to stagnate in the mire of succession politics and Sino-American relations will continue to reflect American apprehension over dealing with an unstable and retrograde Chinese leadership. There is little the United States can do to change this situation.

In these circumstances, the challenge to American policymakers is to formulate a China policy that permits the development of a working relationship enabling the two sides to cooperate when their interests intersect but that also allows the United States to respond to Chinese actions which violate American standards of human decency or undermine the United States' international interests. This will allow Washington to weather the coming storm of Chinese succession politics. The basis of such a policy must be the establishment of greater distance in relations with the Chinese so that the United States will be able to withstand repeated challenges to American interests which do not threaten the basic assumptions and expectations underlying the United States' policy toward China.

The key to this approach is American willingness to confront directly Chinese human rights violations and bilateral conflicts of interests so that the relationship is neither predicated on nor explained by a false assumption of interests shared across a wide spectrum of issues. The expectation must be developed in both the United States and China that conflict is expected and inevitable and will likely occur in a number of different areas. In this way, policy can conform to American interests regarding both human rights and international security, while the Bush administration and its successors can protect themselves from domestic charges that they are displaying excessive friendliness to a repressive Chinese regime. Moreover, insofar as recurring conflict is the accepted norm, such an approach will reduce the United States government's susceptibility to Chinese pressure to compromise in order to preserve stable relations. This was the general character of George Shultz's diplomacy in the Reagan administration, and the Bush administration should return to this policy line.

Given current circumstances in China and throughout the world, however, the Bush administration must give greater prominence to human rights issues in Sino-American relations than the Reagan administration did. American policymakers must place human rights high on the public agenda of China policy. This is the prerequisite to political cooperation with China in the post–cold war era. When current administration officials meet with Chinese officials to discuss various political issues, they will also have to address China's domestic policies and voice support for its democracy movement. Similarly, the president should meet with Chinese dissidents in Washington and, should he travel to Beijing, he should give vocal support to China's democracy movement, go out of his way to make contact with Beijing's more moderate politicians, and try to meet with dissidents at the United States embassy. Essentially, the United States must have a human rights policy in its dealings with China in order to have a successful security policy. In this respect, both agendas were served by the administration's decision to send Assistant Secretary of State for Human Rights and Humanitarian Affairs Richard Schifter to China and by his warnings that China's human rights violations would jeopardize congressional support for continued most-favored-nation status for China. Although Chinese domestic policy may not have been influenced by Schifter's visit, American development of a human rights policy for China sets the correct tenor for the entire relationship.[19]

The Bush administration, however, should not focus on conflicts concerning only human rights. It should also deal forthrightly with other conflicts of interest as well. Hard negotiating and clear expression of American expectations of China will underscore the administration's willingness to tolerate ongoing tension when interests differ, whether in trade issues, arms sales to the Middle East, or other conflict areas. It will also disabuse Chinese leaders of the mistaken notion that, despite the end of the cold war and of Chinese leverage in the "strategic triangle," China remains a major state with global strategic significance. Indeed, it is exactly because the cold war has ended that the United States can adopt a dispassionate posture toward ongoing tension.

Most important, this policy of acknowledging bilateral conflicts and American distaste for Beijing's domestic policy need not interfere with United States interest in developing cooperative relations in distinct areas, such as regional arms control and the resolution of regional conflicts. On the contrary, it will actually facilitate cooperation by accommodating the demands of various influential domestic constituencies regarding other issues and will place the overall bilateral relationship on a realistic footing. But for cooperation to coexist with conflict, American diplomacy must pursue American interests in discrete areas, preventing conflict *or* cooperation in one area from influencing the tenor of relations in other spheres. The imperative of cooperation in Indochina, for example, must not undermine the administration's commitment to seeking respect for human rights in China. The administration should pursue firmness in human rights issues as well as in trade relations and arms sales whenever our interests clash with those of China, but it should not allow differences to interfere with Washington's ability to cooperate with Beijing when American and Chinese interests can converge.

Secretary of State Baker's June 20 discussion of his advice to the president regarding high-level exchanges undermined such diplomacy. By linking diplomatic contacts with China's human rights violations, he set back the entire Sino-American relationship, frustrating the Bush administration's ability to cooperate with Chinese leaders. The harmful secret diplomacy was one result of this mistaken policy. High-level dialogue is frequently necessary to establish policy coordination, and American human rights policy should not obstruct such cooperation.

The risk to such a policy is that Chinese leaders will try to prevent the United States from setting the agenda of Sino-American relations. Whereas Washington might wish to limit conflict to discrete areas, China may insist on linkage, withholding its support for American policy in exchange for American concessions on human rights or trade issues. Yet the advantage to such a policy is that it places the burden on Beijing for retaliation across issue areas, and thus of escalated conflict and general deterioration of relations. Moreover, given the end of the cold war and limited American interest in the Chinese economy, Washington should be able to tolerate the threat of increased bilateral tension with relative indifference.

This dual-track approach to China will affect the character of future Sino-American diplomatic exchanges. In contrast to the diplomatic pomp of the 1970s and 1980s, in the 1990s the level of diplomatic cooperation will be shaped by the immediate requirement of the situation. No longer will American presidents travel to China to sign relatively insignificant agreements; lower-level aides will carry out these assignments. Moreover, in an era of reduced strategic concerns and China's pariah status because of human rights, the public relations benefit to an American president of a Beijing summit has vanished. Indeed, should such a meeting be necessary to secure important Chinese cooperation, the White House would probably prefer a low-key affair in order to minimize the president's embarrassment at seeming to legitimize a barbarous regime.

The era of American fixation on friendship with China must be replaced by a pragmatic American policy that recognizes the merit of a "mixed" (conflictual and cooperative) stance toward the PRC. Both cooperation and confrontation can be appropriate postures, each to be applied toward a different situation. Such an American policy will produce a less congenial relationship, but it will be a relationship free from misleading expectations and one that more accurately reflects the important issues in Sino-American ties, thus enabling American policymakers to maximize opportunities for cooperation in the future.

NOTES

1. See, for example, Sanjoy Hazarika, "Dalai Lama Urges Peaceful Protest against China," *New York Times,* 8 October 1987, p. A-8; "Who May Cry for Tibet?" (Editorial), *New York Times,* 9 October 1988, p. A-30; and "Senator Leahy's Report of the Visit to China and Hong Kong," *Congressional Record,* 11 October 1988, pp. S15501–02.
2. Elaine Sciolino, "Beijing Is Backed by Administration on Unrest in Tibet," *New York Times,* 7 October 1987, p. A-1; Sciolino, "U.S. Official Defends Stance on Turmoil in Tibet," *New York Times,* 15 October 1987, p. A-18; and Sciolino, "U.S. Is Reassessing Response on Tibet," New York Times, 18 October, 1987, p. A-17.
3. Committee on Foreign Affairs, U.S. House of Representatives, *United States Policy toward China,* 101st Cong., 2nd Sess. (Washington, DC: GPO, 1990), p. 18.
4. See, for example, George Bush, *Looking Forward* (New York: Bantam Books, 1987), pp. 128, 249.
5. *Weekly Compilation of Presidential Documents,* 22 January 1990, pp. 91–93. The Bush administration's most comprehensive statement of American concerns for long-term Asian stability is in United States Department of Defense, *A Strategic Framework for the Asian Pacific Rim: Looking toward the 21st Century* (mimeo, 1990).
6. See Baker's Senate testimony in Committee on Foreign Relations, U.S. Senate, *The Future of U.S.- Soviet Relations,* 101st Cong., 1st Sess. (Washington, DC: GPO, 1989), pp. 939–40.
7. For the administration's explanation of the July and December visits, see Deputy Secretary of State Lawrence Eagleburger's testimony in *U.S. Policy toward China,* pp. 3–57, 177–89.
8. *Weekly Compilation of Presidential Documents,* 21 February 1990, p. 228. Also see Robert Pear, "Bush Distressed as Policy Fails to Move China," *New York Times,* 11 March 1990, p. A-15.
9. Note the support for continued MFN status for China in "Half Right on China Trade" (Editorial), *New York Times,* 25 May 1990, p. A-26; "Aim the Policy at Next Generation" (Editorial), *Los Angeles Times,* 7 May 1990, p. B-6; and "Correcting the Tilt to Beijing," *Washington Post,* 11 May 1990, p. A-26.
10. Thomas L. Friedman, "Chinese Official Is Invited to Washington in Response to Gulf Stance," *New York Times,* 28 November 1990, p. A-15; and Robert Pear, "Bush Meeting Foreign Minister, Lauds Beijing Stand against Iraq," *New York Times,* 1 December 1990, p. A-8. The foreign minister's comment is reported by Wen Xian, "Answering States, Qian Qichen Says China Stands for Peaceful Solution to the Gulf Issue," *Renmin Ribao* (Overseas Edition in Chinese), 29 Novem-

ber 1990, p. 1; as translated and reprinted in Foreign Broadcast Information Service, *China,* 29 November 1990, pp. 2–3.

11. On China's arms sales to Iran and Iraq through 1988, see Richard F. Grimmett, *Trends in Conventional Arms Sales Transfers to the Third World by Major Suppliers, 1981–1988* (Washington, DC: Congressional Research Service, Library of Congress, 1989), pp. 15–20.
12. See, for example, the following recent publications: Asia Watch, *Merciless Repression: Human Rights in Tibet* (New York: Asia Watch, 1990); Asia Watch, *Punishment Season: Human Rights in China after Martial Law* (New York: Asia Watch, 1990); Amnesty International, *Massacre of June 1989 and Its Aftermath* (New York: Amnesty International USA, 1990); Amnesty International, *People's Republic of China: Tibet Autonomous Region, Compilation Document* (New York: Amnesty International USA, 1990); and the new monthly journal *Human Rights Tribune,* published by Chinese scholars and professionals. Also see the commentary by Robert L. Bernstein, chairman of Human Rights Watch, "Break Up the Chinese Gulag," *New York Times,* February 17, 1991, Section 4, p. 13.
13. Pear, "Bush Meeting Foreign Minister."
14. For a discussion of China's motives for canceling the agreement, including the importance of cost-overruns, see Barbara Starr and Douglas Barrie, "China Drops F-8 Upgrade," *Jane's Defence Weekly* 13, No. 2 (26 May 1990), p. 996.
15. For a discussion of these aspects of Sino-American military relations, see Eden Woon, "Chinese Arms Sales and U.S.-China Military Relations," *Asian Survey* 29, No. 6 (June 1989), pp. 601–18; and Edward W. Ross, "U.S.-China Military Relations," in Joyce K. Kallgren, Nordim Sopiee, and Soedjati, eds., *ASEAN and China: An Evolving Relationship* (Berkeley, CA: Institute of East Asian Studies, University of California, 1988), pp. 86–108.
16. For a discussion of Sino-American economic relations prior to the Beijing massacre, see Nicholas R. Lardy, *China's Entry into the World Economy: Implications for East Asia and the World Economy* (Lanham, MD: University Press of America and the Asia Society, 1987).
17. Clyde H. Farnsworth, "Chinese Trade Practices Raising Concern in the U.S.," *New York Times,* 26 December 1990, p. A-1.
18. See Allen S. Whiting, *China Eyes Japan* (Berkeley, CA: University of California Press, 1989).
19. Sheryl WuDunn, "American Official Presses China to Free Captives," *New York Times,* 20 December 1990, p. A-16; and WuDunn, "China Keeps Door Closed on Dissent," *New York Times,* 23 December 1990, Section IV, p. 2.

TWO

China and the U.S. Congress:

Policy Determinants and Constraints

Robert Sutter

THE TUMULTUOUS EVENTS in China in 1989, along with major changes in world politics and domestic political developments in the United States, were factors that served to undermine the general consensus that had prevailed in Congress, and between Congress and the executive branch, over United States policy toward China in the 1980s. That consensus had only come about after several rounds of contentious, often behind-the-scenes debate in the Carter and early Reagan administrations about sensitive issues in Sino-American relations. Issues in that policy debate had focused on such questions as continued American arms sales to Taiwan, Washington's emerging military cooperation with the People's Republic of China (PRC), and the importance of United States policy toward China relative to American interests vis-à-vis the Soviet Union and major United States allies and friends in Asia.

By 1983–1984, around the time of President Reagan's trip to Beijing, United States policy hit upon a balance that appeared basically acceptable to the administration and to various leaders in Congress. It notably assumed that China's importance in American foreign policy would be somewhat less than in the recent past, that Japan would remain the key to American security interests in Asia, and that United States policy regarding sensitive issues in relations with Taiwan would not be swayed substantially by pressures from Beijing. Although PRC leaders were not pleased with the reported "downgrading" of the PRC's importance in United States policy, they saw on balance that it was to China's advantage to continue developing relations with the United States and to avoid major action that would disrupt Sino-American relations.[1]

In the late 1980s, prior to the Tiananmen incident, there were grounds for optimism in assessing the course of Sino-American relations and the continuation of the general consensus in United States–China policy. The strategic dimension of that relationship, involving close Sino-American collaboration in opposition to Soviet expansion during the 1970s and early 1980s, diminished considerably in importance as both American-Soviet and Sino-Soviet tensions eased. Yet relations between Washington and Beijing were still seen by both American and Chinese policy planners as strategically important over the long term. Both groups anticipated China's playing an increasingly important role in an emerging multipolar world. The superpowers, the United States and the Soviet Union, were expected to remain at odds and slowly to decline in power relative to other parts of the world. They were thought to be particularly interested in working closely with China and other newly emerging centers of world power (that is, Western Europe and Japan).[2]

China's ongoing economic reforms attracted increasing world attention and support among developed countries and international financial institutions supported by them. Beijing looked forward to growing fruitful economic interaction, technology transfer, and training in China's relations with the United States and Western-aligned countries. Easing Sino-Soviet tensions also opened prospects for broader economic cooperation with the Soviet bloc.

American policymakers for their part pursued the steady development of a multifaceted relationship with China. Trade ties grew to an annual turnover of $13 billion in 1988. Aside from Hong Kong, the United States was China's most important source of foreign investment. Political ties continued to grow with frequent high-level official visits, including those of representatives of the American and Chinese armed forces. United States technology transfer to China was an important element in Chinese modernization plans, and there were 40,000 students from China studying at American universities.[3]

American differences with China involved a wide range of issues that sometimes resulted in episodes of diplomatic or other activity but did not fundamentally challenge the basic forward thrust of American policy toward China. Thus, Chinese arms sales to Persian Gulf countries, especially missile sales to Iran and Saudi Arabia, brought strong rebukes from the administration and Congress. Chinese repression in Tibet first caught the attention of the Congress, but the administration subsequently also joined in taking a firm stand against China's actions. Although the United States and China seemed to share many common strategic goals in Asia, there was increasing unease, especially in Congress, with China's active support of the Khmer Rouge in Cambodia.

The Tiananmen massacre and subsequent Chinese government efforts to exert tighter control over political and economic developments in China repelled American leaders and popular opinion alike. American government reaction in the form of official criticisms and limited sanctions prompted strong Chinese government protests. Many in the United States and China saw prospects of a "downward spiral" in relations, despite extraordinary efforts by the Bush administration in sending two high-level missions to consult with Deng Xiaoping and other leaders in July and December 1989.

Indeed, the Bush administration's actions and congressional reactions to them saw the reemergence of strong congressional-executive friction over China policy. The ability of American leaders to restore a general consensus in policy toward China was also in doubt. It was undermined not only by the tumultuous events in China but also by the major changes in Americans' international outlook brought about by the collapse of communism in Eastern Europe, the breakup of parts of the Soviet empire, and the seemingly more important role of ideology and values in American foreign policy.

Meanwhile, partisan politics once again appeared to be playing a major role in the conduct of American policy toward China. Some Democratic critics in Congress were highly vocal in their strident criticism of President Bush's China policy. Some observers believed that they might be seeking partisan advantage in doing what they could to highlight their criticism of the president's "mistaken" policy and to differentiate the Democrats' view from the administration's position.[4] President Bush reportedly also appealed to partisan loyalties of congressional Republicans to block an attempt to override his veto of China-related legislation in January 1990.[5]

In short, by early 1990 it was clear that any past consensus in American policy toward the PRC had ruptured. Whether the United States could look forward to repeated rounds of acrimonious debate or to the reestablishing of consensus on China policy depended on the following variables:

- The evolution of events in China
- The changes in world politics brought about by the collapse of communism in Europe and increasingly collaborative United States–Soviet relations
- Partisan issues in American domestic politics

By mid-1990 there was a distinct possibility that Sino-American relations could fall to a new low as a result of Washington's refusal to renew most-favored-nation (MFN) tariffs for Chinese imports and Beijing's warnings of probable Chinese retaliation. Though circumscribed by circumstances, leaders of both sides appeared anxious to do what they could to sustain a basic framework of relations that would serve their respective interests. For Chinese leaders, relations with the United States still represented a critical element in their efforts to modernize China. American leaders — in Congress and the executive branch — generally were reluctant to allow revulsion caused by the Tiananmen crackdown or other concerns to lead them to isolate China in ways that could jeopardize stability in Asia and a hoped-for revival of reform in China.

New Challenges for Chinese Policy

Events in China leading to the Tiananmen massacre and the subsequent political crackdown and economic retrenchment vividly demonstrated the fault lines that run through the Chinese leadership over a range of sensitive domestic and foreign policy questions, including relations with the United States. Such division and debate intensify among ambitious younger officials jockeying for power as the older generation of leaders headed by eighty-six-year-old Deng Xiaoping approaches its end. Internal political intrigues add to uncertainties regarding Chinese policies as a result of the reversal of reforms at home and radical changes abroad.

Those in Beijing who made the decision to suppress dissent forcefully clearly recognized that much of the noncommunist world would react negatively. And they almost certainly expected some negative reactions to the intensification of China's concurrent economic retrenchment. Available evidence suggests that Chinese party leaders judged that their continued political control required harsh measures; and at least some felt that sharp negative reactions from the West and elsewhere would pass without long-term consequences to China.[6] Perhaps this prediction would have come true in late 1989 if world conditions had not changed. But events in Eastern Europe and the Soviet Union markedly upset this Chinese calculus.

The dramatic changes in the Soviet bloc had an obvious "ripple effect" in China, encouraging pro-democracy forces and alarming Chinese leaders, who grew even more determined to maintain the party's monopoly on power. In addition, developments in the Soviet bloc abruptly ended Chinese leaders' hopes that they could avoid the "spiritual pollution" of pro-democracy ideals by expanding economic-technical contacts with communist-ruled European countries. By 1990, political ideas coming from Eastern Europe appeared perhaps more directly challenging to the political status quo in China than were the ideas from the West.[7]

Finally, changes in the Soviet bloc also attracted positive attention from Japan and the developed countries of the West, including the international financial institutions and businesses associated with them or located there. Thus, not only did the PRC crackdown alienate foreign interests and capital, but the positive prospects in Eastern Europe served as a magnet to attract these resources instead toward Eastern Europe and the USSR.

Shifts in Global and Regional Politics

On the plane of world politics, the events of 1989–90 began to alter significantly the balance of world forces with which Beijing had dealt reasonably effectively, over especially the previous ten years. Heretofore, the Chinese world view had been premised on an international order heavily influenced by Soviet-American strategic competition. Because of their rivalry, the superpowers would spend resources on weapons, foreign bases, foreign interventions, and in other ways that would weaken them relative to newly rising centers of world power such as Japan, the European Community, and China. Given its size, strategic location, large armed forces possessing nuclear weapons, and demonstrated willingness to use force to pursue its interests in world affairs, China was seen by many at home and abroad as holding a key position in world politics. It was one corner of the "strategic triangle" in Sino-Soviet-American relations — a critical balancing force between the United States and the Soviet Union. Policymakers in Washington and Moscow, therefore, paid close attention to Chinese policies to avoid driving China into the arms of their main adversary. Of course, the zero-sum-game quality of the triangle varied over time; by the late 1980s, American policy architects appeared confident that the slowly emerging Sino-Soviet detente would not have major deleterious effects on Washington's interests. But American — and presumably Soviet — policymakers continued to pay close attention to how China's policy affected their respective interests in the competition for world influence.

By mid-1990, relations between the United States and the Soviet Union had changed to such a degree that observers in China and elsewhere could no longer safely assume that the Soviet-American rivalry would continue as an overriding international factor into the 1990s. Because of events in Eastern Europe and the USSR, it was becoming increasingly apparent to Western leaders that the Soviet Union was unlikely to again pose a major threat to the West for some time. Even though there remained a persistent danger of reversal of policies, should Mikhail Gorbachev be toppled or other possible circumstances intervene, it seemed likely that the United States and its allies would find the Soviet policies more accommodating than confrontative. The United States could increasingly see its interests as better served by encouraging accommodating Soviet policies.

Thus the dynamics of Soviet-American competition and possible collaboration in world affairs, so central to China's world view, were in the process of fundamental change. Chinese officials in the past had portrayed possible collaboration between Washington and Moscow as coming at the expense of lesser powers, especially those in the third world, including China — a concern which appeared to be reflected in recent Chinese media coverage.[8] Beijing leaders almost certainly considered possible logical conclusions coming from recent trends in East-West relations. At a time of rapidly improving relations between the superpowers, both would likely see their interests as best served by avoiding actions with countries of lesser importance (including China) that could complicate the improvement of East-West relations.

Possible Soviet-American Collaboration in Asia

Under these circumstances, both sides — Moscow and Washington — would likely pursue mutual accommodation to deal with international trouble spots. In Asia, these trouble spots include Afghanistan, Cambodia, and Korea. Both sides showed increasing interest in 1990 in cooperating or working in parallel in order to ease tensions or settle conflicts in these areas.

From China's perspective, such American collaboration with Moscow could signal a fundamental change in the common strategic orientation that has defined Sino-American relations since the Nixon-Mao rapprochement. Despite differences over a wide range of issues, China and the United States were able to reach common ground in the early 1970s on their fundamental opposition to Soviet expansion in Asia. This Sino-American understanding continued with varying degrees of activity for two decades. As the Soviet threat to both China and the United States appeared to diminish in the 1980s, both sides adjusted their policies accordingly but still kept in close touch about their respective and often parallel policies vis-à-vis the USSR. Indeed, the December 9–10, 1989, trip to China of National Security Adviser Brent Scowcroft was initially described as one in a long series of American efforts to keep Chinese leaders fully informed about Soviet policies as seen in Soviet-American arms control and summit negotiations.

Taken together with the recent downturn in Sino-American relations, the events in Eastern Europe and the USSR and resulting changes in Soviet policy held out the distinct possibility of a challenge to the basic anti-Soviet basis of Sino-American policy in Asia. If trends in Soviet accommodation of Western interests continue, American policymakers may increasingly see their interests as better served by quiet cooperation and coordination of policies designed to foster an atmosphere conducive to a return to economic and political reform in China and to achieving common Soviet and United States goals of stability and progress in Asia.[9]

Beijing's Response

As Beijing faced these challenges and problems, some United States officials warned of possible dire consequences for future Chinese foreign policy if the United States reacted too strongly to China's internal political repression and economic retrenchment. They warned particularly of Beijing's reverting to the self-imposed isolation of the past in the interest of sustaining Communist party control.[10] But more moderate American views gained ground as Chinese leaders appeared to place limits on reversing the generally moderate foreign policies of recent years, including policy toward the United States.[11] Thus, limits were seen in several areas:

First, much of the basic framework that had governed Chinese foreign policy in the post-Mao period remained intact:

- Chinese leaders continued to place priority on promoting China's wealth and power. All policies, including foreign policy, had to serve this goal. Economic development still represented a linchpin determining their political success or failure. They did not have the prestige of Mao, who could ignore development needs in pursuit of ideological or political goals. These officials had to produce concrete results in order to stay in power.

Thus the continuation of this basic framework suggested that China was not looking for trouble but for help.

Second, broad international trends supported a continuation of moderation in Chinese foreign policy in general and policy toward the United States in particular.

- PRC leaders' awareness of their need to focus on economic development and to pursue open interaction with the world to achieve that goal was underlined by their knowledge of the accomplishments of Japan and many other noncommunist East Asian states, and their knowledge of the negative development experiences of the rigid communist regimes in North Korea and Vietnam.

- Despite sanctions imposed by the West and Japan, the non-communist world, especially the countries of East Asia, made clear that they had no intention of isolating China. Indeed, Taiwan took the lead at this time in promoting trade, investment, and tourism which helped to offset the downturn in investment and tourism by the West.
- Soviet bloc changes meant that China could not turn to these countries for support in economic development if Beijing decided to cut back economic interchange with the West.

Third, internal factors and trends argued for continuity of moderation:

- The PRC leadership appeared divided and in transition from one generation to another. Making significant changes in foreign policy in most areas remained sensitive politically. Past periods of similar leadership transition (1973–1975, 1976–1978) did not see marked changes in foreign policy.
- Leaders who actively promoted reform, interaction with the world, and cooperation with the West were quiet, but they had not been removed from power.
- Even so-called hardliners had proven records of following relatively moderate foreign policies and related defense and domestic policies. Few appeared to favor a return to the policies of isolation, autarchy, or Stalinist control that were tried unsuccessfully in the past.

Finally, the evidence of Beijing's post-Tiananmen foreign policies did not suggest a radical shift from the recent past. Even the results of the economic retrenchment and political repression policies were mixed. Foreign trade and investment continued to grow, although at a less rapid rate than before June 1989. Thousands of Americans and other foreign experts continued to be invited to work with the Chinese in China. The *New York Times* reported that 7,000 Chinese students came to the United States from June 1989 to January 1990.[12] While Beijing put stricter limits on Chinese students studying outside the country, older Chinese or those assumed to be more likely to return to China after training continued to go abroad.

In sum, Beijing's leaders almost certainly felt beleaguered in the face of international criticism and sanctions, and in response to the rapid changes in Eastern Europe and the Soviet Union. But Chinese leaders were cautious. They avoided unduly harsh reactions to foreign criticism, and took few concrete steps in response to world trends that appeared to jeopardize their basic interests.

United States Policy

Chinese leaders' preoccupation with internal control and adverse international trends passed the initiative in Sino-American relations to the United States after mid-1989. President Bush succeeded initially in preserving a general national consensus about China when he announced on June 5, 1989, the steps the United States would take in response to the Tiananmen incident. The president ordered among other measures the suspension of all government-to-government sales and commercial exports of weapons, the cessation of visits between American and Chinese military leaders, and sympathetic review of requests by Chinese students in the United States to extend their stay. He took the additional steps on June 20, 1989, of causing the United States government to suspend participation in all high-level exchanges of governmental officials with China and directing American representatives at various international financial institutions to postpone consideration of new loans for China.[13]

Reflecting the strong reaction of American public opinion, media, and human rights organizations against China's leaders after the Tiananmen events, many in Congress pressed for even stronger measures against China. As debate continued into the summer, however, it became clear that the congressional sanctions against China would leave the president considerable room for maneuver. The lengthy amendment on China to the State Department authorization bill, which passed the Senate in late July, codified the sanctions on China already imposed by the president and added the following actions: (1) suspension of new programs to guarantee American investments in China, (2) suspension of licenses for crime control and detection equipment, (3) suspension of export licenses for American-made satellites scheduled for launch on Chinese vehicles, (4) discontinuation of Sino-American peaceful nuclear cooperation, and (5) new requirements that the president negotiate with the Coordinating Committee for Multilateral Export Controls (CoCom) to suspend further liberalization of export controls for technology to the PRC. The bill provided sufficient waiver authority to be acceptable to the administration. Meanwhile, in July and August 1989, the House and Senate, respectively, passed the Emergency Chinese Immigration Relief Act, which would have made it possible for Chinese students in the United States to extend their stays for up to an additional four years.

The Bush administration and many in Congress privately pressed the Chinese authorities to take actions that would improve the strained atmosphere in Sino-American relations. Suggested steps included easing of martial law in Beijing; showing greater flexibility in the case of dissident Fang Lizhi, who had taken refuge in the American embassy in Beijing; allowing Fulbright professors from the United States to resume work in China; halting periodic Chinese jamming of Voice of America (VOA) broadcasts to China; and allowing the U.S. Peace Corps to begin its volunteer program in the PRC. As gestures to China in the interests of preserving substantive United States–China relations, the administration in late July 1989 granted waivers to the suspension of military sales to allow the sale of four Boeing commercial jets with navigation systems that could be converted to military use. In October 1989, Washington permitted Chinese military officers to return to work at United States facilities where they had been assisting American engineers in upgrading China's F-8 fighter with American-developed avionics systems. On November 30, President Bush let it be known that he would "pocket-veto" the Emergency Chinese Immigration Relief Act, maintaining that the bill was unnecessary since he was ordering into practice many of its provisions.

Although there was considerable grumbling in Congress and the media over the president's "soft" approach to China, the debate over China policy reached a fever pitch following the December 9–10, 1989, visit to Beijing by an American delegation led by National Security Adviser Brent Scowcroft and the disclosure a few days later that a similar American delegation had secretly visited Beijing in July 1989. The administration mustered several arguments for its initiatives:

- Because China and the world were in a period of major transition, the United States needed to sustain a productive dialogue with China to deal with relevant issues.
- Excessive United States pressure against China was adverse to growing American economic interests in China.
- Chinese intellectuals were seen as divided over the wisdom of continued American pressure on the current Beijing leadership. Many opposed it.
- United States allies, especially those in Asia, were seen as generally supportive of American initiatives to improve relations with China.
- The Scowcroft visits provided a face-saving means for the beleaguered leadership in Beijing to pull back from its recent repressive policies.

Critics in Congress, the media, and elsewhere denounced the president's actions and called on Congress to take stronger action when it convened in late January. Arguments focused on several points:

- Political repression in China continued despite some easing of martial law in Beijing in late 1989.
- Resuming high-level contacts and other business with Chinese leaders disassociated the United States from Chinese proponents of greater political reform and democracy.
- Exempting China from normal American treatment regarding human rights served only to solidify the grip of hardliners in Beijing.
- Special American consideration of China was no longer needed in order to ensure Chinese cooperation with the United States against the international danger posed by Soviet expansion. Soviet reforms and the turmoil in Eastern Europe were likely to curb any such Soviet expansion for some time. And China was likely to remain preoccupied internally and unlikely to disrupt Asian stability.

Despite the storm of criticism, President Bush continued his moderate approach during December. On December 19, he waived restrictions prohibiting export licenses for three American communications satellites to be launched on Chinese launch vehicles, and he announced that he would not impose the new restrictions on Export-Import Bank funding for China that Congress had enacted earlier.

As Congress prepared to reconvene in late January 1990 amid a chorus of media comment calling for tougher action against China, it was clear that the president had miscalculated and would have to adjust his policies. For one thing, Chinese leaders had proven unable or unwilling to make gestures to the United States of sufficient importance to justify the president's actions. The Chinese government ended martial law in Beijing, but a major police presence remained. Some prisoners were released, but only a small fraction of those thought to be held. The Chinese promised not to sell medium-range ballistic missiles to any Middle East countries, but this was widely viewed as a repetition of previous promises. By late February, President Bush personally expressed disappointment with China's response.[14]

It was also clear that changes in international and in American domestic politics had restricted the president's flexibility in foreign affairs in general and toward China in particular. He would have much greater difficulty than previous presidents in arguing for secret diplomacy, special treatment, or other exemptions that had marked Washington's treatment of China since Henry Kissinger's secret trip in July 1971.

The American people, media, interest groups, and to a considerable degree legislators traditionally place a strong emphasis on morality or moral values as well as *Realpolitik* or "national interest" in American foreign policy. The Tiananmen massacre sharply changed American views about China.[15] Instead of pursuing policies of political and economic reform, the leaders in Beijing now appeared to be following policies antithetical to American values and therefore seemed unworthy of American support. Rapidly changing Soviet-American relations also meant that there was no longer a *Realpolitik* or national security rationale of sufficient weight to offset the new revulsion with Beijing's leaders and their repressive policies.

Meanwhile, political, economic, and security changes on the

other side of the world attracted wide and generally positive attention from the American people, the media, interest groups, and legislators. Eastern Europe and the Soviet Union were increasingly pursuing policies of reform in their government structures and economies that seemed to be based on the individual freedom, political democracy, and economic free enterprise valued in the United States. As a result, these American groups tended at times to push government decisionmakers to be more forthcoming in negotiations and interaction with their East European and Soviet counterparts in arms control, trade, foreign assistance, and other matters.

This shift in American public opinion regarding China and the Soviet bloc countries was of greater significance than it might have been in the past in determining the course of American foreign policy. Since the start of the cold war, the executive branch had been able to argue, on many occasions quite persuasively, that domestic American concerns with common values should not be permitted to override or seriously complicate *Realpolitik* interests in the protracted struggle and rivalry with the Soviet Union. Now that it was generally seen that the cold war was ending and the Soviet threat dissipating, the ability of the executive branch to control the course of American foreign policy appeared reduced. The administration could no longer argue that the dangers of cold war contention and confrontation required a tightly controlled foreign policy.

Partisan politics also complicated President Bush's ability to sustain a policy toward China that was more moderate than that demanded by much of the Congress, media, and interest groups. Opponents portrayed the president and his backers in the Republican party as more sympathetic to the "butchers of Beijing" than to Chinese students and other pro-democracy advocates. Ironically, partisan politics allowed the president to avoid an embarrassing defeat at the hands of the Democratic-controlled Congress, which took up as its first order of business in January 1990 the override of the president's veto of the Chinese immigration measure. By seeking the support of wavering Republican senators for the Republican president in the face of a barrage of often partisan criticism from Democrats, White House lobbyists were able to gain enough votes to sustain the president's veto on January 25, 1990.[16]

The unanticipated defeat of the Democratic leadership's override effort appeared to have a sobering effect. During the winter and spring of 1990, congressional leaders did not go out of their way to challenge the president's China policy so long as he avoided major initiatives or exceptions in dealing with China. In February, the president signed the State Department authorization bill, which contained a version of the China sanctions language passed by Congress the previous summer, and the administration delivered a hard-hitting report on conditions in China as part of its annual human rights report to Congress.

Most notably, the administration adopted a low public profile on what was expected to be a major issue — the annual waiver of provisions under the Jackson-Vanik Amendment of the Trade Act required for Chinese goods to receive most-favored-nation tariff treatment by the United States. Loss of MFN would lead to immediate heavy duties on China's $12 billion of annual exports to the United States — in effect closing much of the American market to Chinese goods. The last waiver had been granted in late May 1989, and the 1990 waiver was due by June 3 — coincident with the first anniversary of the Tiananmen demonstrations and crackdown.

Congress, the media, and various human rights groups were expected to attack any early administration decision to grant a waiver for China. Faced with that likelihood, the administration delayed, neglecting numerous opportunities to stake out a position on the issue and refusing to appear at public forums addressing the question. This had the effect of forcing Congress, the media, and interest groups to address the issue themselves. After deliberations, many critics of Bush administration policy toward China nevertheless came out in favor of granting, with appropriate conditions, MFN treatment for Chinese exports.[17] As a result, in mid-1990, it appeared that the administration's decision to grant a waiver for China — announced finally on May 24 — would not be stopped by congressional action.

Congressional debate on the issue during the summer saw members come up with a dozen bills. Some would have blocked China's MFN status, but others looked to place conditions on the extension in 1991 of MFN treatment for the PRC. One bill (H.R. 4939), sponsored by Representative Don J. Pease, was approved by the House Ways and Means Committee on July 18, 1990. It continued normal trade relations with China but conditioned extension of MFN treatment in 1991 on several human rights goals, including Beijing's terminating martial law, accounting for detained persons, and easing restrictions on freedom of the press. Anticipating the debate over MFN and anxious to encourage Western-aligned countries to resume aid, loans, and investment, the Chinese government took several steps to improve its human rights status following the Tiananmen incident. In May and June, Beijing announced the lifting of martial law in Tibet, the freeing of several hundred jailed dissidents, and the departure of Fang Lizhi from the American embassy to travel abroad.

At the end of the 101st Congress in October 1990, the House debated both the Pease bill and another bill (H.J. Res. 647), sponsored by Representative Gerald Solomon, that would have repealed China's MFN status. Both bills passed the House by very wide margins, in part because even some House supporters of continued MFN treatment for China recognized that voting for the measures could provide a useful symbolic censure of Beijing's policies but would have little substantive effect given the Senate's likely refusal to address the issue so late in the session.

Prospects

Despite such efforts to prevent further deterioration, there was little sign in mid-1990 that the problems in Sino-American relations over the previous year would be resolved quickly. Those leaders in Washington and Beijing with an interest in strengthening ties between the United States and the PRC seemed likely to continue to face important challenges. Events in China, East-West relations, and American attitudes toward China had changed markedly in 1989–90 and remained fluid. Optimists speculated that strong American interest in China would revive once China returned to a path of political reform and economic liberalization. But prospects for reform in China depend on many factors, not the least of which is the status of China's leadership, now dominated by a clique of octogenarians led by Deng Xiaoping.

There is also no guarantee that American interest in the 1990s in a reforming China would be as strong as that in the 1980s. Changes within the Soviet bloc and in Soviet-American relations have undercut a substantial part of the strategic imperative behind Washington's policy toward China. They have also absorbed

American political and economic interests that in the past might have focused on China. In this new international environment, it will likely be more difficult to generate popular enthusiasm or special government programs for support of United States relations with China.

Until China returns to the path of reform, critics in Congress are likely to make it very difficult for any of their colleagues in the administration or in Congress who might want to restore a more normal relationship with China. Factors impeding a return to a more normal relationship in late 1990 included the sometimes partisan American critics of President Bush's policies, members of Congress who have used the crisis over the past year to press various human rights-related measures against China, continued generally negative American media coverage of events in China, and opposition to China's government from various human rights groups. Issues looming near the horizon that could further complicate the situation included congressional concerns over the rising Chinese trade surplus with the United States (expected to be about $10 billion in 1990) and Beijing's alleged use of prison labor to produce goods sold in the United States.

The factors that appeared to favor movement toward a more normal Sino-American relationship included a gradual resumption of exchanges with China by many United States allies and international organizations, support on the part of at least half of the American people for a "patient" approach that avoids economic sanctions against China, growing recognition in the Congress and elsewhere that China plays a key role in the American-led international coalition against Iraq's occupation of Kuwait, and the Beijing regime's efforts, albeit sometimes muddled, to promote greater diplomatic, economic, and other interaction with the West and other countries.

Under these circumstances, it appeared doubtful that consensus in Sino-American relations could be achieved within the United States government or by the American electorate anytime soon. Congress continued to speak with many voices in China policy, and those in Congress who supported the maintenance of close relations were generally loath to speak out against the critics.[18] President Bush still labored under the impression by many that he was insensitive to the "new realities" of the world order, had ignored human rights, and overemphasized the strategic and economic importance of China. Critics also believed the president had been unduly influenced by so-called "Kissingerian" advisers such as Brent Scowcroft and Lawrence Eagleburger. Moreover, although recent polls show that half of the American public favor avoiding economic sanctions against Chinese leaders, critics of the Bush administration's policy have been firm in setting down markers in favor of some form of continued American sanctions against the PRC.

In fact, the president had been remarkably consistent in following his own views of appropriate policy toward China, which he had laid out in great detail and with notable warmth and eloquence during and immediately after his February 1989 visit to China.[19] Contrary to his critics' charges, the policies advocated there gave strong attention to fostering democracy and freedom in China and reflected a clear awareness of how recent changes in the world security environment had altered American interests vis-à-vis the PRC. Ironically, President Bush had not followed a predilection, seen by his critics, to adjust his policy to changing circumstances, especially American public opinion. He instead staked out a clear position on where he felt Sino-American relations should go and remained generally consistent despite the tumultuous events of the previous year and a half. Under foreseeable circumstances, however, it was unlikely that his critics in Congress and elsewhere would be prepared soon to adjust their views to accord to the president's approach.

NOTES

The views expressed in this paper are those of the author and not necessarily those of the Congressional Research Service or the Library of Congress.

1. For background on the United States policy debate and its resolution, see among others, Robert Sutter, *The China Quandary: Domestic Determinants of U.S.-China Policy, 1972–1982* (Boulder, CO: Westview Press, 1983) and Sutter, *Chinese Foreign Policy: Developments after Mao* (New York: Praeger Publishers, 1986), pp. 176–86.
2. Chinese foreign policy expert Huan Xiang and American commentator Henry Kissinger were notable proponents of this view in the latter 1980s.
3. Steven Levine, "The Uncertain Future of Chinese Foreign Policy," *Current History* 88, No. 539 (September 1989), p. 262.
4. Charges of partisan politics were especially common as Congress reconvened in January 1990 and began efforts to override the president's veto of the Chinese student immigration bill. See discussion below.
5. Discussed in David Zweig's chapter in this book.
6. See discussion of this view in *Crisis in China: Prospects for U.S. Policy,* Report of the Thirtieth Strategy for Peace, U.S. Foreign Policy Conference (Muscatine, IA: The Stanley Foundation, 19–21 October 1989).
7. See, among others, Nicholas D. Kristof, "In Reaction to Rumania, a Hardening in Beijing," *New York Times,* 7 January 1990, p. 16.
8. See for instance, Qian Wenrong, "U.S.-Soviet Cooperation and Third World Apprehensions," *Liaowang* (Overseas Edition), No. 2 (7 January 1990), p. 28.
9. A good example of how the American public and especially congressional views of changed world circumstances could lead to shifts in United States policy possibly detrimental to China occurred in regard to Washington's policy toward Cambodia in 1990. In 1989 and 1990, some in Congress had taken the lead in pressing for a change in policy that would allow for contacts with and assistance to the Vietnamese-backed Hun Sen government, would cut off United States supplies to the noncommunist resistance forces unless they broke with the Khmer Rouge, and would focus American policy on the danger of the Chinese-backed Khmer Rouge's regaining power in Cambodia. Congressional critics of the United States policy on Cambodia often linked the Bush administration's alleged "tilt" in favor of China with its reluctance to work with Hun Sen and the Vietnamese against the Chinese-backed Khmer Rouge.

The congressional pressure, changes in the battlefield situation in Cambodia, and other developments saw the administration shift policy on Cambodia in ways that at least initially appeared detrimental to China. The change in American policy on Cambodia also underlined the difficulty of restoring a close Sino-American relationship on the same anti-Soviet strategic basis that had prevailed in the past. In particular, after consultations with the Soviet foreign minister in late July 1990, Secretary of State James Baker announced that the United States would change policy, approach Vietnam in order to seek an end to the Cambodia conflict, and no longer support the Khmer Rouge-backed coalition government in the United Nations. The action appeared to take China by surprise, and Beijing reacted negatively. (Subsequently, China adjusted its policy to accommodate the shift in American policy.) On one level, the secretary's action showed that the United States government now saw that it had more to gain by collaborating with the Soviet Union, even in apparent opposition to China in an area of Asia of vital interest to China. This marked a change toward a more balanced American policy relative to the USSR, China, and Asia in general from the previous American emphasis on "anti-hegemonism" (that is, anti-Soviet expansion) that had dominated American policy in Asia and provided the main common strategic ground for Sino-American collaboration over the past twenty years. For background, see Robert Sutter, *The Cambodian Crisis and U.S. Policy Dilemmas* (Boulder, CO: Westview Press, 1990).

10. See statement of Deputy Secretary of State Lawrence Eagleburger in hearing before the U.S. Senate Foreign Relations Committee in U.S. Senate, Committee on Foreign Relations, *U.S. Policy toward China,* 101st Cong., 2nd Sess., 7 February 1990, pp. 3–12.
11. See the assessment from various American vantagepoints in Rochelle Stanfield, "It's Beijing's Move," *National Journal* 22, No. 8 (24 February 1990), pp. 445–49.
12. Nicolas D. Kristof, "Students Find U.S. Embassy a Barrier," *New York Times,* 26 January 1990, p. A-9.
13. The administration's actions and congressional responses can be monitored in *Congressional Quarterly Weekly Report.*
14. See the review of American policy toward China at this time by Lena H. Sun, "Stance of Chinese Government Disappoints Bush Adminis-3tration," *Washington Post,* 7 March 1990, p. A-30.
15. See discussion in *Crisis in China: Prospects for U.S. Policy.*
16. Discussed in Stanfield, "It's Beijing's Move," pp. 455–59.
17. Winston Lord, "Bush's Second Chance on China," *New York Times,* 9 May 1990, p. A-31.
18. A notable recent exception was Congressman Jim Leach in remarks

on September 6, 1990. See *Congressional Record,* 6 September 1990, p. E2753.

19. See the weekly compilation of Presidential Documents, The White House, Washington, D.C.

THREE

Sino-American Relations and Human Rights

June 4 and the Changing Nature of a Bilateral Relationship

David Zweig

FOR MANY YEARS, the strategic imperative had protected Sino-American relations. In the early 1970s, the United States and China ended their two decades of hostility and reestablished ties on the premise that a unified front would prevent the USSR from achieving global dominance. Under Henry Kissinger and Richard Nixon, improving ties with China primarily served the goal of squeezing the Soviet Union into helping resolve the United States' impasse in Vietnam as well as restructuring the international system and increasing global stability.[1] Even in the early Reagan years, China's role as a balance to the USSR remained the primary justification for improving ties with a communist China rather than a noncommunist one on Taiwan. The package of issues supporting United States–China ties included anticipated economic benefits to the United States, America's "special relationship" with China, and the general belief after 1978 that reforms were improving the lives of Chinese citizens in a way that was consistent with American values. Western media heralded these changes, lauded Deng Xiaoping, and reinforced popular feelings that America, as China's "big brother," should help China make the transition to a more market-oriented and more democratic society.

All these positive images pushed human rights far down the list of issues in Sino-American relations. Even the Carter administration, which institutionalized human rights in American foreign policy, never let this issue overshadow the strategic partnership.

According to A. Glenn Mower, Jr., both Carter and Reagan subordinated human rights to national security and national interest and demonstrated "a readiness to take advantage of loopholes in national human rights laws in order to extend aid to countries with poor human rights records for political/security reasons."[2] Under such circumstances, the arguments of congressional proponents of human rights, especially on Tibet, anticommunist allies of Taiwan, and human rights activists found little resonance in the White House and State Department.

Yet Sino-American relations were built on a soft foundation. According to Michael Oksenberg, only the strong support of President Jimmy Carter prevented Sino-American ties from falling prey to the lethargy of Washington's bureaucracy.[3] Popular opinion remained quite fickle and susceptible to rapid shifts. Most important, while many congressmen and American policy elites had passively supported American ties with China, no bloc of congressmen actively supported the People's Republic of China. Only in 1979, when Congress passed the Taiwan Relations Act, thereby directly intervening in Sino-American relations, did PRC officials recognize Congress's important foreign policy role, and since then, they have made greater efforts to build ties with members of that body.[4] In the words of one congressional observer, all these factors made Sino-American ties vulnerable to "single-issue politics."[5]

However, events of April–June 1989, culminating in the military assault on Beijing's citizenry, dramatically transformed the nature of Sino-American relations, catapulting human rights into the forefront of issues affecting this bilateral relationship. Popular opinion and media coverage of China switched dramatically, demonstrating widespread disillusionment with the Beijing government. Renewed interest in human rights abuses and increased questioning of the benefits of trade triggered a massive assault on United States China policy. While congressmen wanted to express their outrage at the betrayal of reform in Beijing, proponents of single-issue politics found fertile ground for asserting their particular anti-China grievances. New actors emerged on the scene, further undermining the People's Republic of China as a legitimate partner. Brick by brick, each policy that had contributed to the foundation of Sino-American ties was challenged under the rubric that no regime which murdered its own children deserved the goodwill of the United States government.

In retrospect, the administrations in both China and the United States failed to recognize or accept that the defining nature of bilateral ties had changed. Both resisted challenges to their definition of the relationship and clung to the strategic and economic imperative. As a result, Sino-American relations went into a tailspin. Fortunately, by spring 1990 leaders in both countries recognized that the nature of their ties had changed and that some alteration in their own behavior was mandatory if Congress and Chinese hardliners were not to destroy the relationship. To understand the political process that ensued from mid-1989 through spring and summer 1990, we must understand how the June 4 crackdown changed the nature of relations between Washington and Beijing. This paper seeks to elucidate that change.

Human Rights as an Issue Area

A hierarchy of issues structures bilateral relations in the international system. Elites in two countries can establish ties for several reasons; yet some issues are critical in driving or limiting closer ties. If bilateral relations are to garner domestic support, public perceptions of the relationship in a democratic country must accept the public rationales of the political elites. Without some consensus on the major bilateral ties which structure a state's overall foreign policy direction, domestic challenges will emerge from the media and popularly elected officials who, for various reasons, try to reflect popular sentiments towards the nation's foreign policy. Which issues are dominant in a bilateral relationship determines much about that relationship: which constituencies have the authority to speak on it and with how much influence, the extent to which political elites can be challenged on a particular issue, and the level of popular attention to the issue and the salience attributed to it.

For Sino-American relations, as long as the administration defined the issue as strategic, the critical factor affecting China's status in Washington was China's ability to tie down Soviet forces in Asia. Within the business community, China's economic reforms and its willingness to open its economy to American interests determined the level of support for the relationship. Although many participants in the Democracy Wall movement were arrested in 1979–80, undermining China's human rights record, China received most-favored-nation trade status in 1980. Definition of the issue as strategic and economic, stress on the positive aspects of reform, and the arrival of an improved domestic human rights climate in the 1980s ensured that China's continuing human rights abuses played almost no role in relations between the United States and China.

Chinese and American Views of Human Rights

Fundamental differences between Americans and Chinese on the nature of human rights affect bilateral ties. In the American conception of human rights, "the individual is central" and has a "core of retained rights," including a sacrosanct and inalienable right to participate in self-government.[6] Government power is limited primarily because it cannot infringe on individual rights. If government action "impinges on a fundamental right — essential privacy, political freedom, freedom from racial, religious, or other invidious discrimination — that action will stand only if upon strict scrutiny by the courts it is found to serve a compelling public interest."

In traditional China, "the individual was not central and no conception of individual rights existed in the sense known to the United States."[7] Individual participation in society was not on a voluntary basis and was subsumed in a variety of relations in a "familial, paternal hierarchy." According to Louis Henkin, "the ideal was not individual liberty or equality but order and harmony, not individual independence but selflessness and cooperation, not the freedom of individual conscience but conformity to orthodox truth."[8] The legitimacy of the government did not depend on the consent of the individual or the people, and while morality was a far more constraining force on government behavior for Confucianists as compared to Legalists, "neither Confucianism nor Legalism saw moral laws or individual rights as limiting the power of the state."[9]

Under socialism, individual interests remained subsumed by

collective or corporate ones. While the state in theory is the proletariat's tool for suppressing class enemies and promoting economic development, the individual can find fulfillment only within the collective, and his economic security can be advanced only if the state can promote the general welfare. While almost all rights outlined in the United States Constitution are addressed in the 1982 Chinese Constitution, these rights are subordinated in China to the needs of socialist society and are seen as instrumental in attaining the economic betterment of the whole. In this pursuit, the state is "maximal and pervasive."[10]

American and Chinese views differ as well on the Universal Declaration of Human Rights and basic international norms of human rights. While the United States stresses political and individual rights and since 1980 has downplayed social and economic rights, the Chinese Communist party stresses the latter. Although its various constitutions pay lip service to political and individual rights, government policy always subordinates these rights to socialist economic development and the social stability necessary in their eyes for economic development. Thus the Chinese constantly rebut their critics in the United States Congress, arguing that without economic development there can be no human rights in China and that this development can occur only with social stability.[11] If individual pursuit of political rights threatens that order, the state has the legal and moral obligation to the collective interest to suppress that individual and limit his actions.

Human Rights in Sino-American Relations before June 4

Before June 4, 1989, human rights played a limited role in Sino-American relations. Some members of Congress, angered by China's Tibet policy, tried to make human rights the central issue in bilateral ties after 1987; but pressure on this issue was limited, and forces in Congress who favored strategic and economic ties to the PRC fought an ongoing battle against guerrilla-type attacks on Sino-American relations.[12] Until the crackdown in Beijing on June 4, both the Reagan and Bush administrations succeeded in ensuring the predominance of strategic and economic issues.

Congressional activism on human rights policy reflected an overall assertiveness in foreign policy begun with the War Powers Act of 1970 and followed by specific human rights initiatives beginning in 1973.[13] Congress regularly speaks out to express disappointment with foreign governments on human rights and to pressure the president to act. In its concern that states which mistreat their citizens not receive its help, Congress instituted legislation linking all countries' human rights policies to American development or security assistance.[14] The American legislature also invoked specific sanctions against selected countries violating acceptable human rights standards. Finally, President Carter institutionalized human rights as a critical component of American foreign policy by creating a Bureau of Human Rights and Humanitarian Affairs in the State Department in 1977 and legislating that the State Department submit to Congress an annual Human Rights Report on the situation in every country in the United Nations.[15] All these strategies affected the politics of human rights before and after June 4.

Overall, the situation in Tibet had been the only consistent congressional issue linking human rights and China. Although a hearing on human rights in China in 1987 found that abuses continued, especially in Tibet, Senator Claiborne Pell, a staunch supporter of Tibetan rights, reported himself that the human rights situation in China had improved.[16] Nevertheless, congressional advocates of human rights, especially for Tibetans, kept human rights on the agenda of Sino-American ties.[17] When protests led the PRC to crack down on Tibet on October 1, 1987, Congress denounced the action, called upon President Reagan to meet with the Dalai Lama, and threatened to link arms sales to China's human rights record, while Representative Tom Lantos called for Tibetan observer status at the United Nations.[18] State Department assertions that the PRC's government had the right to keep order in Tibet, since it was part of China, triggered strong congressional and media attacks on administration policy, forcing the State Department to devise new ways to address human rights in its dealings with China.

Congress was attempting to make human rights the primary issue in Sino-American relations with its amendment to the Foreign Relations Authorization Act of December 1987, which made PRC treatment of Tibet "an important factor" in the conduct of relations between the United States and China. And when the Chinese government responded in March 1989 to major riots in

Tibet by killing many protestors and instituting martial law, Congress was ready for a fight.

The administration's position on human rights before June 4 reflected trends in previous presidential administrations; with several proteges of former Secretary of State Kissinger now serving under George Bush, the United States did not consider human rights an important component of Sino-American relations. In a December 1988 policy address by Paula Dobriansky, deputy assistant secretary of state for human rights and humanitarian affairs, China was not mentioned once.[19] Her speech graphically outlined the Bush administration's thinking on human rights:

> In pursuing human rights policy, we also should continue to balance human rights concerns with other national security imperatives. . . . Our approach should be balanced and receptive to cultural and ethnic heritages of other countries. Yet under any circumstances, we should not ignore egregious human rights violations that cannot be excused by any cultural differences.

In an extremely sensitive passage, she asserts that

> the peculiarly American concept of human rights may appear alien and even dysfunctional to many foreign cultures and societies. In particular, many Third World traditional cultures emphasize corporate group rights. . . . In public policy matters, the United States should be mindful of this cultural diversity and not try to impose indiscriminately its own concept of morality and ethics on anybody.

Yet in terms of attention, the PRC did not escape the State Department's scrutiny. As events heated up in Tibet in 1987 and exploded in Beijing in 1989, the State Department's Human Rights Report responded accordingly (see table 1).

Due to its limited emphasis on human rights and its continued concerns over strategic alignments, the Bush administration did not press the case of Fang Lizhi, a leading Chinese dissident, who had begun a major campaign in early 1989 to gain the freedom of political prisoners. When he was not admitted to the president's banquet during an official visit to Beijing in early 1989, only a mild protest was registered. While many Americans recognized Fang's

Table 1
Country Reports on Human Rights Practices, 1985–1989
Report lengths in pages

	USSR	PRC	Taiwan	Canada	UK
1985	15	16	14	5	13
1986	18	15	13	3	10
1987	24	20	14	4	10
1988	23	21	16	5	17
1989	18	24	14	5	12

Source: Department of State, *Country Reports on Human Rights Practices for 1985, 1986, 1987, 1988,* and *1989.* Report submitted to the Committee on Foreign Affairs, House of Representatives, and Committee on Foreign Relations, U.S. Senate. The reports are published in February following the year studied.

---

importance and China's continued human rights abuses, the Bush administration was not going to get involved in the case of one dissident.[20]

Yet administration officials assert that there had been little pressure on them except from Congress to raise the profile of human rights in Sino-American relations. They pointed to the fact that human rights groups had not criticized the China section in the annual Human Rights Report — the administration's official position on human rights. In fact, the 1986 critique of the State Department Human Rights Report does not list China among the thirty-nine countries which human rights groups discussed.[21] According to officials in the Bureau of Human Rights and Humanitarian Affairs, there had never been any criticism of the report by the human rights community, and prior to June 4 very few people concerned about human rights ever visited the bureau. Nevertheless, even though human rights groups had been far more concerned with the softness of the 1986 report on Latin America and the Israel-occupied territories, China was addressed in the June 1988 and January 1989 critiques.

On the other hand, human rights groups had criticized the 1986 report for dropping the section, "Economic, Social and Cultural Situations," which reflects the American government's rejection of a state's efforts to improve living standards as part of a state's responsibility to respect human rights.[22] The economic approach to human rights represents China's position, and the inclusion of this assessment in the reports suggests a more favorable view of human rights progress in China among human rights groups throughout most of the 1980s before the 1987 crackdown in Tibet, as Deng's reforms significantly improved the economic, social, and cultural conditions of hundreds of millions of Chinese. Activists still opposed China's abuse of individual and political rights, but they did not raise this issue with the Bureau of Human Rights and Humanitarian Affairs.

Public opinion and media coverage did not place too much emphasis on human rights. According to one study, human rights received a dramatic boost in media attention during Carter's early years and did not return to pre-Carter levels under Reagan.[23] However, once "the content of the debate about human rights shifted more toward oppression in the Soviet Union and the meaning and consequences of international terrorism," human rights abuses were more likely to fade from media attention. American media significantly increased their reporting on human rights in China in 1987, when abuses were on the increase, and expanded their coverage in 1989 (see table 2).

There was also little change in public opinion towards human rights as a foreign policy goal during the Carter and Reagan years, excluding the issue of apartheid.[24] Most citizens, while supporting the protection of human rights abroad, decrease their concern when it is suggested that such protection might interfere with other foreign policy goals, such as containing communism or keeping good ties with strategically and economically important countries. China benefited from such views before June 4.

PRC Views: Human Rights and Sino-American Relations before June 4

China confronts a serious dilemma in dealing with the United States and other democratic countries on the issue of human rights. As mentioned above, cultural and political differences created very different views on human rights in China and the United States. Because foreign powers infringed on China's territorial integrity for a century before 1949, China's leaders are extremely

Table 2
Frequency of Articles Referring to Human Rights, 1983–1989

People's Republic of China

	1983	1984	1985	1986	1987	1988	1989	1990†
Washington Post	31	40	22	47	62	72	242	188
Los Angeles Times			41	47	82	61	251	184
Associated Press			101	97	157	148	493	472

Soviet Union

	1983	1984	1985	1986	1987	1988	1989	1990†
Washington Post	150	156	210	339	410	448	482	284
Los Angeles Times			280	353	427	420	480	266
Associated Press			811	987	1131	1142	1152	761

†projected from first ten months' data

sensitive about national sovereignty. China supports United Nations positions opposing interference in other countries' domestic affairs — hence China's strong embrace of the "Five Principles of Peaceful Coexistence" and its emphasis on noninterference in another country's internal affairs.

China's leaders also believed that the world cared little about human rights in China. Deng's famous statement that "China locked up Wei Jingsheng and no one cared" reflects that perspective; the world's lack of response to his jailing confirmed it.[25] And while the U.S. Congress made Tibet the core of its human rights dispute with China, in Chinese eyes Tibet represents issues of national security and national unity, as an autonomous Tibet could become a focus for foreign infiltration. Moreover, even India recognized Tibet as a part of China.

The widely accepted view that there are universal standards of human rights to which all states must subscribe, however, legitimizes interference in a country's affairs when it commits human rights abuses. In other arenas, China has relaxed its rigid views on sovereignty — it allows on-site inspections by the International Atomic Energy Agency. In the human rights arena too, China must recognize that how it treats its people affects how governments deal with it.

Sino-American Relations and Human Rights after June 4

When the Chinese government used armed force, killed hundreds of citizens to end the occupation of Tiananmen Square, invented a "class conspiracy" to justify it, arrested thousands of political activists, and executed dozens of workers without proper appeal, it transformed the core of Sino-American relations. World-wide revulsion erupted as millions watched on television an apparent massacre in the square where only a few weeks earlier idealistic youths had demonstrated for democracy. Public emotion moved human rights to the top of the list of issues determining Sino-American ties for many Americans, for the media, and for most members of Congress.

Any American who opposed China for any reason could now put his case against China on the public agenda. The Tiananmen crackdown strengthened the hand of those who resented the double standard applied to China's human rights abuses.[26] The media went on an anti-China tirade that lasted until mid-1990. In some academic circles, one could not ask questions about the government's motives without first denouncing the current Chinese regime as the most barbaric government in world history. This one act of repression expanded the scope of active opponents of Sino-American ties and increased the number of people within the United States who wanted to punish China. American supporters of good relations with China who tried to understand the government's actions or who felt that such a crackdown was not surprising, given the nature of the regime, were forced into silence. When they expressed their views they were roundly denounced.

Yet President Bush added oil to the flame of righteous indignation by refusing to recognize that human rights had become the heart of the Sino-American relationship. Rather than strongly denouncing the Chinese government's actions and publicly recognizing the seriousness of China's human rights violation, he tried too quickly to walk a line between expressing dismay and maintaining good ties with the regime that had shot its own people.[27] As a result, he risked losing control of the issue, and Congress pressed forward with a host of sanctions. The president found his credibility and authority under attack by an American media that pointed out the double standard, made more glaring by the collapse of communism in central Europe. Human rights organizations found good grounds for criticizing the president's lack of response to individual suffering and even torture.[28]

Under these pressures, the president was forced into a reactive mode, constantly responding to congressional actions in ways that made it appear that he was acting on behalf of the Chinese government and defending China's interests rather than promoting American foreign policy interests, including human rights. He chose to adopt secretive tactics to keep lines of communication open with Beijing, and when these were discovered, it appeared as if he were working at the beck and call of the "perpetrators of the Beijing Massacre." His decision to veto the Pelosi bill and the subsequent announcement of the Scowcroft mission allowed the Democrats to challenge the president's personal capabilities and turned China policy into a highly partisan issue, politicizing Sino-American relations to a degree unknown for two decades. Moreover, when the president did respond to domestic pressure to prove his "human rights credibility," he took positions that were sometimes more harmful to China's interests than the policies of his congressional opponents.

The president's efforts to keep control of China policy caused serious divisions within the administration. According to administration sources, some senior officials in the State Department and the White House concluded that although stressing the strategic relationship and engaging China's leaders in dialogue was correct, the domestic climate made a public defense of this position politically infeasible. State Department officials who reportedly had qualms about the China policy also discouraged administration officials from talking publicly about it. As a result, the administration had to defend its China policy until early 1990.

The White House also felt that reducing public attention to China and avoiding exacerbation of bilateral strains would slow the decline in Sino-American ties. But in fact this strategy reinforced congressional criticism that the administration did not know what it was doing. A perception developed in Congress that the administration's reticence to defend its policy implied that the administration itself viewed the policy as indefensible. According to some sources, only after Under Secretary of State Lawrence Eagleburger's public testimony in early February did many members of Congress become convinced that the administration had a real policy and that it might get the Chinese to move forward on critical issues of interest to the United States.

President Bush's apparent insensitivity to the human rights dimension of China policy, his conflicts with a Congress pressing that agenda, and perhaps the media's anger at having been "duped" by the Chinese into believing that democracy was coming in China led the American press to swing from characterizing "Deng as the open-door westernizer" to presenting "Deng as the Butcher of Tiananmen."[29] Editorials and articles railed against the president, and due to the desire of the press to prove that the president's policy was wrong, they distorted many stories during this period. They refused to recognize the role played by the Scowcroft visit in stemming the tide of leftism in late 1989.[30] They understated the significance of the lifting of martial law in mid-January, and the formidable politics behind that move was never acknowledged. Every release of several hundred detainees was portrayed as a cosmetic act to win the favor of foreigners; yet for those who were released and for the people in China life was improving.[31] Had the media presented the lifting of martial law as a victory for moderate forces, or taken the prisoner releases more seriously, they would have had to recognize the utility of the Bush strategy, including visits to China by Nixon and Scowcroft. Yet for journalists and members of Congress, these visits symbolized administration insensitivity to Chinese suffering and the willingness of the American government to ignore human rights in the pursuit of strategic ties. Given the apparent immorality of this strategy, how could they accept the fact that it might succeed?

Once major newspapers and television news editors decided that the story in China was the suppression of human rights and the struggles of the brave Chinese people to throw off the oppressive yoke of the Chinese Communist party, few stories appeared even into mid-1990 that did not focus on arrests, popular disillusionment, and anti-government hostility. While some moderation in the political climate in China began in mid-February, no prominent American newspaper ran such stories. According to a survey at Harvard University's Kennedy School's Barrone Institute, reports written by Western and Japanese embassy officials in Beijing for their home governments were far more upbeat than the articles that were appearing in the American press.[32] Some American journalists in China admitted that they had become so disillusioned by the government's crackdown that they could not bring themselves to write such stories, although they knew a favorable political shift was occurring. They also knew what their editors would run. As a result the media presented to the American public only a partial picture of post-June 4 life in China.[33]

Finally, once China policy became a human rights issue, new actors entered the policy debate. The most important group was the Chinese students living in the United States, who used the issue of human rights both to attack a government they abhorred and to ensure their own security in America. Other actors, such as immigration lawyers and human rights activists who had previously been far more concerned with Central America, joined the battle over China policy.

Chinese Views of Human Rights and Sino-American Ties after June 4

Events on June 4 significantly changed China's foreign policy by altering leadership attitudes toward the international system, increasing the influence of some actors who had previously played a minimal role in Sino-American ties, and silencing many former advocates of good relations between Beijing and Washington. The international response to the Tiananmen crackdown intensified the threat perception of China's old guard and convinced them that the U.S. Congress and China's enemies in the United States were allied with domestic forces aiming to topple CCP rule. While many Chinese leaders may have seen the violent nature of the crackdown as harmful to party interests, they did recognize that some forceful political action had become necessary to ensure the continued dominance of the CCP. The Western reaction to that decision suggested that the West did not recognize the party's right to self-preservation. Economic sanctions imposed on China undermined the Communist party's ability to ensure economic development and challenged the utility of China's "open door policy," the two of which form the basis of legitimacy of Deng's reformist regime.

The Tiananmen incident let some leaders reintroduce "class analysis" into foreign policy, which painted a conspiratorial picture of the Western critique of China's human rights behavior. Western criticism of Chinese human rights abuses was not simply "interference" but was seen as one tactic in the long-term strategy of "peaceful evolution" by which American politicians and diplomats had for the past forty years sought to overthrow the party and undermine China's global status. In the United States, China's leaders witnessed the ascension of actors who had for years resisted Sino-American ties, such as the human rights lobby, the anti-family-planning forces, anticommunists and pro-Taiwan forces, and those who opposed China's growing challenge to American economic interests. As the shift of emphasis allowed for these people to take center stage in Congress, it made it appear in China as if long-term American opponents of the PRC were now in a position to challenge it on all fronts.[34]

This shift in attention to human rights threatened China's leaders internally as well. While one day they may regret the verdict made on June 4, it became impossible for China's leaders to accept that the efforts to ensure party leadership and maintain the stability necessary for economic development could be first and foremost an infringement on people's human rights. Most important, Deng did not see that his decision to use force was wrong in that it would arm his opponents and undermine party rule.[35]

The attack on China in the United States also silenced many Chinese advocates of Sino-American ties and gave power to those who sought to undermine these links. Before June 4, Deng retained the final say on all aspects of China's United States policy; after June 4, other leaders and institutions could attack many of the linkages in the American-Chinese relationship. For example, in August 1989, when one of the old guard who rose to power in May–June criticized the Foreign Ministry for allowing its staff to be trained in the United States under funding by an American foundation, the training program was canceled. Officials in China's Foreign Ministry, who themselves seemed to believe that the CCP had used excessive force, stressed in all sincerity that the criticism of China's human rights policy would only be seen as interference in China's internal affairs and could never be recognized as legitimate.[36] After the June 4 crackdown, officials in the Chinese embassy in Washington began to use "class struggle" and "class analysis" in their reports to the State Education Commission on the Chinese students.[37] These reports could only reinforce the belief in China that class enemies were trying to undermine Sino-American relations. Finally, Chinese in Washington were unable to launch any effort to improve China's position in the United States. Only in August 1989 was the embassy informed of the government's official position on the Tiananmen crackdown and the public position they were to take. Moreover, most of them could not immediately defend publicly a policy they initially so strongly opposed; they preferred not to approach Congress rather than try to explain what for them was an unexplainable policy.

Thus, China could not respond to the new salience of human rights in Sino-American relations. For domestic reasons, as they tried to quell anti-government hostility, the leadership could not admit the human rights nature of the issue; to do so internationally would have justified the foreign attack on the government's legitimacy. The rise of Li Peng as the head of the Foreign Policy Leadership Small Group further complicated the issue, for if China accepted the Western critique that China had abused its people, the prime minister, who had been the major target of the demonstrators and who had declared martial law, would be the most likely leader to fall from power. Similarly, public recognition of human rights abuses would threaten Deng's authority, since he had sent in the troops.

Thus if the Sino-American relationship was to get unstuck, President Bush had to send a clear, unambiguous message to China's leaders that, although he deplored their excessive use of force, he was not part of what appeared to them to be a global conspiracy to overthrow the CCP. Scowcroft's visit, and the inclusion in the party of a personal friend of the president's, helped to defuse the fear in China of a global threat. Once that relaxation occurred, and once China recognized that sanctions would not undermine China's ability to export, China could take tentative steps to release its political prisoners, which it hoped would deflate the attack on China's human rights record. While officially they continue to deny any human rights abuses, Chinese leaders' actions since the spring of 1990 show that they recognize the importance of human rights in relations between Washington and Beijing and the need for China to respond to those concerns.[38]

Case Studies

This section will examine several critical issues in Sino-American ties since June 4, and illustrate how the question of human rights affected politics in Washington and Sino-American relations. For each case, variations in the nature of the issue — whether it was a human rights issue, a partisan political one, an economic one, or simply declaratory policy — as well as the timing of the policy debate, what issues had been fought out before, the perceived stakes involved, and who had legitimacy to speak on the issue, all affected the policy process and its outcome.

The Sanctions Bill: Negotiating an Acceptable Amendment

The negotiations on this bill occurred before a major split had developed between the administration and Congress, so the level of acrimony was not high. Second, control over the policy remained in the hands of people who were concerned about expressing outrage at China's gross human rights abuses but who were also interested in maintaining economic links that were beneficial to American business and political links with China that were in America's national interest. The issue came down to whether the president could maintain control over the nature of the sanctions. Through negotiations, he was able to do so.

According to some congressional staffers, relatively weak support for China on the Hill meant that supporters of stable Sino-American relations were constantly warding off guerrilla attacks from a variety of fronts. China and the White House were not without friends in Congress who could beat back congressional efforts to undermine Sino-American ties.[39] For example, when some congressmen tried to block the launching of American satellites on Chinese rockets, supporters of China in the House of

Representatives had been able to protect this new form of Sino-American cooperation. But after June 4 all bets were off. According to one Republican staffer, "Between the best efforts of the Chinese government and the policy of the President of the U.S., we were left with no recourse but to support sanctions." Even Republicans who favored continuing most-favored-nation status for China in the belief that American business in China advanced human rights more than cutting trade, had to support sanctions. A "feeding frenzy" on China ensued in Congress. Much of the reaction was based on genuine outrage, as most members felt that Congress as an institution had to demonstrate its horror at the events in China. Yet it has to be admitted that few could afford to be seen as inactive on such a public moral issue. A slow response on this apparently clear-cut human rights question would allow future electoral opponents to attack incumbents for ignoring constituent concerns.

Amendments to the Foreign Assistance Authorization Bill poured into the *Congressional Record.* Losers of earlier battles on China-related issues tried to reverse verdicts. Opponents of the Chinese satellite launch, who had lost the battle once, put forward an amendment opposing it as violating the prohibition on military sales and transfer of technology to human rights offenders. New initiatives, such as Congressman John Edward Porter's efforts to put through a Hong Kong resolution — which would not have passed before June 4 — were accelerated through Congress.[40]

The immense number of proposed amendments forced House Foreign Affairs Committee staffers to pile up all of them and bargain over them as they put together an omnibus China Sanctions Amendment. This way they hoped to satisfy those who had listed amendments without having all the amendments put forward one by one in Congress. The decision on which amendments were included fell into the hands of people who, while desirous of sending a clear signal to China, would not let human rights abuses scuttle two decades of China rapprochement. The majority and minority sides of the House committee tried to limit the impact of sanctions on American business interests. Sanctions on the export of "dual use" technology were excluded, as were sanctions on the high-value goods readily available from other sources. In the words of one staffer, "If you start to put a human rights yardstick next to trade, you wind up trading with yourself."

Included, too, was an exemption from sanctions for the sale of "inertial navigation systems" — a code word for Boeing planes whose sale was pending.[41] While the sanctions sent a strong message to China, significant aspects of the economic relationship were protected.

A deal was also struck on the wording of the "waiver authority." The White House wanted the broadest terminology possible, which would allow the president to lift individual sanctions and protect American business interests. Initially, the House bill provided for the president to waive sanctions only in the interest of "national security."[42] The Senate's version, however, allowed the president to lift sanctions if it was in the "national interest."[43] No final deal was struck in the House/Senate conference committee until General Scowcroft, head of the National Security Council, promised Congressman Solarz that the president would not veto the bill over the China amendment if it included the broader waiver authority.[44] Although Solarz angered Democrats who felt "national interest" gave the president too much leeway, a compromise was achieved which allowed the president to authorize the sale of Boeing planes and satellites.

Yet in his effort to match congressional activism, President Bush pressed his global allies to impose sanctions on China which were more onerous than those imposed by Congress. Besides the initial sanctions of ending military sales and high-technology exports to China and stopping high-level governmental exchanges, the administration put strong pressure on bilateral and multilateral lending agencies to freeze their activities with China. Thus the flow of funds to China from international lending agencies dried up completely. By July 1989, the G-7 had frozen $10 billion in aid and loans from the World Bank and Japan as well as another $780 million in World Bank loans slated for the end of June. These restrictions, more than anything imposed by Congress, hurt the Chinese economy by halting many critical, centrally controlled development projects. Thus while congressional anger toward the president was not inconsequential on the sanctions issue, the two parties worked together, and supporters of President Bush in Congress cooperated with their colleagues who opposed him. A sanctions bill acceptable to the administration was passed, and no major split occurred between Congress and the president.

David Zweig

The Pelosi Bill: China Policy and Political Partisanship

The politics of the Pelosi bill differed greatly from the sanctions bill. New actors on China policy emerged, especially Nancy Pelosi and the Chinese students. The protracted debate involved issues of freedom from persecution and freedom of thought, values which lie at the heart of the American ethos. The president's secret diplomacy infuriated Congress and the media, making this a highly partisan issue. His tactics also cost him support within the administration. In the end, the nature of the fight politicized China policy in a way that could take years to overcome.

At the outset, the events surrounding this bill followed a somewhat similar pattern to the development of the sanctions issue. In response to events in Beijing, congressional actors moved quickly to "give concrete form" to their anger. Many staffers had been frustrated by the plethora of non-binding, declaratory resolutions that had appeared following the Tiananmen crackdown and wanted something meaningful.

Popular emotion was intense. Numerous members of Congress who had not previously been involved on China policy were under pressure to act. Nancy Pelosi, a second-term Democrat from San Francisco, had not been active on China but had supported Central American refugees. So when Chinese constituents called her to do something, members of her staff contacted immigration lawyers with whom they had worked on the issue of Central American refugees and wrote the Pelosi bill (H.R. 2712). Chinese students, who previously had not played a role in Sino-American relations, became what one congressional staffer called "an unbelievably effective lobby." Three days after the drafting of the Pelosi bill, a group of Chinese students who knew the content of the bill deluged Pelosi's office with letters, faxes, and phone calls. Pelosi's office then directed them to contact their own congressmen. Overnight the bill had 250 cosponsors. Chinese students from every state came to lobby Congress. Every campus sent representatives, and they worked almost every congressional district in the country. No doubt, some had reason to fear the Public Security Bureau or investigations within their place of work if they returned to China; others thought that their presence in the United States during this period might later be used against them in promotion decisions if they returned to the PRC. Yet the students overstated the threat to their security and were willing to sacrifice future Sino-American educational exchanges to ensure their access to permanent residence status.[45]

The human rights issue gave some members of Congress an important opportunity for national attention. Although Congresswoman Nancy Pelosi had not been active on Chinese human rights, she had found an important issue on which to expand her influence. By the time this question was settled, she had been appointed chairperson of a new informal congressional committee on China policy. Another congressman who had tried to help the students, Steve Gunderson, of Wisconsin, was less successful in finding the right approach. He had put forward an amendment to set up a committee to help the Chinese students with financial matters, but when the staff working on the omnibus sanctions bill discovered that the Institute for International Education was already doing this with private funds, Gunderson's initiative was dropped in the House-Senate conference committee.

The administration once again appeared to be on the wrong side of a clear-cut issue of human rights when the president chose not to sign H.R. 2712. With thousands of people in China being arrested for exercising their right to influence government policy, how could the president fail to protect Chinese citizens in the United States who had pursued that same right? Even though the president followed his pocket veto of H.R. 2712 by instituting a presidential directive that offered protection to an even greater number of Chinese citizens, his decision to introduce only limited sanctions soon after June 4 made many congressmen and students fearful that at some future point he might succumb to Chinese pressure and revoke his own directive. During the Christmas recess, Congress and the Chinese students felt justified in doubting the president's word. While he had included a moratorium on high-level exchanges in his sanctions package, the president announced to the shock of Congress and the world that Scowcroft, Eagleburger, and other Americans were visiting Beijing. In fact, it was soon revealed that in July, only one month after the Tiananmen crackdown, these same diplomats had gone to Beijing at the president's request. In the environment of public mistrust fueled by the president's obvious efforts to justify his secret diplomacy by manipulating words such as "exchanges" and "visits," Congress decided to protect the students and fight the president's veto.

Some Democrats saw the president's apparent insensitivity to human rights and his refusal to openly confront the Chinese as a way to embarrass him, and they turned this issue into a personal and partisan battle, with Senate Majority Leader George Mitchell leading in accusing President Bush of having "kowtowed" to the Chinese.

When the House met after Christmas, it quickly overrode the veto, leaving the battle to be won or lost in the Senate. Seeking support from conservative Republicans, the president portrayed this as a partisan issue, arguing that the Democrats wanted to use the controversy to weaken him. His staff made a video of all the times Senator Mitchell had accused the president of "kowtowing" to the Chinese and showed it as an illustration of the Democrats' strategy to Republicans they hoped to persuade. The issue of human rights and China policy got lost in the battle.

The president pulled out all stops to prevent the override of his veto, adding his own partisan efforts to rally right-wing congressional support. In the words of one supporter of the Pelosi bill, this was "the most serious lobbying effort by the administration ever." Reports suggest that administration officials targeted senators who had potential ethics problems, including Dave Durenberger, Alfonse D'Amato, and John McCain, and pressured them not support the veto override. In the end, eight undecided senators went along with the president, and his veto was sustained.

The battle over the Pelosi bill also highlighted splits within the administration, particularly between the White House and the State Department. In justifying the presidential veto of this bill, the administration spoke with several different voices, leaving both its critics and its allies befuddled. Initially, the State Department and Chief of Staff Sununu both said that the president opposed the bill because it might cause the Chinese to cancel exchanges and therefore prevent other Chinese from coming to the United States. Another State Department official asserted that the veto was to protect exchange programs worldwide. Yet when the president justified this policy, he did so arguing that he "opposed Congressional micromanagment of foreign policy."

A recent explanation links the veto to the Scowcroft visit. According to administration sources, the Chinese were furious about this bill and threatened to cancel the trip unless the bill were vetoed. Deng could not meet Scowcroft unless the administration distanced itself from a Congress which seemed bent on overthrowing the CCP and abetting a "brain drain" to the United States. Deng reportedly sent a message that he wanted to get out of the bind that the crackdown had imposed on Sino-American relations; the defeat of the Pelosi Bill was part of that effort to help him.

Yet to prove that he could protect the students as well as Congress could, the president's directive went beyond the Pelosi bill on two counts: the president's directive concerning work authorization applied to *all* PRC nationals who were in the United States on June 5, 1989, whereas congressional proposals covered only individuals in a lawful student exchange or having visitor status. Thus the president also protected people whose visas had expired. Second, in the section concerning forced abortion and coerced sterilization, the president's directive offered protection "to all foreign nationals, regardless of their country of origin," while H.R. 2712 covered only PRC nationals.[46] This outcome left both Congress and the Chinese angry at him. According to Chinese sources, President Bush had told Chinese officials that his student policy would be more favorable to the regime. But the furor over his veto forced him to introduce a policy that was quite pro-student, leaving the Chinese feeling betrayed and angered. It also angered members of Congress and their staffs, with whom he had fought a fierce battle, and left them wondering why he had reacted so forcefully in the first place.

Human Rights Report

The Human Rights Report was the administration's first public recognition after June 4 that there was a major human rights problem in China that had to be addressed. The 1989 report was much tougher than its 1988 predecessor. According to officials in the Bureau of Human Rights and Humanitarian Affairs, the deteriorating human rights situation in China led them to make the report more honest. Thus the report finds that Chinese "authorities clearly used excessive deadly force" against "peaceful demonstrators" in Tiananmen Square.[47]

However, the tenor of the report changed dramatically. While Chinese efforts to improve human rights in China — by introducing new laws — were emphasized in previous reports and problems in implementing human rights policy were downplayed, the

1989 report focused on abuses that had been going on for several years. For example, it criticized China for not succeeding in "stopping abductions and the trading of women and children" and stated that "there is no evidence" that discrimination against women had been reduced. While previous reports had highlighted Chinese legal strictures against torture and human rights abuses, had accepted Chinese contentions that they were working to improve human rights in China, and had even stated that they expected the "liberalizing trend" would "continue," the 1989 report admitted that torture is "persistent and consistent," and spoke of "slippage" on human rights. Whereas the 1988 report found no forced labor outside prisons and labor camps, the 1989 report observes that few Chinese at all have any significant degree of choice in their employment, something the State Department knew all along but never stressed. Thus any implication ended that the Chinese government had taken progressive measures and that only implementation was lagging. Finally, concerns were put aside about the sensibilities of the Chinese ruling elite, which had influenced past reports. The report chastised a "few senior leaders" who to maintain power killed citizens and carried out a crackdown and "a massive disinformation campaign aimed at rewriting history."

According to officials in the bureau, the tougher language was also due to the fact that since June 4 they had far more information than ever before. The sharper critique on population policy was due to the fact that Congressman Chris Smith, a pro-life activist, had supplied more information. However, other administration officials said such information had always been available, particularly since the information Congressman Smith and others provided consisted mostly of unsubstantiated allegations from the Chinese press in 1981–84. The State Department had simply rejected the information until after June 4, when it became necessary to use it. Previously the State Department had just updated the report, resisting pressures to beef it up; but it had been easier to resist these pressures before June 4, 1989. Perhaps, too, after the Tiananmen crackdown, the drafters of the Human Rights Report were themselves less willing to resist these pressures.

The report was first drafted in Beijing in October, then edited in the State Department, mostly by the China desk and the Bureau of Human Rights and Humanitarian Affairs. While many working-level officials anticipated high-level pressure to dilute the strong language in the embassy's draft, such pressure did not materialize, so the report's tone remained essentially as written. Three plausible explanations for the lack of pressure include high-level inattention to the report in the crush of other business, warnings from Congress not to water down what was known to be a tough embassy draft, or a decision that China's limited response to the Scowcroft visit did not justify a softer tone. Yet while the document was part of the public realm and surprised the Chinese by its frankness, it was only declaratory policy. Though a really tough criticism of China, it had no teeth and was unlikely to harm American business interests or the strategic relationship. It did, however, play a role, as several witnesses in the congressional hearings on MFN cited the report as proof that China's human rights situation "has deteriorated in virtually every area."[48]

MFN: Economic Interest and the Emergence of a Coalition

The fight over MFN followed a different pattern. There was a battle over the definition of the issue, as the president wanted to make it an economic issue and detach it from human rights. But to do so, the president had to expand the range of participants in the debate. The high price of the Pelosi bill battle meant that, without significant help from Beijing and from American supporters of strong ties to China, the president preferred not to act alone on this issue. But Congress, the Chinese students, the human rights community, and an important sector of the American community interested in China policy were intent on maintaining the linkage and saw MFN as an important economic lever with which to send a message to Beijing on its human rights policy. The president advised the Chinese that if they wanted to keep MFN, they had to defuse the saliency of their human rights policy. Fang Lizhi's release was Deng's contribution to this policy debate.

To mobilize support, the president decided to warn American and Hong Kong businessmen, as well as the Chinese, that he might not exercise a veto to ensure continuation of MFN.[49] As a result, actors who had an economic interest in the policy, but who had not been involved in the sanctions or Pelosi bill debates, moved to the fore. The U.S.-China Business Council prepared a very persuasive document showing the impact of increased tariffs on imports from China for American retailers and consumers. The presidents of the American Chamber of Commerce in both Hong Kong and Beijing spoke at the congressional hearings. Also, the heads of many important trade organizations, including wheat exporters, toy manufacturers, and the American Association of Exporters and Importers, all presented material to the House committees addressing the MFN issue as an economic one. In his presentation to the House Subcommittee on Asian and Pacific Affairs, M. David Lampton, president of the National Committee on U.S.-China Relations, argued that ending MFN sent a message that "the United States is insensitive, if not hostile to the economic aspirations of all China's people."[50] Liberals who had bashed the president for his China policy shifted sides on this issue, expressing their concerns about the impact of revoking MFN on both China's and Hong Kong's economies and their belief in keeping the door to China open.[51] Even some Chinese dissidents began their own lobbying efforts to stress the economic costs to China of revoking MFN.[52]

The timing, too, was different. By the time of the debate on MFN, the bottom floor had been reached in Sino-American ties. Much of the emotionality of the summer of 1989 had apparently passed, particularly among the American public. Also, the Chinese finally realized that they could not expect help from the president without some give on their part first. Numerous Americans warned Chinese Foreign Ministry officials and higher-level leaders that the president had used up all his cards defeating the Pelosi bill and that they would have to contribute something on human rights — such as more prisoner releases or the release of Fang Lizhi — if they wanted the president to protect bilateral ties.[53]

The Chinese did release more prisoners and lifted martial law in Tibet, so that by May 1990, when the president had to make his decision on MFN, the Chinese government claimed that only 437 prisoners arrested after June 4 remained in jail. Then in early July, at Deng's bequest, the Chinese government allowed Fang Lizhi and his wife to leave China. China's leaders seemed finally to have learned that Sino-American relations had become a human rights issue.

To some extent, splits began to emerge within the Democratic leadership, as Senator George Mitchell continued to press the Chinese human rights issue. Meanwhile, Speaker of the House

Thomas Foley, whose constituency in Washington state has extensive trade relations with China, began to approach it from a foreign trade perspective.[54]

Nevertheless, anger in the House and continued lobbying by Chinese students who opposed China trade made saving MFN an uphill battle.[55] In some ways the administration appeared to be out of touch with the mood of Congress. For Congress, the issue was whether to reject the president's authorization of MFN or to accept his determination to waive the Jackson-Vanek amendment, but with conditions.[56] Thus although Richard Solomon, assistant secretary of state for East Asian and Pacific affairs, argued that the president's decision on May 24, 1990, to continue MFN unconditionally was in the national interest — focusing on the positive role of MFN in promoting American business, China's human rights, Hong Kong's future, and continuing Sino-American dialogue — Congressman Solarz warned him to argue instead for a conditional one-year extension as the best deal the administration was going to receive from Congress. If, however, the administration worked for a full extension, he said, "You run the real risk of ending up with an immediate termination of MFN."[57]

Congressman Solarz was correct. House Speaker Foley, who wanted to preserve MFN, failed to get the House Rules Committee to send the MFN bill to the House floor with no opportunity for amendments. He even went back to the committee and demanded that it reconvene to ensure that no challenges could be raised against it. In the end, the House rejected the president's certification of MFN status for China, but the Senate, distracted by the budget crisis, never met on it. Thus, the president's certification was allowed to stand. MFN for China remains highly contentious, as efforts failed to make it only an economic issue. China's human rights policies remain key to congressional actions and Sino-American foreign policy.

Conclusion

What will be the future role of human rights in Sino-American relations? Is it here to stay as a significant issue? How important is external pressure in improving China's human rights policy?

Without a strong lobby in Congress to protect China policy,

ties between the United States and the PRC remain vulnerable to single-issue constituents who either oppose China's human rights policy or use it to advance their own particular causes. And while China policy was relatively immune to impact from the human rights issue for most of the past ten years, in the post-June 4 era Sino-American ties will remain highly vulnerable for several reasons. A new coalition of opponents to China has evolved composed of right-to-life advocates, liberal human rights activists, trade protectionists, and anticommunists, who for different reasons share a common interest and act in ways that can further weaken Sino-American relations. Moreover, the shift in the strategic global environment and the declining Soviet threat has reduced China's strategic importance to the United States. The disillusionment of American business with China and the current economic retrenchment and go-slow approach to economic reform in China also undermine some of the economic rationales for the relationship.[58] Finally, the ballooning trade deficit with China — in 1990 it was $12 billion — will give ample ammunition to those who question why the American government continues its double standard on human rights abuses in the Soviet Union and China. All these factors will be counterposed to Chinese and administration efforts to downplay the human rights component in Sino-American ties.

But there is good news in this. China clearly abuses its people's human rights. Most members of China's old guard care little about human rights and see it only as a bargaining chip in their ties with the United States. Police at the local levels are free from any effective monitoring and the courts regularly lock people up without proper proceedings. Serious work will be necessary to reverse the negative impact of the post-Tiananmen crackdown on the progress that had been made in human rights under the Deng reforms. Until a free press is instituted, Chinese people will be forced to rely on outside pressures, such as strong public criticism, formal diplomatic protests, and even some economic sanctions, as well as their own internal public opinion, passed up through various channels to state leaders, to improve the human rights climate in China. Therefore, while Congress's political activism in support of Chinese human rights — such as their rejection of MFN and efforts to pry Tibet free from Chinese control (which will trigger recalcitrance) — is likely to be counterproductive, the increased salience of human rights in Sino-American relations should help improve China's domestic human rights environment.

In part this shift may already be under way, for something has changed in the way the Deng regime deals with its internal political enemies. While it still executes some of its working class foes and deals harshly with those whose organizational skills really challenge communist power, most of the Chinese intellectuals who were arrested in June–July 1989 were released within a year.[59] Had this been 1957, the time of the Anti-Rightist Campaign, or the Cultural Revolution, almost all of these political prisoners would have stayed in jail for ten to twenty years. While China argued that it would not yield to external pressure, greater economic interdependence has decreased China's ability to withstand economic sanctions and international opprobrium. Fang Lizhi's release is the proof.

While Mao could close China down, today's hardliners could not do so even if they desired it, because of Deng's certain resistance to any such prospect. Moreover, the vested interests in many parts of the country, including among some very important leaders, favor continuing interaction and openness. While the Chinese government denounced the 1989 Human Rights Report, for the first time it responded officially to the substance of the report by providing a written critique. Some — though not all — State Department officials are hopeful that this exchange will lead to a productive dialogue on human rights issues. The reception in China in December 1990 of Assistant Secretary of State for Human Rights and Humanitarian Affairs Richard Schifter, who presented a list of 150 names of political activists currently under arrest to the ministries responsible for perpetuating most of China's human rights abuses, is a further sign of a shift in the way China handles the public side of the human rights issue.

One hopes that China's leaders understand the human component of human rights, but it is doubtful. They instead appear as determined as ever to hold onto power. As their children become more entwined in the economy and in benefiting from their control over it, they too are likely to back political and military suppression, even as they wish that their support were not required. In the short run, a fundamental shift in China's real view of human rights is unlikely. Should new serious challenges to CCP dominance emerge, human rights abuses will follow. When they do, the U.S. Congress, pushed by the new anti-PRC coalition, may find popular support among the American body politic and society in the post-June 4 era for new sanctions and new limitations on Sino-American relations. At such moments, the president will be hard pressed to preserve good Sino-American ties.

Yet openness and reform have their virtues. We should anticipate a change as China recognizes the fundamental nature of its response to human rights and the need to improve its performance if it wishes to keep Western loans and technology flowing into the PRC. Ten years of Deng's reforms have had a significant impact. For a decade Deng told the Chinese intellectuals that they were part of "the people" and had the right to participate actively in China's modernization drive. Their views and China's ties to the outside will have their impact. In the words of one of the author's Chinese friends, a well-known political hardliner, "The world has become internationalized and China cannot go on its own as in the 1950s and 1960s and ignore what the world thinks about it. We have to be concerned and try to deal with these issues. China cannot go back on its open policy. The people would not accept it, and this has led to changes in China, in people's views and people's demands." Let us hope he is right.

NOTES

Funds for research and travel for this paper were provided by the Hewlett Research Grant, Fletcher School of Law and Diplomacy, Tufts University. Research assistance was provided by Alexias Feringa Thurman, Wayne White, and Yang Yi. Special thanks goes to Kenneth Lieberthal, Hurst Hannum, Alfred Rubin, and especially William Tow for their helpful and challenging comments. All errors are my own.

1. Henry Kissinger, *White House Years* (Boston: Little, Brown and Company, 1979), p. 164.
2. A. Glenn Mower, Jr., *Human Rights and American Foreign Policy: The Carter and Reagan Experiences* (New York: Greenwood Press, 1987), p. 153.
3. Michael Oksenberg, "The Dynamics of the Sino-American Relationship," in Richard Solomon, ed., *The China Factor* (Englewood Cliffs, NJ: Prentice Hall, 1981), p. 198.
4. According to one Chinese official, despite a great emphasis on building ties with Congress, both by inviting congressmen and their staffs to visit China and by delegations from China's National People's Congress to America, the ideological and political differences over Taiwan, Tibet, human rights, and birth control, as well as limited financial resources, make it quite difficult for China to win over congressmen.
5. Much of the information collected for this paper comes from a series of confidential interviews conducted in early August 1990 with administration officials, congressional aides, and Chinese officials.
6. Louis Henkin, "The Human Rights Idea in Contemporary China: A Comparative Perspective," in R. Randle Edwards, Louis Henkin, and Andrew J. Nathan, eds., *Human Rights in Contemporary China* (New York: Columbia University Press, 1986), pp. 14–16.
7. Henkin, "Human Rights Idea in Contemporary China," p. 21.
8. Ibid.
9. Andrew J. Nathan, "Sources of Chinese Rights Thinking," in Edwards, Henkin, and Nathan, eds., *Human Rights in Contemporary China,* p. 127.
10. Ibid., p. 161.
11. According to a noted specialist on human rights, Hurst Hannum, the assertion that economic development took precedence over individual rights was quite common in the 1960s and 1970s. But as the international regime on human rights became more legitimate, this argument was abandoned by most states except China.
12. Author's interview, 1990.

13. David P. Forsythe, *Human Rights and U.S. Foreign Policy: Congress Reconsidered* (Gainesville, FL: University of Florida Press, 1988).
14. See Stephen B. Cohen, "Conditioning U.S. Security Assistance on Human Rights Practices," *American Journal of International Law* 76, No. 2 (April 1982), pp. 246–79.
15. As a result of these two pieces of legislation, every United States embassy has a human rights officer in the political section who is responsible for, among other tasks, writing the first draft of the human rights report, and therefore is known within the host country as someone who can be involved in checking up human rights abuses.
16. Gary W. Vause, *Tibet to Tiananmen: Chinese Human Rights and United States Foreign Policy,* University of Maryland Occasional Papers Series in Contemporary Asian Studies, no. 6 (Baltimore: University of Maryland School of Law, 1989), p. 15.
17. The most active is Congressmen Tom Lantos, a staunch supporter of Tibetan independence, who sees the suppression of Tibetan efforts for self-rule as a holocaust. For Lantos, any violator of human rights must be taken to task, but he is now particularly irked by the double standard which allows China to escape precepts imposed on countries such as the USSR. In September 1987, with the help of the Congressional Human Rights Caucus, he brought the Dalai Lama to Washington and created tensions in Sino-American relations when his statements to Congress recognized the Dalai Lama's government-in-exile. The Dalai Lama was accorded some trappings of a head of state, which Lantos claims was a conscious action to advance the claim for Tibetan independence. See Vause, *Tibet to Tiananmen,* p. 37.
18. Ibid.
19. Paula Dobriansky, "Human Rights Policy: Future Opportunities and Challenges," *Current Policy,* No. 1143 (Washington, DC: United States Department of State, Bureau of Public of Affairs, Office of Public Communications, January 1989).
20. For Ambassador Winston Lord and particularly his wife, who was actively involved in promoting human rights in China through regular contacts with leading Chinese intellectuals, human rights in China took on an extremely personal component, since many of the people abused by the government were regular attendees at ambassadorial functions. Bette Bao Lord described many of her ties with government intellectuals who suffered human rights abuses during the Cultural Revolution in her recent book, *Legacies: A Chinese Mosaic* (New York: Knopf, 1990), especially pp. 40–69.
21. Watch Committees and Lawyers Committee for Human Rights, *Critique: A Review of the Department of State's Country Reports on Human Rights Practices for 1986,* April 1987, submitted to the State Department.

22. According to the 1986 Human Rights Report, the State Department dropped this category because "the concept of economic, social, and cultural rights is often confused, sometimes willfully, by repressive governments claiming that in order to promote these rights they may deny their citizens the rights to integrity of the person as well as civil and political rights." *Critique,* pp. 3–4.
23. Anne E. Geyer and Robert Y. Shapiro, "The Polls — A Report: Human Rights," *Public Opinion Quarterly* 52, No. 3 (Fall 1988), pp. 386–98.
24. Ibid.
25. The desire to maintain communist power and the entire CCP system, which stresses suppression of all political challenges, means that many CCP officials have little respect for individual human rights. Particularly when political liberalization creates instability, most CCP leaders would support tightening the political system. For Deng Xiaoping's comment on Wei Jingsheng, see "Central Document" (Zhongfa) No. 1, 6 January 1987, in *Chinese Law and Government,* Spring 1988, p. 19.
26. According to people close to Congressman Lantos, many moderates on the issue of human rights who had previously not wanted to believe his claims about abuses in Tibet were convinced by the June 4 crackdown that he had not been exaggerating.
27. Perhaps the conflict in the United States was inevitable, given the popular and congressional anger and the president's commitment to maintaining relations with China. Could the president have taken stronger actions and have still pursued a dialogue with the Chinese leadership in a way that allowed him to be well positioned for reestablishing meaningful ties when the Chinese finished their internal and anti-foreign post-Tiananmen paroxysm? For a comprehensive critique of administration policy, see Human Rights Watch, *The Bush Administration's Record on Human Rights in 1989,* January 1990.
28. Asia Watch, *Punishment Season: Human Rights in China after Martial Law* (New York: Asia Watch Committee, 1990), pp. 59–68.
29 James C. Thomson, "Jilted Again: The U.S. Media's Courtship with Democracy in China," *Gannett Center Journal* 3, No. 4 (Fall 1989), p. 91.
30. According to several Chinese sources, tension on Beijing's streets relaxed immediately after Scowcroft's visit was announced in the *People's Daily.* After Scowcroft asked for the lifting of martial law Deng called on Jiang Zemin, who worked for one month before he could do so. Most important, it proved to Deng and the old guard that President Bush was not working with the Congress to try to overthrow CCP rule in China. Without the Scowcroft visit, martial law would not have been lifted in China so soon after Ceausescu's execution.
31. The Chinese government contributed to this cynical view that pris-

oner releases were cosmetic by neither announcing the number of arrests nor publishing the names of released prisoners. Western journalists remained unsure as to the percentage of prisoners who remained in jail. Also, while the lifting of martial law took the troops off the streets, the number of People's Armed Police reportedly increased.

32. See a report by Michael Berlin at a round-table seminar, Fairbank Center, Harvard University, 4 June 1990, in author's possession.
33. For my own, more optimistic views, see David Zweig, "Bloody, but Unbowed," China Focus 1, No. 3 (November 1990), p. 4.
34. This perspective was confirmed by well-informed Chinese colleagues, who argued that Chinese leaders feared the sanctions as an extension of the effort to overthrow them or change China's political system. Therefore, for these leaders, the criticism of China's human rights policy became major interference in China's internal affairs.
35. After all, one of the main issues of the student movement which Deng had resisted was the revocation of the April 26 editorial in the People's Daily. If Deng could not accept that he was wrong on that decision, he clearly could not recognize his error in calling for the use of force.
36. Interviews in Beijing by the author in March 1990.
37. Interview at the Fairbank Center, Harvard University with a former employee of the Chinese embassy in Washington.
38. At a meeting in March 1990, officials from the Foreign Ministry, Education Commission, Ministries of Public Security and State Security, and the Organizational Bureau and Propaganda Department of the Central Committee, recognized that Sino-American relations had collapsed since the Tiananmen crackdown. They recognized that lifting martial law and releasing political prisoners had limited impact. While they recognized that some Americans, including President Bush, wanted to use a carrot-and-stick approach, maintaining dialogue while denouncing the "June 4 event," they saw releasing prisoners as one of the few "cards" in their hand. See Memorandum from Dr. Haiching Zhao, *Secret Documents from the Chinese Government Relating to Foreign Policy and Chinese Students in the United States and Canada,* 10 May 1990.
39. When congressional supporters of American launch companies tried to block the sales, Defense Department officials argued that the sale to China was tied to efforts to pressure Beijing to be more responsible and not sell destabilizing missile systems to Middle East countries. Once Defense Department officials presented the issue as one of national security to members of the House Subcommittee on East Asia and the Pacific, opponents of the sale could not challenge it.

40. Still, Congressman Lantos was unable to use this omnibus sanctions bill to press for withdrawing MFN from China; the MFN issue belongs to the Ways and Means Committee, which would have challenged the amendment as overstepping jurisdictional lines. Had the amendment included sanctions on MFN, White House supporters in Congress were prepared to use their contacts on Ways and Means to stop the amendment.
41. The member who put this point in the bill did so to save Boeing, but did not tell people why it was being put there. This was the first sale to go through after June 4.
42. Initially, Democrats pressed the House Subcommittee on Asia and the Pacific for a conditional waiver, dependent on the Chinese meeting a list of human rights improvements. But under pressure from presidential supporters on the committee, the bill included only the proviso that either China meet a set of human rights conditions or the president could determine that it was in the interests of national security.
43. One cynical source said that "national interest" means what is politically possible. Yet the term really reflects the ongoing battle between national interest — defined as military security or economic benefits to some American companies — and human rights as to which should be more salient in determining United States foreign policy, as well as a struggle between the president and the Congress over who controls export policy.
44. Republicans on the House subcommittee had worked all along to get a bill that the president would not have to veto, feeling that a weaker bill was clearly better than no bill or a vetoed bill — which would send the Chinese the wrong message. Their ability to threaten Solarz that the president might veto the bill was part of their strategy to get a bill through that would allow the president to protect American business interests in China.
45. Many people in China felt that the students in America were "crossing the river and blowing up the bridge" (*guo he che qiao*) as a way to ensure that they would be allowed to stay.
46. Alexis Feringa Thurman, "The American Response to Tiananmen: Perceptions and Problems," Unpublished Paper, Fletcher School of Law and Diplomacy, Spring 1990, p. 9.
47. See U.S. Department of State, *Country Reports on Human Rights Practices for 1989,* Report submitted to the Committee on Foreign Affairs, House of Representatives and Committee on Foreign Relations, United States Senate. Special thanks to Wayne White for his analysis of the changes in the reports.
48. See Hearings before the Subcommittee on Human Rights and International Organizations, Pacific Affairs, and on International Eco-

nomic Policy and Trade of the Committee on Foreign Affairs, House of Representatives, *Most Favored Nation Status for the People's Republic of China,* 101st Cong., 2nd Sess., 16 and 24 May 1990, p. 7. See also the comments by Congressman Smith which went into the record, pp. 94–95.

49. Author's interview in Washington, August 1990.
50. *Most Favored Nation Status for the People's Republic of China,* p. 22.
51. "Don't Punish the Wrong China" (editorial), *New York Times,* 27 April 1990, p. 34, and "Keeping China's Door Open" (editorial), *Boston Globe,* 15 May 1990, p. 15.
52. The most important of these groups was the China Information Center in Newton, Massachusetts, which had always been seen as a center of anti-China dissidents. Chinese at the center lobbied in favor of MFN in direct conflict with the more radical Independent Federation of Chinese Students and Scholars. Although some of them even supported the president's veto of the Pelosi bill if it increased the likelihood that China would allow more students to go overseas, they too had been intimidated by radical student groups and did not speak out until the MFN debate.
53. A delegation from the United States National Committee on U.S.-China Relations, led by its director, Mike Lampton, made this point in Beijing during March 1990. In the author's own meetings with Zhang Yijun, the director of the North American and Oceania Bureau of the Chinese Foreign Ministry, and with the head of that ministry's American desk in March 1990, both raised the question of whether President Bush had any capital left to help China on MFN. I asserted that the president could not help China if the PRC failed to extend an initial concession to the United States on the human rights issue.
54. Clifford Krauss, "Democratic Leaders Divided on China Trade," *New York Times,* 9 October 1990, p. A-5.
55. The Chinese student organizations reportedly favored "conditional renewal" but feared that if they took that position Congress might give China unconditional renewal. So they advocated overturning MFN expecting or hoping to get Congress to agree to "conditional renewal." Author interviews in Washington, August 1990.
56. See comments by Stephen Solarz in *Most Favored Nation Status for the People's Republic of China,* p. 266.
57. Ibid.
58. Lynn Chu, "Chimera of the China Market," *Atlantic* 266, No. 4, (October 1990), pp. 56–68.
59. The stiffest sentences, thirteen years each for Wang Juntao and Chen Ziming, stem from their long histories of political activism and their abilities to create unofficial political and social organizations.

Part Two

Functional Collaboration

FOUR

The Future of China's Industrialization Program:

Why Should the United States Care?

Dorothy J. Solinger

WHETHER THE UNITED STATES SHOULD CARE about the strategy China chooses in its quest for industrialization is a question which suggests responses on two different levels. We may ask first of all about the impact of *the specific content of any given policy* for the United States — the implications for the bilateral economic relationship of some particular plans the Chinese might pursue. Or, secondly, we might look more broadly at the global level, in light of the new world order appearing on the scene, with its novel emergent regional trade blocs.

To deal with the first inquiry, American business ties with the People's Republic of China (PRC) are assumed to be enduring; in answering it, we do not challenge the fundamental reality of the Sino-American economic relationship. What can be questioned, however, is how this or that move of the Chinese affects particular American industries or commercial concerns. Thus, in thinking on this level we aspire to be well informed about exactly what approach Beijing is emphasizing in its industrial policy at any given moment. To grapple with the second question, though, we may legitimately inquire, Why should we be involved or concerned with China at all?

This chapter addresses the question of American involvement on both the policy content and international systemic levels of analysis. Initially, it focuses on the content of Chinese industrial policies. There appears to have been in China vacillation between two sides of a "dualistic" approach over the past two years. The fluctuation started with a strong commitment to an industrial policy favoring exports and reducing imports, promoting austerity and domestic investment in the basic sectors. This then was followed by a spate of reformist jargon and a few seeming reformist initiatives later on.

This dualism — the coexistence of reform and a belt-tightening, inward-looking reaction — is clearly a Chinese response to contradictory impulses emanating from the PRC's political elite. On one hand, there has been a sense of external threat — economic, political, and ideological. Its roots are two: a fear of "spiritual pollution" from the capitalist world and also a miffed withdrawal in the face of international economic sanctions imposed by the capitalist nations in the aftermath of the Tiananmen crackdown.

This threat perception, along with anxieties about the inevitable negative offshoots of any serious economic reform program (which many in China thought was pressed far too rapidly, causing inflation, uncontrolled foreign trade activity in some localities, and an excess of processing ventures along the Chinese coast as some of the undesirable byproducts of accelerated reform) produced an isolationist backlash. Indeed, there arose a desire to punish the part of China that had experimented most with market practices and was most linked to international markets, particularly the southeastern part of the country. The Eighth Five-Year Plan, published in the autumn of 1990, is predicated on the notion that China must bolster its domestic capital goods, raw material, and infrastructural sectors to ensure its very viability against these threats.

Simultaneously, the Chinese regime's desire to involve outsiders in continued reform never completely dissipated following the tragedy of Tiananmen but has intensified since mid-1990, in the hope of attracting more foreign trade and investment. There are obviously still those in China who truly believe that economic liberalization and involvement in world markets will be essential to revive the still-stagnant Chinese economy that emerged from the PRC's austerity program in late 1988. There are also those who realize China's urgent need for help with producing high-quality exports that can gain hard currency to replace foreign loans and repay old loans soon to come due.

Despite China's bid to build networks with the outside word, to date the recitation of reformist goals has not caused Deng's regime fundamentally to veer away from the basic program installed in the wake of panic over reform's effects in 1988–89. As will be argued below, economic policymakers have selected an economic development package reflecting decisions about a set of five dichotomous choices that are all interrelated. All of them center around the promotion of a sharply delineated industrial policy that gives privileges to domestic heavy industry and exports.

After laying out the background that led China to poise itself between two opposed economic strategies in the late 1980s, and then after indicating the specific solutions picked, this chapter will look more closely at the content of the dominant strategy of these two, the basic-industries-cum-austerity approach. Next, the implications of this Chinese approach for the United States will be assessed by reviewing the several roles in which Americans encounter and deal with the PRC and its economy. The various dimensions along which Chinese policy can change have somewhat disparate consequences — whether the United States is considered as, for instance, an importer, an exporter, or an investor. The chapter concludes by advancing some brief observations about the second, the global, level on which China's growth plans might or might not affect the United States.

China's Economic Policies: 1988–90

Background: A Decade of Reform and the Tiananmen Incident

China's typically wavering course in designating a strategy for industrial growth over the past two years has resulted from a series of reactive reappraisals. First there was the autumn 1988 stocktaking of the economic reforms that had been the mainstay of policy through the 1980s, but which were suddenly felt by many to have produced startlingly ominous effects. Then the Chinese were compelled to cope with the imposition of economic sanctions by the Western powers and Japan following the Tiananmen massacre of June 1989. Most recently, the austerity program that materialized from these two jolts spawned its own set of consequences, and a loosening of some of the shackles binding the economy followed.

The Thirteenth Party Congress of the Chinese Communist party, held in October 1987, provided the final podium on which then-Party General Secretary Zhao Ziyang held forth as the chief promoter of economic reform, a cause he had been championing from his successively more prominent and prestigious positions in the party and state since the late 1970s. That meeting seemed to outside analysts to represent a culmination of the almost decade-long campaign to loosen the strictures of the planned economy. Its slogan — that China was still just in the "primary stage of socialism" — appeared to serve as an alibi for all manner of experimentation with market-type practices. The reasoning popularized by this plenum was that any measure that stimulated the economy would, at least theoretically, prime the productive forces for an eventual transition to a later, more orthodox stage of socialism.

Thus in 1987 and 1988 trials of enterprise bankruptcy, stock markets, enterprise mergers and "enterprise groups," and materials exchange markets began to proliferate within the state-run economy. These were accompanied in the unofficial sphere by an all-too-healthy out-of-plan marketplace, with its double-track pricing system for goods of all types, and by a wide berth given for the private and collective sectors of the economy.

Along with this loosening in the domestic economy, in early 1988 a pet plan of Zhao's, the "coastal zone economic development strategy," opened several coastal provinces to foreign investment and technology, giving a boost to the labor-intensive, non-state-owned processing industries so prevalent along the southeast coast, especially in Guangdong and Fujian provinces.[1] This policy added extra energy to the already explosive development of these processing ventures, as Hong Kong capitalists moved their operations over into the mainland to take advantage of preferential tax rates, cheap labor, and more plentiful land than they had access to at home.

These firms were able to pay higher prices for the raw materials they needed than state concerns could afford, constrained as they were to charge state-set prices for their goods. Because of their flexibility, the non-state firms were then able to siphon off supplies the government intended for its larger and more essential factories.[2] The most common way of describing the dislocations that ensued was to say that "the development of the processing industries far surpassed the capacity of the energy, transportation, and raw materials industries."[3] Another not insignificant issue was that middlemen with the right contacts were profiting from diverting these commodities away from the official track and reaping profits from the differential between the prices at which they could purchase them and the prices they could go on to command for them on the market.

Also in 1988, the already notable decentralization scheme of 1985 was taken even a step further. The earlier reform had turned many commodities previously handled by the trading corporations attached to the central Ministry of Foreign Economic Relations (MOFERT) over to the corporations' provincial branches. In the 1988 liberalization the central government relinquished controls over export licenses to provinces or even to lower levels of administration, while local governments were allowed to retain 80 percent of the foreign exchange revenue they earned beyond base levels set in 1987.[4] These new stipulations released the localities from following priorities for foreign trade that might have ben entertained in Beijing and set them off into sprees of unregulated profit-seeking, often at the expense of the state's crucial resources.

A third innovation in 1988 was the decision made in the spring, reportedly by Deng Xiaoping but pushed ahead by Zhao Ziyang, to free up the prices for many commodities formerly regulated by the state. Rumors of this plan reached the populace in force in the ensuing months, causing immediate inflationary shocks.

The 1980s were a decade that had seen much official speculation feeding off the double-track pricing system, and it also witnessed both mass incomes (wages and bonuses in state industry, profits in the private sector, and from free market and other entrepreneurial activity in the countryside) and state subsidies (for prices and for enterprise losses) rising steadily, far beyond productivity.[5] On top of this, by late summer a racing inflation rate — already appraised to be in the neighborhood of 20 percent — shot up higher than ever.[6] Some estimates ran as high as 50 percent for key foodstuffs in the major cities; a more likely unofficial evaluation put overall figures at 30 percent by year's end.[7] Bank runs and hoarding of staples broke out in alarming proportions in August, accompanying and further feeding the inflationary spiral.

Combined with a continuously growing deficit in the state budget, [8] these developments triggered among the majority of the leadership a rapid rethinking of economic strategy followed by a swift reining in of the economy. By September, a rigorous austerity program, called an "economic adjustment" or "economic rectification," was installed. The measures included a sudden and severe freezing of prices; a transferral of the power of approval for foreign trade activity back to the central level; an effort, as in the past, to guide economic behavior through setting quotas and norms in the capital; a closing off of credit; large cuts in currency issuance; a scaling back of capital construction targets; and the cancellation of projects already conceived.

Thus, many reasoned, the economic reform and opening to the outside world which had been the hallmark of the 1980s had exceeded the bounds of what the economy could sustain. It had thrown the system seriously out of balance, causing excess demand; an inadequacy of supplies, resources, and financial power; and rampant price rises.

Not surprisingly, this draconian retrenchment bred its own array of difficulties. In the succeeding months the sluggish market, capital shortage, closure of some enterprises (with an attendant rise in unemployment, reportedly doubling, to about 4 percent by the end of 1989[9]), and general slowdown in economic activity only heightened the state deficit, pegged at 9.535 billion yuan for 1989.[10] The deficit increased as enterprises found themselves unable to pay their bills, and inter-enterprise debts skyrocketed to 100 billion yuan by 1989.

State subsidies used to compensate enterprises suffering losses amounted to 60 million yuan, and, combined with subsidies on prices granted to state firms and foreign traders, the central government was compelled to invest a total of 100 billion yuan in state enterprises that year.[11] Within a year of the onset of the austerity program, the Chinese economy had fallen 2.1 percent below its level a year earlier; [12] profits of state-owned enterprises continued to drop into the first half of 1990, and this then ate even more into state returns.[13]

These troubles coincided with, and of course were exacerbated by, the economic sanctions that came in the wake of the killings of June 1989. Just as the Chinese political elite had been struggling to "rectify" what in their eyes had been an overly liberalized economy, the international reprisals for the Tiananmen massacre rendered their job of making do on a shorter string much more challenging. Cutoffs of loans and investment and a reduction in the PRC's overall trade volume added to the chronic lack of working capital. This went on to affect foreign firms as well as domestic ones. Simultaneously, the state's demand for foreign firms to rely on local sourcing became harder than usual to fulfill, with the generalized stagnation of domestic production.[14]

Probably partly because of the austerity program and also in part as a result of lessened foreign interest, China concluded 25 percent fewer contracts for importing technology in 1989 than in 1988, and the value of contracts went down by 15 percent.[15] Import controls and increased licensing requirements checked purchases as the government tried to limit spending.[16] The state also re-centralized and tightened up on approval mechanisms that had been decentralized only a year before.[17] Total foreign trade fell by 3.2 percent in the first five months of 1990 (exports rose, but imports declined).[18]

It was not so much government sanctions as the specter of ideological rigidity and political and social instability that affected investment in the aftermath of Tiananmen. Already by the third quarter of 1989, foreign investment had dropped 25 percent as compared with the same period the year before;[19] in the first half of 1990, it was down by 22 percent as compared with the same period the year before.[20] In Guangdong province, investment dropped 20 percent in the first quarter of 1991,[21] while 46.6 percent of the foreign-funded enterprises were losing money.[22] Quite unfortunately for the Chinese, these several sorts of drop-offs came about just as major payments fell due (in 1990) on the foreign debt of $40 billion which China had chalked up over the past decade.[23]

In short, over the two years from 1988 to 1990 the leadership in China had to come to grips with two occurrences which amounted to major challenges. One of these was a deeply disquieting realization that, by their form of reckoning, the reform program which had seemed so rosy only shortly before had wrought difficulties too massive for even this old-line leadership to ignore; the other was an international pariahhood perhaps even more severe than the one from China had recovered only a decade or so before. Both of these crises resulted in economic contractions, one chosen and the other in part imposed. How, concretely, did the leadership essay to meet these challenges?

Dorothy J. Solinger

Economic Strategies and Solutions in the Post-Tiananmen Period

Five different responses met the disillusionment with reform and the post-Tiananmen economic crisis in China. The first and most persistently and energetically pursued of these has been the effort to impose an industrial policy upon the country's industrial agenda, and upon the PRC's foreign economic contacts as well. Two other policies announced more or less simultaneously entailed encouraging exports and placing faith — and some policy emphasis — in technological upgrading and high-tech schemes.

During 1990, experiments from the reform period reemerged, first with the promotion of enterprise groups and mergers and the opening of two securities exchanges, and later with signs of a generalized loosening up, including lowered interest rates, release of locked-up loan capital, and permission for previously blocked new capital construction to go back onstream.

The plan to enforce an industrial policy surfaced around November 1989, when the Thirteenth Central Committee's Sixth Plenum put forward a thirty-nine-point plan favoring large enterprises and reducing the autonomy that had been thriving in the south. Raw-material distribution was to be allocated centrally, as in pre-reform days, with priority accorded the major state firms. The southern coastal provinces were to suffer a reduction in their ability to approve projects, handle their finances, and retain foreign exchange.[24]

A project in the same spirit was announced in March 1990. This one granted concessions to what were entitled "double-guarantee" enterprises. For some four or five dozen large-scale state-owned concerns in the northeast, the state planned to ensure the delivery of energy, raw materials, communications, and transportation in exchange for finished products, profits, and tax payments to the state. The enterprises involved accounted for about 90 percent of the coal and steel output, and all the petroleum, electrical power, non-ferrous metals, motor vehicles, and electricity-generating equipment produced for distribution by the state from three provinces of Liaoning, Jilin, and Heilongjiang.[25]

Both of these programs reflect the concept of the industrial policy that the state began promulgating in late 1989. It is premised on strengthening the basic industries, which policymakers believe the processing industries had been squeezing out in the reform period. Around the beginning of 1990 all of the state's administrative apparatus was turned toward providing preferential treatment for firms in the key sectors of transportation, energy, and raw materials production. Agencies ordered to act on these priorities included the Ministry of Materials and Equipment; the People's Bank; the tax, commercial, statistical, and price departments; and, at the head of it all, the State Planning Commission, which was newly equipped with an Industrial Policy Bureau.[26]

In the realm of foreign economic relations, by the second half of 1989 China was cutting its imports of consumer goods.[27] The *China Daily* announced in the spring of 1990 that, in the first ten months of 1989, Shenzen alone had rejected 196 foreign-funded projects that failed to meet the criteria of China's structural adjustment.[28]

In early 1990, the Bank of China offered preferential treatment for foreign-funded enterprises that produce exportable goods as well as for firms working in the basic sectors, those whose products could be used as import substitutes, and those with advanced technology that could update existing industrial facilities. MOFERT and the foreign exchange control departments also prepared detailed rules for carrying out the policy.[29]

At a symposium on trade and investment between the mainland and Taiwan held in early July 1990, the State Planning Commission released a list of priorities for foreign investment which again included advanced technology, export-oriented industry, and new equipment and materials. At the same time, it expressed a lack of interest in low-grade light industry and textile products, general machinery and electrical goods, and domestic-oriented durable electronic products.[30]

Accompanying this policy of sectoral choice was a distinct regional strategy, clearly geared like its sectoral twin to reorient industrialization away from the bases of the reform era. Reportedly a compromise plan was struck in March 1990, according to which the southern regions would receive only the minimum of economic encouragement from the central government, while largess would go instead to other regions, namely the northeast, some inland provinces, and the prosperous eastern provinces.[31]

Later news items had it that Guangdong and Hainan had been instructed to slow down and that Shanghai would reap the benefit.

Apparently the new strategy gave little berth to the processing and assembly operations that had flourished so mightily in the Pearl River Delta during the heyday of Zhao Ziyang's policies.[32]

Linked to the general industrial policy, the second prong of the post-crises policy was focused upon enhancing the quantity of China's exports while reducing imports. Especially in the aftermath of the freeze in foreign lending that followed the Tiananmen crackdown, as an economist at the U.S. International Trade Commission explained, "The Chinese are desperately trying to increase their exports. . . . It [China] must now depend almost entirely on export revenues for hard currency."[33] In the first four months of 1990 exports had risen by 14.62 percent to $15.58 billion.[34] In part this was China's way in the late 1980s and early 1990s of putting into practice Mao's old prescription of self-reliance in the face of adversity. As late as March 1990, Politburo Standing Committee member Song Ping reminded the nation that even while China continued opening up it should also enhance self-reliance in the face of economic sanctions.[35]

The other way the Chinese leadership hoped to maintain — or, more precisely, attain — an augmented self-reliance was through increasing its technological capabilities. Along with attention to the basic industries, economists hoped to apply advanced technology and equipment to upgrade China's competitiveness in world markets.[36] The 1990s are also slated to see a major overhaul of the computer industry in China, both to meet growing domestic demand and to export parts. Investment and preferential treatment will go to the largest government-owned (as distinct from the so called *minban,* ("people-managed") computer companies in the next five years.[37]

Yet one more sign of this interest in technological enhancement appeared when the press boasted of some thirty high-tech zones scheduled to become an important part of the national economy. These were to receive preferential support to attract foreign and joint ventures, it was announced.[38] The press report claimed that in the past year, enterprise zones had begun to merge into group corporations to take advantage of economies of scale.

This mention of enterprise groups harks back to the heady days of reform when such concerns were vaunted as capitalistic practices that could invigorate the economy. Beginning in the spring of 1990, when they were heard of once again, those forming enterprise groups were instead instructed to build them in fields that satisfied the structural requisites of China's industrial policy.[39]

But the clearest signal that reform policies were to be experimented with once again was the announcement of the opening of the securities exchanges in Shenzen and Shanghai.[40] It seems that the rigors of the austerity program had so deflated the economy that those who had first called for retrenchment had eventually to cede to liberalizers, if not on the same scale as during the 1980s.

Already at the National People's Congress held in March, Premier Li Peng advocated more play for the role of the market. He also asked for easy money policies to bolster the sluggish economic activity the country had been experiencing for a year and a half at that point.[41] As a Hong Kong journalist reported, "The conservative leaders have not been able to turn the clock back completely on a decade of market oriented reforms."[42]

The first step back toward lifting restraints came in the form of financial assistance disbursed from the center. Between January and April 1990, loans totaling more than 55 billion yuan were issued to help large and medium enterprises boost production and purchase materials needed to produce daily necessities and items for export.[43] Going a step further, by the end of May 1990, a new appraisal of development policy had become official.

Along with a statement that industry had only grown 0.5 percent in the first four months of 1990, the *China Daily* reasoned, "The current growth rate may be too low and affect State revenues and unemployment."[44] The article used this circumstance to legitimize a return to a more stimulatory policy: "A series of measures have been adopted to fine tune economic leverage to let a revitalized market pass greater incentives to industry." These measures included an increase in loans, a cautious expansion of capital construction, a moderate scaling down of interest rates, and some major moves to induce foreign investment.[45]

Here we see, then, that the Chinese leadership was essentially floundering in economic and industrial policy during the two years from autumn 1988 through autumn 1990. Initially startled by what many of its prominent members perceived as chaos wrought by reform, these leaders nonetheless returned, if quite gingerly to date (late 1990) to some of the tenets of reform policy in a little over a year and a half, in the face of consequences that overly stringent austerity measures had produced. Or, as some have reasoned, the attempt to rely strictly on a centrally coordinated industrial policy emphasizing particular sectors and regions perhaps was no longer possible once the reform program had reshaped the economic structure and heightened the provinces' sense of entitlement to go their own ways.[46]

China's Industrialization Strategies: Choices and Implications

For the two years from September 1988 through August 1990 Chinese decisionmakers approached their economy and its direction in terms of five divergent choices. It is possible to consider these five dimensions separately, but in fact they belong to a total package. Choices along one dimension structure the choices in other dimensions, at least if one adopts the framework and development philosophy embraced by the conservative leadership in charge of the national economy after August 1988.

The dimensions along which these men made their selections are these: first, there is the decision to stimulate the economy and to be expansionary as opposed to adopting a reliance on austerity measures. The second election concerns the mode of organization of economic behavior, that is, whether the economy is to be primarily plan-driven or mainly market-driven, with key decisions centrally controlled or decentralized.

Third, sectoral choice within industry may be either for heavy industry, giving priority treatment to the basic industries such as transport and communications, raw materials and energy, or for light industry, primarily consumer goods production or the processing industries. The larger, state-owned enterprises benefit under a pro-heavy industry policy, while the collective and private sectors, with their much smaller firms, are privileged under a pro-light industry policy. Related to this is the fourth pair of alternatives, this one concerned with regional orientation. The main options here are for coastal as against inland regions. And finally, there is the question of foreign involvement, whether to encourage it or to fall back upon some modified version of self-reliance, and also how and how much to guide such involvement.

After late 1988 Chinese decisionmakers by and large chose a

package all of whose ingredients derive from the choice of the austerity approach. This program was meant to deflate the policies that the politicians in charge of the economy from that time onward believed had proven too expansionist and too inflationary. All of the other choices flowed from that one; they have been tightly bound together as corollaries of the austerity program, according to this particular Chinese leadership perspective.

In the world view of these officials, austerity is best handled by concentrating resources and decisions in the capital to the extent possible and by reintroducing administrative modes of steering economic activity. The "double guarantee" program described above seems to be an only slightly disguised effort to reinstitute the authority of the state plan, in order to bind enterprises to meet targets set for them by bureaucracies. Those determined to restore balance and stability to the economy considered that the upheavals and overheating in the economy under the reign of Zhao Ziyang were the consequences of a reformist program that entailed excessive dependence upon market-type practices. Thus, cooling off and tightening up were seen as best achieved through a return to centralized, plan-motivated tactics.

These tactics could be most effectively pursued, the reasoning went, by an appropriate sectoral policy. In this case, for China's political elite this meant diminishing the amount of consumer goods produced in China — which ate up supplies and strained capacity — as well as those imported into China, and instead propping up with state largess the factors of production, the basic sectors. This was in part an economic choice in the period of austerity. But it was later also spurred by political events: after the June 1989 crackdown and the imposition of sanctions that followed, the leadership, feeling isolated and threatened, became pronouncedly more serious about ensuring that China's infrastructure and energy supply could meet its own needs, and that its transport and raw materials were put into the service of essential, state-designated projects.

Illustrating this thrust is a list of major construction projects the state hoped to foster in 1990. Among them were plans to increase coal production capacity by 24 million tons, add 8 million kilowatts of power generating capacity, increase ethylene production capacity by 1.2 million tons, and complete 852 kilometers of electrified railway.[47]

The regional strategy went hand in glove with the promotion of basic industries. More than 60 percent of China's exports are produced in the south, where private, village, and foreign-managed plants operate on market principles.[48] The experience of having developed such a quasi-capitalist environment rendered this area especially suspect in the eyes of the aged leaders, and they have turned away from it in distaste. As a Hong Kong commentator explained it:

> The SEZ's were abandoned by the Center after June 4 [1989] . . . [They] became a site for rampant bourgeois liberalization in the reform era and after June 4 turned into a place of escape and an underground railway.[49]

As noted above, Guangdong province, where Hong Kong and Taiwan capitalists had opened small, low-tech factories to process light industrial products,[50] saw its foreign-funded firms losing money and its investment from abroad curtailed; and it had to suffer restrictions on its consumer-oriented imports,[51] even as the central government also recentralized control over some sixty or seventy export commodities.[52] Moreover, the labor-intensive operations that thrived in Guangdong were downplayed in the interest of revitalizing sections of China where heavy industry has a firm foundation, such as the northeast, Shanghai, and the Yangtze valley. In that time of desperate scrambling for export-derived income, a vice-minister in the Ministry of Foreign Economic and Trade Relations explained the logic behind the shift as follows:

> Most of our foreign cooperation efforts with direct investment are in processing. . . . The shortage of energy and raw materials has impeded the productivity of foreign-invested enterprises. . . . We must try our best to ensure the steady development of exports.[53]

A prominent example of this changed regional policy is a plan that had been on the drawing board for some years. This scheme, to develop an industrial zone named "Pudong" on farmland in eastern Shanghai, was finally launched in the spring of 1990. Although the project is intended ultimately to turn Shanghai into a prosperous financial center and a major harbor, the first stage of its development will be aimed at laying down the infrastructure.

This plan symbolizes a basic shift in regional planning for the nation as a whole. For one thing, this is the first time since 1949 that the central government has created a special zone in the industrial heartland of the country. Also, Shanghai's growth is meant to stimulate development of the entire upper and middle Yangtze valley, bringing new dynamicism not just to Shanghai's neighbors, Jiangsu and Zhejiang, but to Anhui, Hubei, and Sichuan as well. These areas are notably rich in raw materials and are linked to Shanghai through a railway trunk line.[54]

All of these first four choices were taken in part as a response to China's predicament in its foreign ties; each choice also has implications for the slant at which China's door will be opened in the near term. Various unsettling factors — the $40 billion foreign debt China had to begin repaying during 1990, the economic sanctions imposed after June 4, the drop-off in foreign investment, and the realization that the preponderance of foreign investment projects in the 1980s had done relatively little to enhance China's modernization in any basic way — all combined to dispose the leadership to steel itself for greater self-reliance by strengthening its own basic industry.

These circumstances also led China's leadership to try regulating and steering the use of future investment from Beijing once again — hence the recentralization of foreign trade decisionmaking and the effort to subsume foreign investment within the scope of the industrial policy that accompanied this recentralization. The Bank of China and the Ministry of Materials and Equipment, among others, instituted priority incentive programs for foreign-funded firms that advance the basic sectors, that produce export goods, and that channel funds into upgrading China's domestic industry, especially in the areas of machinery and electronics, so that the country can be more competitive on the world market.[55] The Chinese government also made clear that investment was no longer welcome in sectors such as textiles or hotels, or in projects for which there would be no investment in technology.[56]

Moreover, foreign investment was suddenly encouraged in Shanghai, which in 1989 led the nation in volume of foreign currency trading, at $1.29 billion. Beijing also reduced the foreign exchange earnings retention rate in the special economic zones — previously 100 percent — down to only 80 percent, while Shanghai was permitted to keep 33 percent of its revenue from foreign trade in 1989, as against only 25 percent in 1988.[57]

Thus, the decision to retrench taken in autumn 1988 had repercussions for a string of related fundamental options. That these choices — for more centralized administrative control, for the basic sectors, and away from the coast — may steer the economy for at least the first few years of the 1990s is a reasonable assumption, since they have been enshrined in the Eighth Five-Year Plan, scheduled to govern investment policy through 1995.[58]

Implications for the United States

After reviewing the options and alternatives in development strategy among which the Chinese have selected in the past two years, we are now in a position to address the question of American concerns about the course China charts in a certain period in its industrialization program. But the response is best formulated by disaggregating: a specific Chinese strategy such as the one set forth above has different implications depending on whether one considers the United States as importer and buyer of Chinese goods, as exporter and seller to the Chinese market, or as investor and joint venture partner.

The United States as Importer

As a purchaser of Chinese goods, the United States must confront two main concerns. The first of these is individual commodities — whether protectionism is called for, either because of the imports' competition with American-made goods, because of the possibility of Chinese dumping, or because of the competition between Chinese-made items and those made in other East Asian countries with which Washington is allied. The other issue relates to the United States' overall balance of trade with China, that is, whether the current deficit in Sino-American trade relations bodes badly for the American economy or at least for particular sectors within it.

Specifically, how has the industrialization strategy implemented by China over the past two years affected these two areas, competition and deficit? U.S. Department of Commerce statistics do show a mounting Chinese trade surplus with the United States, if re-exports from Hong Kong are added in. According to the reckoning of the United States government, this trade deficit in China's favor grew from $3.5 billion in 1988 to $6.2 billion in 1989.[59] Also, in the first eight months of 1989 there was a 50 percent increase in China's exports to the United States, according to the Department of Commerce.[60]

Then, in the first two months of 1990, China's trade surplus with the United States rose 79.2 percent higher than it had been during the same period in 1989.[61] This imbalance can be explained by the fact that Chinese exports rose 19.1 percent while imports from the United States were down by 9.6 percent in the first five months of 1990.[62] These figures clearly resulted from China's recent intensive push to promote exports and cut down on imports, as it responded to the economic difficulties outlined earlier in this chapter.

The austerity program of late 1988 matters to the United States for another reason. The revived centralization of decisionmaking affects the type of commodities whose production will be given preferential treatment within China and the type of products that will be exported. Some aspects of China's sectoral policy could reduce the output of some of China's key exports to the United States. For instance, toys, luggage, and shoes together jumped from 2.3 percent of total exports in 1983 to 17.6 percent of the total in 1988.[63] However, these items are light industrial products and thus not priority trades under the new industrial policy.[64] And to the extent that these commodities are produced in the smaller-scale, collectively run firms on the southeast coast, they will also be more neglected than before by central government investments and benefits. Other categories of Chinese exports, however, such as industrial equipment and consumer electronics, will be favored under this policy, and these already had climbed from nearly nothing to almost $1 billion by 1985.[65]

Yet competition is less a problem at present than the trade surplus or any shifting composition of exports that might occur. Quotas limiting the growth of textile imports from China into the United States — once the chief irritant as a competitive import — to only 3 percent a year were set in 1987, and these will hold through 1991. Moreover, though textiles remain a potential source of long-term Sino-American friction, the Chinese have admitted that the retrenchment has rendered textiles "much less competitive" internationally during 1990. This was because of their poor quality, caused by the provision of insufficient funds to the industry. Moreover, the small amount of funds that were available needed to be spent for expensive raw materials.[66]

Worldwide, Chinese textile imports in the first half of 1990 were 39 percent below what they were in the same period of 1989.[67] Given this downward trend, which has benefited other Asian cotton exporters, including Taiwan, our greater restrictions on textile imports from Taiwan and South Korea (much higher than China's to begin with, but limited to only 1 percent annual growth in the 1987 agreement) may be more palatable than before.

As for dumping, the list of items recently under scrutiny does not at this time include any major commodities. They are sparklers (fireworks), heavy-forged handtools such as axes and picks, industrial nitrocellulose, cloth headware, tapered roller bearings for bikes and cars, and some cookware. Although some of these items could continue to be problems under the current industrial policy, China is not yet at a point where its high-tech products make any real impact (even at a billion dollars in 1989, Chinese electronic exports still comprise only a tiny share of the United States market).[68] And it is this type of product that most concerns those worried about foreign dumping.[69]

Thus, in the United States' role as an importer, China's present industrial policy emphasizing basic industries and exports could pose certain challenges to American businesses. If so, however, it is more because of Washington's rising trade deficit with the PRC than it is because of any specific product competition between the Americans and the Chinese.

The United States as Exporter

As sellers to the Chinese market, American business interests face similar issues related to the package of retrenchment policies of the past two years. As the government shut out many imports and reduced credit to domestic companies after late 1988, Chinese purchases that would have taken place under the regime of Zhao

Ziyang have not occurred. American exports to China, which had expanded by 16 percent to $5.7 billion in 1989, dropped a percentage point during the first two months of 1990, to $876 million, as against the same period the year before.

Another effect of the austerity program has been the need to obtain agreement from the central Chinese government, under more stringent rules, for certain types of trade proposals. In the main, these are proposals for which local officials had been considered competent to dispense approval — and had done so much more liberally — in the past.[70]

But the sectoral priorities of what the Chinese call their "economic rectification" need not necessarily hurt all American exporters. Some will probably stand to gain, once some loosening of the frugality sets in. Two of the major exports to China from the United States in past years — aviation and power-generating equipment — fit well into China's priority list today, and both have continued to see good sales.[71] Other American goods supplied to China over the past decade include machinery, locomotives, computers, and instruments, and these should continue to be in demand during the Eighth Plan.[72]

For instance, with the current emphasis on infrastructure and communications, the United States is in a position to respond to applications made beginning in mid-1990 from over a dozen cities to import technology and equipment for subway and light rail transit systems.[73] In short, if concentration on the basic industries can be decoupled from its original bond to the austerity program, there could be even greater scope for some American sales than under Zhao. Significant downgrading of the retrenchment policies, however, will probably be contingent on the resumption of loans from the West on a large scale.

The United States as Investor

The same stringency that dictated a reduction in imports also worked to scale down American investment in China after mid-1989. In part this reduction took place because American investors became less interested in starting up new projects than they were before the jolt in June.

The Chinese central government, through MOFERT, also began exercising much stricter controls over investment than before.

The Chinese started to approve projects more selectively than previously, in the interest of ensuring that those that go forward turn out exportable goods and provide modern technology for China's own industry and that they meet the specifications of China's industrial policy. The State Council's Leading Group on Foreign Investment also announced that all foreign-invested projects competing with domestic producers must obtain MOFERT approval, as must projects in the non-priority sectors, such as consumer goods, textiles, and hotels.[74]

As a result of these disincentives, American investment in China dropped in 1990: in the first quarter of the year, according to MOFERT, American companies signed sixty-five investment contracts worth $48 million, which is far below past levels. (In the first half of 1989, by contrast, American corporations signed contracts worth $382 million, which was about a threefold increase over the same period in 1988.)[75]

But again, the longer-term picture may be more promising as large-ticket investments are ultimately more compatible with an infrastructural and high-tech development plan than with a consumer-goods-first approach. Americans, for instance, will be supplying tunneling equipment and signaling devices to help in the Pudong development program.[76] A prospective joint venture with the U.S. Dresser Industries Group was expected to be signed in 1990 for producing mining equipment (eight 154-ton dump trucks for the Dexing mine in Jiangxi province).[77] The focus on upgrading Chinese high-tech has led to contracts with AT&T and Motorola for the production of TV and audio equipment chips and semiconductors, respectively.[78]

Indeed, in general the late 1980s saw the earlier cooperation in tourism and light industry between China and the United States shift to aviation, electronics, power, telecommunications, automobiles, building materials, coal mining equipment, and offshore oil exploration and development.[79] A final consideration is that if the Chinese succeed in improving their communications and transport infrastructure and their energy production, American investors in China will certainly be among the beneficiaries in the long run.[80]

To summarize, China's austerity program led to short-term losses for American business, partly because it coincided with a period of troubling political instability and distasteful governmental policies which cooled American interest in new investment and exchange. Problems for Americans also arose because of the tightness both for purchases and for credit. But the priority list that accompanies the austerity program, originally designed at least partly as a component in a kind of refurbished "self-reliance" strategy, may well outlast that program and turn out to serve American business very well. This will depend upon the willingness of the United States and other industrialized nations to come forward with loans once again.

In Global Terms, Why Should the United States Care?

Most of this chapter has concentrated on ascertaining where the Chinese see themselves heading at this time, why they are moving in a certain direction, and what the implications might be for the American economy. To arrive at an answer to the second, global-level question raised at this chapter's outset — whether we should or need concern ourselves about China — inherently transcends economic issues. Strategic concerns of a new sort can also dictate that we pay attention to China.

Even though, as the discussion above has shown, the United States can offer the kind of technology and equipment that the Chinese basic industries development program demands, other countries possess specific advantages in meeting these demands that may be more suitable to the Chinese economy than what American firms can offer. This is especially the case in a time like the present, when the Chinese economy is short on capital and when the United States and other Western nations are reluctant to resume loans to China. At such a time, China's specific strategy of industrialization is less the issue; its feeling of relative poverty and isolation becomes the more salient point.

Potentially most worrisome among the various other nations whose commercial, investment, and technological dealings with the Chinese might rival our own are the Soviet Union and Japan. In 1990, both nations jumped into gaps created by the United States' policy of sanctions directed against the PRC.

In 1990 alone, as if to prove the sincerity of Japan's commitment to China despite the actions of other countries, the Japanese private sector and government were quite active. Japanese companies set up ventures in a new industrial development zone in Ningbo,[81] Japanese banks and enterprises formed groups to survey the new Pudong industrial zone,[82] and two of Japan's financial institutions and one of its biggest industrial companies formed a new joint venture-leasing company in China to finance the imports (presumably from Japan) of machinery and raw materials that China so desperately needs.[83] Japanese firms are also involved in the upgrading of China's computer capabilities.[84] As an American journalist explained, the Japanese government and its private sector "regard China as holding immense strategic importance as a major market and a low-cost production base."[85]

Most significantly of all, Japan reinstituted its stalled massive low-interest loan program — which is to fund Japanese projects in China, including railways, port centers, and phone lines — before any of the Western nations returned to the loans-for-China business. As the *New York Times* commentator who reported on this move viewed it, this was done "implicitly to encourage China to see Japan as its most reliable ally among the industrialized nations."[86]

The Soviet Union has also been busy courting the PRC. Perhaps as an entering wedge, the two nations agreed in 1990 to establish the first Sino-Soviet joint venture in China, a linen mill, to be situated in Inner Mongolia.[87] On a far grander scale, a ten-year agreement was signed during Li Peng's trip to Moscow in April 1990. This will entail joint concerns in the high-tech and nuclear power areas, in fuel and power industries, and in transport and communications.[88] The agreement took place after a period of growing collaboration, beginning with a 1985 set of technological cooperation agreements for constructing and reconstructing industrial projects, followed by an additional seventeen projects in 1987–88 and the building of a railway from Xinjiang into the Soviet Union in 1988.[89]

The latent threat behind Soviet technological assistance appears when that assistance becomes defense aid: Moscow has offered to help in the modernization of Chinese defense plants on generous terms. Since many of these plants — like many of those in other industrial sectors, especially in basic industry — started with Soviet technology transfers in the 1950s, and since Soviet equipment is now far easier for the Chinese to absorb than more sophisticated and more expensive Western technology, the financially strapped Chinese military is eager to accept it.[90]

Neither the Japanese nor the Soviets put specific strings on their loans and aid to China. The danger for the United States in such cooperation and exchange is obviously not merely losing out on specific economic deals. A more acute risk is that increased wooing by either or both the Soviet Union and Japan may well pull China into some kind of condominium with one or the other of them in a way that could largely shut out the United States — perhaps limiting it to its own little North American trade bloc — from Northeast Asia's future economic growth and geopolitical framework. A Hong Kong analyst has recently asserted that "in the U.S. effort to check the Soviet Union and Japan, China has an irreplaceable role to play."[91]

In these times when the alignments and commitments of the major powers float in a still unpredictable flux and world affairs are taking on a multipolar character, what counts for the United States is not what kind of industrialization program China follows. Certainly, over time, there is room for American business interests to take part, whatever the situation. What really counts, then, is not the answer to the first question — of our caring about the specific substance of Chinese industrialization programs. More central is our finding answers to the dilemmas of China's economic vulnerability and political soul-searching in the context of that country's future global relationships — the second level of analysis we have considered here. The Chinese economy must remain vigorous enough and linked enough into the economies of a number of other countries that it need not fall into the role of "junior partner" to another major East Asian power. To avoid that outcome, the United States needs to be ready to support and to remain involved in China's industrialization program, whatever shape it may take.

NOTES

1. *Japan Economic Journal,* 19 May, 1990, translated and reprinted in Foreign Broadcast Information Service, China (hereafter cited as FBIS-CHI), 4 June 1990, Annex, p. 10.
2. Martin Weil, "China's Exports: On the Edge," *China Business Review* (hereafter CBR) 17, No. 1 (January–February 1990), p. 43.
3. One place among many where this phrasing may be found is in Liu Zepu, "China's Economic Rectification and Sino-U.S. Economic and Trade Relations," *Foreign Affairs Journal* (Beijing), No. 16 (June 1990), p. 4.
4. Weil, "China's Exports," p. 38.
5. See "The Chinese Economy in 1988" (Abridged translation of a State Statistics Bureau report analyzing China's economic performance in 1988), *Beijing Review* (hereafter *BR*) 32, No. 6 (12 February 1989), p. 22, which states that there was an 80 billion yuan gap between purchasing power and goods available in 1988; another report noted that the purchasing power generated by excess issuance of currency by the state had exceeded the supply capacity by more than 20 percent as of late 1988 [*Renmin Ribao* (People's Daily), 8 December 1988, translated in *FBIS-CHI,* 20 December 1988, p. 32].
6. In 1987, an additional 20 billion yuan in banknotes was issued to cope with rising demands for cash. See the article by Chuang Ming, "Reform on the Mainland Is Facing the Danger of Retrogression and the Revered Mr. Deng Appears to Be Personally Stemming the Anti-Arab Tide," *Ching Pao,* 10 December 1988, pp. 14–17; as translated and reprinted in *FBIS-CHI,* 16 December 1988, p. 26. By December 1988, it was estimated that the currency in circulation could rise by another 35 percent for that year. See "Year End Special Article," by the Midterm Research Planning Team for Economic Reform under the Development and Research Center of the State Council. "Reform Is Where the Hope of the Individual of the Whole Nation Lies — Thoughts about Certain Major Problems of Economic Reform," *Renmin Ribao,* 8 December 1988, p. 15; translated and reprinted in *FBIS-CHI,* 20 December 1988, p. 32.
7. According to "The Chinese Economy in 1988," *BR,* No. 6 (1989), p. 23, in 1988 retail prices rose by 18.5 percent and the consumer price index by 20.7 percent, figures, the magazine claimed, "never witnessed since the founding of New China in 1949."
8. The deficit went from 7.06 billion yuan in 1986 to 7.95 billion in 1987 and 80.5 billion in 1988. These figures are in Zhongguo Tongjiju (China Statistical Bureau), ed., *Zhongguo Tongji Nianjian 1989* (Chi-

nese Statistical Yearbook) (Beijing: Zhongguo Tongji Chubanshe, 1989), p. 657.

9. John Kohnt, "Reformers Find 'Comfort,' See Glimmer of Hope," *South China Sunday Morning Post* (hereafter *SCMP*), 3 June 1990, reprinted in *FBIS-CHI,* 5 June 1990, p. 29.
10. This figure is from a *Xinhua* report, "National Economic Report Issued," 21 March 1990, pp. 12–14; translated and reprinted in *FBIS-CHI,* 22 March 1990, p. 12.
11. These figures came from an interview with noted Chinese economist Li Yining in Fan Cheuk-wan, "Austerity Relaxation Urged to Avert Crisis: Li Yining," *Hong Kong Standard,* 29 March 1990, p.7; reprinted in *FBIS-CHI,* 4 April 1990, p. 36.
12. *Japan Economic Journal,* 31 May 1990, in *FBIS-CHI,* 4 June 1990, Annex, p. 9.
13. James Sterngold, "Calls for Economic Changes Rise among Chinese Officials," *New York Times,* 30 July 1990, pp. A-1, D-5.
14. Richard Brecher, "The End of Investment's Wonder Years," *CBR* 16, No. 5 (January/February 1990), pp. 28–29.
15. Zhang Peidong, "Foreign Trade Grows Steadily," *BR* 33, No. 27 (2–8 July 1990), p. 30.
16. Brecher, "End of Investment's Wonder Years," p. 11.
17. John Frisbie and Richard Brecher, "What to Watch For," *CBR* 16, No. 5 (September/October 1989), p. 11.
18. Staff Reporter, "Falling Imports Cause Dip in Foreign Trade," *China Daily* (hereafter *CD*), 11 June 1990, p. 2; reprinted in *FBIS-CHI,* 13 June 1990, p. 38.
19. Brecher, "End of Investment's Wonder Years," p. 27.
20. Sterngold, "Calls for Economic Changes Rise among Chinese Officials."
21. Elizabeth Cheng, "China's Changing Tide," *Far Eastern Economic Review* (hereafter cited as *FEER*) 147, No. 26 (28 June 1990), p. 68.
22. Daniel Kwan, "Some Guangdong Firms Face Bankruptcy," *SCMP (Business Post)* 12 June 1990, p. 1; reprinted in *FBIS-CHI,* 13 June 1990, pp. 36–37.
23. Robert Pear, "Bush Distressed As Policy Fails to Move China," *New York Times,* 11 March 1990, pp. 1, 16.
24. Weil, "China's Exports," p. 43.
25. Robert Delfs, "Promises, Promises," *FEER* 147, No. 12 (22 March 1990), p. 51.
26. See "Li Peng Urges Banks to Aid Economy's Regulation," *Xinhua,* 16 January 1990, pp. 27–28; translated and reprinted in *FBIS-CHI,* 17 January 1990, p. 28, and "Good Beginning Noted for Industrial

Policy," *Xinhua,* 15 March 1990, p. 32. A *Xinhua* report from early June claimed that "since February the State Council has adopted a series of measures to boost the economy, including increasing investment in the basic industries." See "More on Improving Economy," *Xinhua,* 2 June 1990, translated in *FBIS-CHI,* 8 June 1990, p. 33.

27. "New Trends in Resuming Loans to China" (editorial), *Wen Wei Po,* 2 March 1990, p. 2; as translated and reprinted in *FBIS-CHI,* 6 March 1990, p. 1.
28. Qu Yingpu, "Changes Expected in Foreign Investment Mix," *CD* (Business Weekly Supplement), 2 April 1990, p. 1, reprinted in *FBIS-CHI,* 4 April 1990, p. 39.
29. "Good Beginning Noted," *FBIS-CHI,* 15 March 1990, p. 32 (from the previously cited *Xinhua* report); "Materials Minister Discusses Supply, Demand (Interview with Minister of Materials and Equipment, Liu Suinian, by Staff Reporter Yuan Zhou)," *CD,* 5 February 1990, reprinted in *FBIS-CHI,* 5 February 1990, p. 24; and "Central Bank to Support Foreign Ventures," *CD,* 23 March 1990, p. 2; reprinted in *FBIS-CHI,* 29 March 1990, p. 40.
30. *FBIS-CHI,* 3 July 1990, p. 54.
31. David Chen, "Compromise Reportedly Reached on Economy," *SCMP,* 3 March 1990, p. 8; reprinted in *FBIS-CHI,* 6 March 1990, p. 38.
32. Elizabeth Cheng, "Now It's Bund Aid," *FEER* 147, No. 11 (15 March 1990), pp. 38–39.
33. Reported by Robert Pear, "Bush Distressed as Policy Fails to Move China."
34. "More on Improving Economy," *Xinhua,* p. 33.
35. Zhu Guoxian and Zheng Zhanguo, "Song Ping Urges Self-Reliance," in a *Xinhua* report, 21 March 1990, as translated and reprinted in *FBIS-CHI,* 22 March 1990, p. 12.
36. "Economic Experts Discuss Development Goals," *Xinhua,* 9 March 1990, as translated and reprinted in *FBIS-CHI,* 12 March 1990, p. 31.
37. Tai Ming Cheung, "All Together Now," *FEER* 147, No. 31 (9 August 1990), p. 53.
38. "Preferential Treatment for High-Technology Zones," *Xinhua* (in English), 12 May 1990; reprinted in *FBIS-CHI,* 14 May 1990, p. 50.
39. Speech by Zhang Yanning at the National Meeting on Economic Restructuring: "Further Deepen Enterprise Reform and Strengthen Enterprise Management," *Zhungguo hingji tizhi gaige* No. 2, 23 February 1990, pp. 22–30; translated and reprinted in *FBIS-CHI,* 23 March 1990, supplement, pp. 30–39.
40. Sterngold, "Calls for Economic Changes"; Elizabeth Cheng, "Counters Revolution," *FEER* 149, No. 30 (26 July 1990), pp. 54–56; and "Li

Yining: Stock Market 'Essential' to Reform," *Jingji Ribao,* 23 June 1990, p. 2; as translated and reprinted in *FBIS-CHI,* 20 July 1990, pp. 40–42, on economist Li Yining's reasons for his advocacy of setting up stock markets.

41. Yasunori Matsuo, "Door Swings Open Once Again to Japanese Economy," *Japan Times,* 31 May 1990, p. 7; reprinted in *FBIS-CHI,* 4 June 1990, Annex, p. 9.
42. Kohnt, "Refomers Find 'Comfort,' See Glimmer of Hope."
43. *Xinhua,* 2 June 1990; translated and reprinted in *FBIS-CHI,* 8 June 1990, p. 33.
44. "Commentator Reviews Retrenchment Policies," *CD,* 25 May 1990, p. 4; reprinted in *FBIS-CHI,* 30 May 1990, p. 54.
45. See also Bao Xin, "'Fine Tuning' Economy, Rectification Viewed," *Liaowang* (Overseas Edition), No. 21 (21 May 1990), p. 1, translated in *FBIS-CHI,* 8 June 1990, p. 36.
46. Matsuo, "Door Swings Open Once Again to Chinese Economy." The Chinese themselves admitted the difficulty of imposing industrial policy from the center. See Zhan Gaoshu, "Reform: Are There More Heavily Fortified Positions to Storm?" *Jingji ribao* (Economic Daily), 20 June 1990, p. 1; translated and reprinted in *FBIS-CHI,* 13 July 1990, p. 29. This article pointed to the greatly weakened control capability of the central government, now that its financial revenues have declined relative to total national income, and the far smaller proportion of industrial products now under mandatory planning as compared with successful past readjustments. The article mentions the one in the early 1960s; what they say also applied to the effective readjustment of 1979–82. For the latter, see Dorothy J. Solinger, *From Lathes to Looms: China's Industrial Policy in Comparative Perspective, 1979–82* (Stanford: Stanford University Press, 1991).
47. "69 New Energy-Saving Projects Approved," *Xinhua* (English language report), 13 June 1990, reprinted in *FBIS-CHI,* 15 June 1990, p. 30.
48. Roger W. Sullivan, "Letter from the President," *CBR* 17, No. 3 (May/June 1990), p. 6.
49. Xie Xiao, "Strategic Transformation in the Mainland Economy," *Zheng ming* (Contend), No. 152 (June 1990), p. 68.
50. Cheng, "China's Changing Tide," p. 68.
51. "New Trends in Resuming Loans to China" (editorial), *Wen Wei Po,* 2 March 1990, p. 2; translated and reprinted in *FBIS-CHI,* 6 March 1970, p. 1. Another source states that there has been a drop in most imports; consumer goods imports in particular fell more than 25 percent in the first five months of 1990, but imports of rubber, coal, crude oil, copper, and iron ore have all risen to varying extents, with

crude oil topping the list with a 109.2 percent increase. See Wu Yunhe, "Government Plan to Support Agricultural Development," *CD,* 11 June 1990, p. 2; reprinted in *FBIS-CHI,* 13 June 1990, p. 39.

52. Cheng, "Now It's Bund Aid," p. 39.
53. Staff Reporter, "Li Longqing, Vice Minister of Foreign Economic Relations and Trade on Foreign Trade," *Zhongguo tingji tizhi gaige* No. 3 (23 March 1990), pp. 7–8; translated and reprinted in *FBIS-CHI,* 26 April 1990, p. 45.
54. See Nicholas D. Kristof, "Showing the World That China Is Still in Business," *New York Times,* 15 July 1990, Section III, p. 10; Cheng, "Now It's Bund Aid," pp. 38–39; Willy Wo-Lap Lam, "Shanghai Industrial Zone Plan Approved," *SCMP,* 10 April 1990, p. 11, reprinted in *FBIS-CHI,* 11 April 1990, p. 37; "Pudong Beckons to Investors," *BR* 33, 20 (14–20 May 1990), p. 10; and Bao Xin, "Letter from Beijing: New Development of Opening to the Outside World in China," *Liaowang* (Outlook) [Overseas Edition], 18 June 1990, p. 1; translated and reprinted in *FBIS-CHI,* 25 June 1990, pp. 27–28.
55. Ren Kan, "Imported Technology to Aid Key Projects," *CD* (Business Weekly), 28 May 1990, p. 1; reprinted in *FBIS-CHI,* 30 May 1990, pp. 51–52.
56. Qu Yingpu, "Changes Expected in Foreign Investment Mix," *CD* (Business Weekly Supplement), 2 April 1990, p. 1; reprinted in *FBIS-CHI,* 4 April 1990, p. 39; Brecher, "End of Investment's Wonder Years," p. 27; Cheung Lai-Kuen, "Controls on Foreign Owned Processing Operations," *Hong Kong Standard* (Business Section), 15 January 1990, p. 1; reprinted in *FBIS-CHI,* 17 January 1990, p. 30; and p. 28 (from *Xinhua*).
57. Cheng, "Now It's Bund Aid," pp. 38–39.
58. See Lo Dic, "Changes in Development Targets," *Hong Kong Standard,* 20 January 1990, p. 11, and Tammy Tam, "New Investment Priorities," *Hong Kong Standard,* 20 July 1990, p. 11; both reprinted in *FBIS-CHI,* 26 July 1990, pp. 31–33. The Seventh Plan put consumer goods and coastal development at the top of the list, with energy and basic raw materials, machinery and electronics as secondary concerns; the Eighth Plan instead emphasizes transport, communications, energy, and basic raw materials first, and then machinery and electronics.
59. Susumu Awanohara, "No More Favors," *FEER* 147, No. 14 (19 April 1990), p. 12.
60. Weil, "China's Exports," p. 42.
61. Sheryl WuDunn, "China Awaits Word on Trade Status," *New York Times,* 13 May 1990, p. 16.

62. Xie Liangjun, "Falling Imports Cause Dip in Foreign Trade," *CD*, 11 June 1990, p. 3; reprinted in *FBIS-CHI*, 13 June 1990, p. 38.
63. Weil, "China's Exports," p. 42.
64. The *People's Daily* reported in October 1990 that China indeed expected to export light industrial goods in increasing numbers, but that there had been a shift from the production of labor-intensive products to technology-intensive products and a switch from low-grade goods and raw materials to high-grade goods and finished products. This is discussed in *Renmin ribao* (People's Daily), 5 October 1990, as reported by *Xinhua* and translated in *FBIS-CHI*, 9 October 1990, p. 39.
65. Ibid. See also Liu, " China's Economic Rectification," p. 8.
66. Oddly, this announcement comes after a year in which textiles accounted for more than one-fourth of Chinese exports to the United States ($3.2 billion of a total of $12 billion, according to the U.S. Department of Commerce statistics). See Robert Pear, "Bush Distressed As Policy Fails to Move China." The Department of Commerce data is found on p. A-16.
67. Xiao Xiang, "Textile Exports Profits Plummet in First Half," *CD*, 24 July 1990, p. 2; reprinted in *FBIS-CHI*, 25 July 1990, p. 38.
68. Weil, "China's Exports," p. 42. See also Susumu Awanohara, "Rights or Duties?" *FEER* 147, No. 18 (3 May 1990), p. 43.
69. Author interview with official at the Office of Investigations, U.S. Department of Commerce, 9 August 1990.
70. WuDunn, "China Awaits Word," p. 16.
71. "Seventeenth American Meeting Discusses Reforms and Strategies," *CBR* 17, No. 4 (July/August 1990), p. 20.
72. Liu, "China's Economic Rectification," p. 8.
73. Li Hong, "State Plans Major Urban Development Projects," *CD*, 17 May, 1990, p. 1; reprinted in *FBIS-CHI*, 17 May 1990, p. 26.
74. Brecher, "End of Investment's Wonder Years," p. 27.
75. *CBR*, 17, No. 4 (July/August 1990), p. 20; WuDunn, "China Awaits Word."
76. Cheng, "Now It's Bund Aid," p. 38.
77. Ren Kan, "Imported Technology to Aid Key Projects."
78. Tai Ming Cheng, "All Together Now," p. 53.
79. Liu, "China's Economic Rectification," p. 10.
80. On this, see Reto Braun, "Unisys Crafts a Hi-Tech Partnership," *CBR*, 16, No. 6 (November/December 1989), p. 42.
81. Geoff Crothall, "Guangdong's Ningbo Coast to Host Enterprises," *SCMP*, 18 April 1990, p. 4; reprinted in *FBIS-CHI*, 23 April 1990, p. 44.
82. "Pudong Beckons to Investors."

83. "Sino-Japanese Joint Venture to Finance Imports," *SCMP* (Business Post), 19 July 1990, p. 1; reprinted in *FBIS-CHI,* 19 July 1990, p. 13.
84. Tai Ming Cheng, "All Together Now," p. 53.
85. James Sterngold, "Tokyo Said to Tell China It Will Go Ahead on Loan," *New York Times,* 19 July 1990, p. 12.
86. Ibid.
87. *New York Times,* 16 July 1990, p. C-9.
88. Francis X. Clines, "Soviets and Chinese Sign Broad Pact," *New York Times,* 25 April 1990, p. A-3.
89. Gu Guanfu, "China, USSR Strengthen Economic Cooperation," *BR* 33, No. 17 (23–29 April 1990), p. 14.
90. Tai Ming Cheng, "Comrades in Arms," *FEER,* 147, No. 27 (19 July 1990), p. 30.
91. Ju Pei-wen, "Deng Xiaoping Talked with Pao Yu-Kang on the General Situation in China and Mubarak Conveyed to the CPC the U.S. President's Message," *Kuang chiao ching* (Wide Angle), No. 214 (16 July 1990), pp. 6–11; translated and reprinted in *FBIS-CHI,* 25 July 1990, p. 2.

FIVE

American Trade Policy Toward China

John Frankenstein

SINCE THE EVENTS OF JUNE 1989, there have been fundamental changes in American attitudes towards the People's Republic of China. Much of the American and international goodwill so carefully and successfully cultivated by the regime of Deng Xiaoping over the decade of the 1980s was squandered in Tiananmen Square. These changes have been reflected in many aspects of Sino-American relations. One area of particular prominence has been American trade policy; the intense discussions over China's most-favored-nation status, with its overtones of constitutional crisis, and China's inclusion in the trade barriers watchlist are only two symptoms of the shift.

Certainly we are a long way from the kind of wonderment that allowed an American reporter visiting a Chinese market in the 1970s to remark favorably upon customers' "buying such things as shoes with the brand name 'Pixie'" — an enthusiasm that did not include the recognition of the romanized Chinese word for "leather shoes." Rather, in today's papers we are more apt to see advertisements for protectionist trade legislation featuring manacled hands and the caption, "Slave labor, China's competitive advantage in America's textile market."[1]

There was more to the catalyst for this change in attitude than the blood shed on Beijing's streets, the countrywide arrests that followed, and the loud accusations of foreign subversion trumpeted by the Chinese regime's mouthpieces. Subsequent events appeared to be even more severe. The regime moved to recentralize control over the economy and foreign trade apparatus, suspended credit and supplies to the burgeoning private and collective sectors of the economy, made tentative moves toward recentralizing agriculture, resurrected old political methods of quashing dissent, and took various steps to reestablish Sino-Leninist orthodoxies. Indeed, in the fall and winter of 1989 virtually every aspect of the so-called Decade of Reform seemed to be under attack from the center in some way. If by mid-1990 there appeared to be a slackening of the pressure and a return to some of the reform policies, this was more a response to a faltering economy than it was to any political change of heart.[2]

The repression brought instant international condemnation. The crackdown was for many in the United States and elsewhere a shocking reminder of the age-old Chinese political imperative of internal control and of the deeply rooted autocratic mentality of the Chinese political class. The love-hate duality that has so marked Sino-American relations once again switched polarity: the same Chinese rulers who had been hailed for trying to bring the benefits of a market economy to their people were now seen as reactionary thugs who would order tanks to roll over unarmed, peaceful students. Some quick (and easy) punishment would be necessary, and trade policy would be a handy tool.

Thus most of the steps the Bush administration took to signal its displeasure were economic: besides the suspension of high-level government contacts, they included a freeze on World Bank and Asian Development Bank loans, cancellation of Foreign Military Sales (FMS) contracts, suspension of talks aimed to further liberalize technology transfer, and a halt to Overseas Private Investment Corporation (OPIC) insurance for investors in China. The effect of all these moves, both Chinese and American, was to bring relations to their lowest point since the early 1970s. Recent statements by Bush administration officials suggest that Washington's China policy is now in a maintenance mode, more devoted to keeping lines of communication open than driven by any particular geostrategic grand scheme.[3]

Here events have gotten ahead of strategists. The collapse of communist regimes in Central Europe and the political and economic crisis in the USSR have rendered moot the competition among Washington, Moscow, and Beijing. Old threats have been neutralized. Indeed, internal crises have called into question the very legitimacy of the current leaderships in both Moscow and Beijing.

Just the same, the late summer 1990 crisis in the Persian Gulf has created new impetus for cooperation among the three superpowers. One fruit of this new era was in fact Chinese and Soviet support of — or at least acquiescence in — the Western position on the invasion of Kuwait by Iraq, a major arms customer for both the PRC and the USSR. Another result appears to be agreement on the Cambodian civil war. These, plus the eventuality of a power transition in China itself as its aging ruling group goes on to meet Marx and Mao, suggest that the natural inclination of the Bush administration to take the low-key communications road with China, despite the powerful emotions stirred by the Tiananmen events, is not inappropriate. But it is equally important to realize that the strategic rationale and thus the nature of the Sino-American relationship has changed, and new formulations will be required.

Before we start the policy review process, and before we evaluate the problems that policy should address, we need a few numbers upon which to base our judgments. When we talk about Sino-American trade, what are we really talking about?

The Numbers

According to United States government statistics, total Sino-American trade (in current dollars) went from $5.4 billion in 1982 to $17.9 billion in 1989, an increase of 230 percent.[4] While the growth is impressive, more than three times greater than the growth of America's global trade during the same period, the total amounts represent just between one and two percent of global United States trade. In 1988, for example, the Sino-American trade volume of $14.3 billion was about equal to United States trade with the Netherlands. That same year, American exports to China ($5.04 billion) represented 1.6 percent of total American exports, and the United States' imports from China ($9.3 billion) represented 2 percent of total American imports.

But over the same period, the United States ran a deficit in its trade with China, as Chinese exports to the United States grew much faster than American exports to China. While the latter increased 73 percent between 1982 and 1989, dampened in part by China's 1988 austerity measures, Chinese exports exploded by 383 percent over the same period. The 1982–89 cumulative Sino-American deficit equals $16.7 billion; in 1989 alone the deficit was $6.3 billion. In 1988, when two-way Sino-American trade represented 1.8 percent of the United States total global trade, the American deficit with China represented 3 percent of the total American trade deficit. It is just this disproportionality — and its rapid growth — that had made Sino-American trade relations a potential (and attractive) target for those Washington policymakers and legislators concerned with the overall American trade deficit.

None of this should be taken to be the basis for a pleading for protectionist measures against China, but it is useful to note that, overall, the United States is in the red in its trade with the PRC. Indeed, according to government statistics, in 1989 the United States became China's largest single export market, taking about 20 percent of China's exports, while American exports to China equaled 10 to 13 percent of Chinese imports (depending on whether American or Chinese statistics are used). Thus, at an aggregate level the United States is far more important to China than China is to the United States.

Commodity Composition

The importance of the American market to China becomes even more obvious if we look at the commodity composition of Chinese exports. The United States is the major market for China's highest value-added exports — the items that could lead China down the path of export-led growth taken by the Asian Newly Industrializing Economies (NIEs). Table 1, calculated from a melange of official United States and PRC statistics, gives a rough idea.

How important are these exports in the American marketplace? According to the U.S.–China Business Council (USCBC), Chinese manufacturers account for almost 15 percent of the imported clothing market, and China is the United States' largest single supplier of imported clothing. Moreover, the PRC has cornered 10 percent of the American footwear market, and one-third of its toy market. These are not trivial percentages.

Table 1
Chinese Exports to the U.S., 1989

Item	Value (U.S.$ Million)	% of Value of Total Exports to U.S.	% of Value of Worldwide Exports	% of Commodity Exported to U.S.
Clothing	3,116	26	6	50
Toys, Sports Goods	1,510	12	3	65
Telecommunications Equipment-	1,088	8	2	95
Footwear	770	6	1	70
Yarns and Fabrics	653	5	1	10
Petroleum	559	4	1	15

(Note: The third and fourth columns in this table give only approximate percentages due to differences in the bases of American and Chinese calculations of value.)

How important is the Chinese market to the United States? Although the relative value of the Chinese market for total American exports is not terribly high, the United States does make a substantial contribution to Chinese imports, and the Chinese market is not an insignificant market for some American firms. The U.S.–China Council reports that China accounts for 20 percent of United States grain exports and about 18 percent of United States fertilizer exports. China is also a major and regular customer of American aircraft makers and other commodity suppliers. It is not unimportant that the United States has a critical share in many of China's leading import sectors: grain (China's third largest import commodity), textile yarns (fourth largest), fertilizer (seventh largest), transport equipment (eleventh largest), and organic chemicals (fourteenth largest). (See table 2.) Even in other leading sectors where Japan or other countries dominate, such as steel and iron, the United States is making inroads.

However, before we proceed, it is useful to put China into proper export perspective. In 1988, other Asian customers of the United States included those listed in table 3.

Table 2
U.S. Exports to China

Item	Value ($U.S. Millions)	% of U.S. Exports to China	% of Chinese Imports of Commodity
Grain	1,127	19	38
Aircraft	536	9	35
Fertilizer	487	8	21
Specialized Machinery	361	6	6
Textile Fibers	355	6	16
Organic Chemicals	286	5	20

(Note: The third and fourth columns in this table give only approximate percentages due to differences in the bases of American and Chinese calculations of value.)

In sum, these aggregates and trends suggest that for China (and for American firms involved in exporting from China), the American market is quite important. On the other hand, while the overall Chinese market for the United States is small, for some sectors of the American economy China is not a trivial customer, even if other economies elsewhere in the region are better ones. At the same time, however, both sides must realize that there is nothing on the mutual trade list that either side could not obtain elsewhere: the United States is not the only supplier of grain and aircraft in the world; similarly, inexpensive clothing and cheap toys can be fashioned just as easily in Thailand, the Philippines, and Indonesia as they can be in the special economic zones in Guangdong and Fujian provinces.

These numbers also reflect a key part of the Sino-American trade policy dilemma. The United States' trade policy, despite nationalist and protectionist tendencies, remains fundamentally devoted to the liberal economic ideologies of profit seeking and Ricardian free trade. Chinese policy, on the other hand, is still based on Leninist-Stalinist economic planning and control of

Table 3
U.S. Customers in Asia

Country	Value ($U.S. Millions)	% of U.S. Exports
Japan	37,732	12
Taiwan	12,131	4
South Korea	11,290	4
Singapore	5,770	2
Hong Kong	5,691	2
India	2,498	1
Malaysia	2,139	1
Philippines	1,880	1

international trade. China's trade strategy is technology transfer for import substitution; exports provide the hard-currency earnings that allow this quasi-autarchic policy. In both cases, special interests that feel imperiled by free trade — certain American industries and unions, parts of the state bureaucracy in China — sometimes raise powerful voices. When we add in the political emotions stirred by the events of June 1989, plus the need to define a new strategic world, we can see that finding the common ground here necessary for the fashioning of successful policy is certainly not a task for the faint-hearted.

Policy Tools: A Broad View

In view of these different economies and different goals — the Chinese saying, "Same bed, different dreams" comes to mind — how can such a relationship be managed? Trade policy has, of course, many facets, involving many different actors and targets. In the abstract, we can see that there are numerous import- and export-side options and tools available, and that these tools are effective at various levels of the economy.

On the import side, there are various forms of protectionist measures, ranging from broadly applied high-tariff walls to more focused quota and orderly marketing schemes. In keeping with American adherence to the General Agreement on Tariffs and Trade (GATT) and a commitment to free trade, there is the MFN option. And finally there are import-encouraging preference plans.

There are also export-oriented policies. At a broad level, these involve trade promotion and development programs; trade and investment insurance and financing plans, including aid credits and loans from multilateral agencies; and sector-specific schemes. There may be national security (and trade protectionist) reasons to attempt to limit some exports. And from another angle, there are negotiations and encouragements to aid commercial and investment activities; these last involve direct interaction with host regimes and host regulations.

The overall aim of trade policy should be benefits, not punishments. But there are also limitations to trade policy. Opportunities for strong leverage are rare, substitute goods and sources are available on the world market, there may be unforeseen and unintended consequences to trade measures, and the potential to extend leverage and compliance from the trade sphere to the larger strategic political arena is weak — witness the usual failure of economic warfare and embargoes unreinforced by other actions. In other words, we should not expect too much from trade policy measures.

The Chinese Case: Imports

MFN Status

How do these broad categories apply to the Chinese case? Certainly the most widely discussed option has been the debate over whether to extend, for yet another year, China's MFN status.

As we have discussed above, the impetus to rescind that status came directly from the events of June 1989. However, the administration was able to sustain MFN status for China, and it might be useful to review briefly the arguments in its favor.[5] There are essentially three categories of argument here: the reasonable, the indirect, and the disheartening. The reasonable arguments include:

- *Macroeconomic harm.* Because suspension of MFN would raise tariffs substantially on Chinese exports to the United States — overall, by a factor of five, according to USCBC — prices would rise, and some China-produced goods would become uncompetitive, thus costing American consumers more and potentially reducing the number and variety of goods available in the marketplace. Not only would consumers suffer, so would American firms handling this trade. According to the USCBC, the impact would be particularly strong on low-priced, low-margin consumer goods: based on 1989 imports, tariffs would go from $431 million to $2.04 billion on apparel and from $180 million to $1.59 billion on toys.
- *Risks to American interests in China.* If the United States acted against China, it would be reasonable to assume that China would cut back on purchases of American goods, and of course tariffs and other restrictions on American goods would be raised substantially. Leading American exports to China can be found elsewhere, and for some items — grain and aircraft, for instance — the market is fiercely competitive. Furthermore, American investments could be put in jeopardy. The Chinese might not appropriate them outright, but they could make their operations very difficult and could slow if not stop further American investment in the country.

Indirect reasons for maintaining MFN include:

- *Affected parts of the Chinese economy.* Hardest hit by withdrawal of MFN would, in fact, be the most progressive sectors of the Chinese economy, namely the foreign invested, the collective, and the private entrepreneurial sectors. According to the USCBC, two-thirds of American imports from China came from these sectors.
- *Effect on Hong Kong.* Hong Kong is the major source of investment for the kinds of Chinese factories supplying the American market. Almost three-quarters of American imports from China transit Hong Kong. Obviously, Hong Kong would have

much to lose should tariffs on Chinese goods rise. Any negative economic effects — and subsequent negative political and social effects — in Hong Kong would also have second-order consequences for the United States since it is the largest industrial investor in the territory.

- *Diminution of American access and influence.* The argument is made that the United States' business presence enhances people-to-people contact and has a demonstration effect for the liberalizing trends in China. One should be cautious here; it is always easy to overestimate one's own positive influence. But it is undeniable that foreign business people have remarkable access and penetration in China — from remote sites in Xinjiang, to closed rocket-launching centers in Sichuan, to the gritty coal pits of the northwest. (One must also wonder at the impression given the Chinese man in the street by the glitzy hotels, so out of context even in Beijing, that service that market.)

Unhappily, this argument is also used negatively by reactionary Chinese who are concerned about foreign subversion, the corrosive effects of bourgeois liberalism, and malignant plots to pervert Chinese socialism. The ambiguities of learning from the West — an old theme in the drama of China's modernization — have yet to be resolved in many Chinese minds. The issue was clearly expressed (but not resolved) by the nineteenth-century mandarin, Zhang Zhitong, in his slogan, "Chinese learning as the base, Western learning for use" — in other words, what came from the West had utilitarian value only as it could be grafted onto an unchanging and distinctly Chinese stock.

Understanding this point is crucial since it is at the heart of Chinese policy toward the West. Even those Chinese who condemn Marxism-Leninism and call for the complete rejection of China's "feudal" past, urging instead full-scale Westernization and adoption of Western-style democracy, tend to skate around this issue and find China's salvation more in the good traditions of the Chinese people than in Western political imports.[6]

The disheartening arguments in favor of continuing MFN status are discouraging not so much because of their content but rather because they suggest a truly unacceptable ignorance of the real world of international trade. Here the argument revolves around the semantics and overtones of the term MFN for the uninformed — of privilege, special treatment, and concession. Of course, far from being special, granting MFN status is routine and part of the American commitment to the GATT and an open international trading system. As the USCBC and others pointed out in the spring of 1990, even Iraq received MFN status from the United States. What is disheartening about this particular argument is not its content — though lifting of MFN for China would in fact do violence to usual American practice — but rather that the supporters of China's continued MFN status feel it necessary to emphasize to legislators, editors, and other opinion leaders exactly what MFN does mean. It is difficult to fashion policy if the policies themselves are not understood.

If in fact punishment is the goal, perhaps the most effective tool would be restrictions on investment and access to capital, especially "soft" or low-interest loans, rather than trade restrictions. But trade cuts are easily understood and can be made into public issues. The effect of investment and capital blockages, which would have to be coordinated at international and multilateral levels, are less readily explained in the public arena, even though they might carry more economic weight, since they get at the heart of China's import substitution policy.

Protectionism

Protectionism in several forms can be found in Sino-American trade policy. The most controversial involves import quotas for textiles.

Textiles are China's largest export to the United States. At the same time, American textile interests, both labor and management, have been quite successful in promoting protectionist measures, including the Multifiber Agreement (MFA) and several accords with China that have progressively limited the growth of (but have not stopped) Chinese textile exports to the United States. The most recent of these, signed in December 1987, limits growth to 3 percent a year and expires in 1991.

The Chinese almost always take an adamant line against these restrictions and sometimes adopt rather unhelpful Leninist rhetoric in framing their arguments. They also sometimes make the argument that these restrictions have a negative effect in the

United States as well, since a decline in Chinese export earnings means less foreign exchange, which in turn means less buying abroad. They feel particularly aggrieved by American pressure here, even though, over all, their own exports to the United States have grown dramatically.[7]

Regardless of the argument, from the macroeconomic perspective such an agreement only raises costs and reduces variety to consumers (and to the monitoring agencies). When the agreement comes up for renegotiation, however, one can expect to see more manacled hands on American newspaper pages.

Other Protectionist Rules

Two areas of American policy, in particular, appear to be in need of clarification. Dumping and country-of-origin rules pose particlar difficulties here. Dumping, of course, means selling goods at prices below the cost of production. However, because China is a heavily subsidized non-market economy, "market value" for products based on factors of production cannot be reliably established. Thus the U.S. Commerce Department has to establish another basis for determining price — ostensibly in a country at a similar level of economic development. Needless to say, much controversy can arise from this, since economic conditions vary by region and sector around the world. The Chinese have complained that these rules are applied capriciously and unfairly by American authorities; one Chinese writer wondered why, in a case involving enamelware, production costs of similar items in the Netherlands and other advanced European countries, and not those of third world countries, were chosen as the basis against which Chinese product prices were measured.[8]

Country-of-origin rules are also not clear-cut. Under American regulations, items transiting a third country must undergo "substantial transformation" if they are to be considered exports from the third rather from the originating country. But there is some dispute over what constitutes "substantial transformation." At present, with China's MFN status confirmed, this is not an immediate issue, but should that status be lost, it will certainly become an issue because of the large percentage of Chinese products modified in Hong Kong or products originating outside China but undergoing some processing there.

Preferences

Although the United States has in the past supported tariff concessions — and thus export incentives — under a Generalized System of Preferences scheme for developing countries, China is not included in such a scheme (though most developed countries extend GSP to China). The Asian Newly Industrializing Economies (NIEs) — Taiwan, South Korea, Hong Kong, and Singapore — are successful graduates of GSP, and other similar schemes, such as the Caribbean Basin Initiative, are on the books. In an Asian context, of course, GSP was part of a larger anticommunist strategy. While the appeal of Marxism-Leninism appears to have diminished, strong reasons for encouraging the growth of the developing economies — greater global prosperity, less civil disorder, and so on — still exist. From time to time Chinese officials have raised the matter of China's exclusion from such plans, but in the current climate inclusion of China in a GSP scheme seems highly unlikely.

United States Export Policy

The United States has encouraged American exports to China and has taken steps to liberalize export laws, allowing a broad range of high-technology goods formerly embargoed to be freely exported to the PRC. In 1983, President Reagan shifted China into the "friendly, non-allied country" trade category (Category V). In 1985 the Coordinating Committee for Multilateral Export Controls (CoCom), the group that oversees high technology exports to communist countries, began to liberalize its control lists significantly. The upshot of these changes has been a major reduction in the time required to obtain a license to export to China (CoCom approval previously would take a year or so) and a major increase in approvals of high technology American exports to the PRC. In 1982, there were just over 2,000 applications, valued at $500 million; by 1988, the numbers had jumped to 5,700 applications, valued at $2.9 billion.[9]

Still, the Chinese have often — and sometimes ingenuously — complained about these controls. More important, American firms also are hampered by them and have been active in trying to get them reduced. This in turn has led to bureaucratic turf battles between the Department of Commerce — favoring reduction of restrictions — and the Department of Defense — which usually favors keeping and perhaps even extending the restrictions. For the moment, the economic arguments seem to be carrying the day. Here the key issue is the lack of United States monopoly on most of the technology. Further liberalization is on the horizon, and China should benefit: no CoCom participant wants to miss out on the opportunities previously embargoed, in Central Europe and further east.

There is, however, an interesting twist to the technology control issue. Not only are American technology exports to China controlled, but Chinese investments in the United States are also subject to technology scrutiny. For instance, in 1990 the China Aero-Technology Import-Export Corporation was ordered to divest itself of Mamco Manufacturing, an aircraft parts maker in Seattle, on national security grounds; Seattle business people, however, privately expressed puzzlement to this writer over the rationale.

Trade Watch List

In the spring of 1990 the U.S. State Department and U.S. Trade Representative issued their annual National Trade Estimate (NTE), which includes material trade barriers. China was listed among the nations with significant trade barriers.[10] The following are the issues identified by the United States government as having significant impact:

- *Import licensing.* Termed China's "principal means of import regulation," China requires importers to jump through multiple bureaucratic hoops to obtain licenses to bring in a broad range of commodities. Between 40 and 50 percent of all Chinese imports (by value) are covered by these regulations. Because multiple permissions must be obtained, sometimes from ministries that produce similar products inside China, the process is complex and fraught with conflicts of interest. Other regulations exist which limit import of some goods to certain ministries or bureaucracies, and some goods — mostly high-technology consumer goods — are subject to severe restrictions if not outright bans, depending on the political whims and economic winds of the moment. Certainly the process, like other Chinese bureaucratic procedures, is not transparent, even to the Chinese; there are reports that local permissions have been rescinded by the central authorities.

- *Import substitution lists.* The Chinese authorities require Chinese companies to source items domestically if a Chinese product is deemed by the central authorities to meet the demands that would have been met by a foreign good.
- *Tests and inspections.* Nine categories of big-ticket machinery and electronic products (such as cars, air conditioners, and televisions) must, since August 1989, undergo product quality testing (paid for, of course, by the exporter). In addition, some 491 products must pass inspection before being allowed into the country. And finally, agricultural pesticides must undergo expensive testing ($5 million per chemical, according to the industry) from which domestic Chinese products are exempt.
- *Tariffs.* Although Chinese tariffs can be high, they do not, according to the NTE, "play a major role in regulating trade." The biggest problems with the Chinese tariffs are that rates change suddenly and arbitrarily and that sometimes it is not possible to confirm a rate change with the Customs Office.
- *Intellectual property protection.* This is a major issue for American firms doing business in China. Patents in China do not extend to chemical or pharmaceutical products, China's trademark law does not include protection for service marks, and China's copyright law and practice does not provide "adequate" protection, especially for computer software. Copying and pirating of all sorts of protected materials is widespread. This entire area is difficult to deal with since what would be considered protected intellectual property in the West is, under the Chinese system, often a free good, and changing habits of mind on these issues is not easy.
- *Services.* According to the NTE, services "face significant administrative restrictions" in China. Lawyers and accountants are precluded from working with local Chinese firms, insurance companies are effectively barred from the Chinese market, and the activities of American shipping companies are also limited.

- *Investments in China.* Despite the October 1986 reforms, investment must be approved through a complex process and ultimately must respond to Chinese political rather than economic priorities. Only "productive" investments — that is, investments that meet the objectives of Chinese planners — are apt to be approved. Expatriation of profits is also difficult; foreign exchange regulations are tight. Among other issues facing foreign investments is the lack of effective formal mechanisms for the resolution of disputes.

Chinese Business Practices: Issues and Challenges

These problems become more manifest when we look at the micro level of Chinese business operations. There have been numerous studies, ranging from the analytical to the descriptive, of foreign business operations in China and their difficulties. All suggest that matching the goals of profit-seeking Western enterprises with the bureaucratic and political goals of Chinese state enterprises is difficult at best. Many of the difficulties arise from differences in the business culture, an area in which government policy can have little effect, although communication through the joint organizations set up by the Chinese and American governments — the Joint Commission on Science and Technology, the Joint Economic Committee, and Joint Commission on Commerce and Trade — and private groups such as the American Chamber of Commerce can help. But one still has to deal with the fact that virtually all Chinese enterprises are part of the country's bureaucracy and thus must respond to state and political, rather than economic, demands; foreign influence here is apt to be small. Indeed, in the view of a Chinese trade lawyer, the facet of the Chinese trade environment that foreigners least understand is that "the economy remains under state control and thus the state can legitimately intervene in any business deal at any time under any pretext."[11]

Among the more salient and most frequently cited issues are problems with Chinese technical infrastructure (plant, equipment, communications) and human resources, particularly inadequate training and education of managers, engineers, and workers. (Many of the foreign engineers working in China interviewed by this author, however, expressed their admiration for what Chinese workers can do on their obsolete equipment.) Differing time horizons cause conflict, and language problems abound. Local (and usually required) inputs are of poor quality, if indeed those inputs are even available. Other issues cited in these studies involve management control, training, and differing expectations on a range of issues, including delivery schedules, post-sales follow-up, and adequacy of fees for technology.[12]

Studies have identified policy actions which could be pursued in resolving problems. Some are:

- Easing of restrictions which result from American laws on technology transfer
- Easing of Chinese foreign-exchange regulations and limitations
- Easing of Chinese laws and regulations concerning
    - Imports
    - Labor practices
    - Patent protection and other intellectual property issues
    - Local content
    - Required counterpurchase/buybacks
    - Access to the Chinese market

A study this writer conducted in 1988 on business environment issues, a follow-up to a small study done in 1984 in Beijing, indicated that Chinese measures taken in the intervening period, plus the generally more liberal domestic economic and political atmosphere of the time, had substantially improved the climate for foreign business.[13] Political and bureaucratic interference was down, access to end-users had improved, and executives felt that they were getting a fairer shake in their dealings with the bureaucracy. However, many of the issues noted in earlier studies persisted — an ambiguous negotiating environment, uncertain and changeable rules, bureaucratic hassles of all sorts, double standards of contract compliance, and, above all, a definitely non-North American approach to time management. Just the same, it was clear in summer 1988 that much mutual learning had gone on, and a transitional economy appeared to be developing.

The austerity and recentralizing measures imposed in the fall of that year obviously have slowed if not halted what foreign business people would see as positive change. The international freeze on credit and the redirection of domestic credit back toward subsidizing inefficient state industries at the expense of joint ventures and the private/collective sectors have slowed industrial growth and imports. The heightened control has also exacerbated pre-existing bureaucratic difficulties, and many Western business people have lost their enthusiasm for continuing to work in China's demanding environment.

Policy Options

The point here is not to repeat the familiar litany of problems in the Chinese business arena. After all, as we have seen, the Chinese themselves have complaints about American policies and practices. Rather, the key question to ask here is the degree to which policy can respond to these issues. Some problems, it would seem, can be directly addressed; in other cases, countermoves may be appropriate, especially if the damage can be quantified.

However, many of these complaints seem to describe not only real and long-recognized problems but also the very nature of the Chinese business environment. It is a politicized, bureaucratized system that responds to political requirements of the leadership. Furthermore, it is a system obsessed with bureaucratic secrecy. Secret *neibu* (internal) regulations are part of the Chinese technique of control. It is a *deliberately untransparent* system, and not only foreigners but even Chinese bureaucrats and business people are often at a loss in doing business in such an environment.

Thus it is not clear what policy initiatives the United States government might take to effect change at the micro level, especially since Washington stands behind some of the international measures taken against China following the June 1989 events and may not be likely to receive a hearing. Furthermore, unless and until the United States makes some kind of move on the textile issue, which has now been elevated beyond the substantive to the symbolic level, and perhaps on dumping and technology transfer regulations, we are apt to be privy to a spectacle of pots calling the kettle black.

However, there are some options. As international sanctions ease, Washington could keep up the normal diplomacy of urging Beijing to fit its business practices in with those of the international business community. There is more to this than simply benefiting Western business. If China aspires to become a member of the GATT, many of its trading and business practices will have to be adjusted to fit the rules of the international trading community. This argument might not find much of an audience among members of the present Beijing regime, and there certainly is no guarantee that any successor group will be open to this argument, although one might expect to find authorities to the south, close to Hong Kong and Taiwan, sympathetic. But it is an argument that, if combined with some further liberalization on the American side and continued American firmness on crucial points, might have some effect.

However, we have to come back from the policy arena to determine our main concerns. The data suggests that in the aggregate, Sino-American trade, while certainly interesting and perhaps significant for some sectors and at the level of the firm, is less important *economically* than we might like to pretend.

The real importance of the Sino-American relationship is political and strategic. China, after all, not only contains a billion people, a large domestic economy, and large conventional armed forces, but also sports strategic, nuclear-tipped intercontinental ballistic missiles (ICBMs). This political weight, plus its position as the cultural heartland of East Asia, raises the level of relations with China to the highest degree. The West may once have seen China as some kind of counterweight to an aggressive Soviet Union; that characterization is no longer viable, and some writers, such as Robert Delfs, argue that China is now "less relevant on the world scene with the collapse of any threat from the Soviet bloc."[14] Perhaps, rather, it is the concept of the "strategic triangle" that is no longer relevant, though certainly no one can deny China's role as a power in a region that has led the world in economic development over the past twenty years. Events in the Middle East, too, remind us that China has significant relations with that region as an arms supplier not only to Iraq but also to Saudi Arabia and other countries, plus important, if denied, ties with Israel.

The challenge now is for the United States to formulate a strategy and policy that will include China — a country with strong isolationist tendencies and a country perhaps on the edge of interesting, if not profound, domestic political changes as the makers of the old cold war environment disappear — as a positive contributor to a new world order that will be emerging in the 1990s. Trade policy will have an important role to play here, but to be effective, it must have some cohesion and must be linked with wider United States policy. "Constructive engagement" with Beijing merely maintains the status quo; we need also to clarify our own vision of China as a significant actor in the post–cold war environment.

Postscript

Since the above was written, the crisis in the Persian Gulf has escalated into warfare, and the positions of major international players on a range of issues have hardened. Political trials in China have continued, with long sentences handed out to dissidents, thus reviving human rights concerns in the United States. Sino-American trade disputes have also intensified, stimulated by a broad range of domestic and international issues, including China's lukewarm enthusiasm for American actions in the Gulf and American domestic economic difficulties.

The key issue, however, is the the ever-growing American deficit in trade relations with China, which reached $10.4 billion in 1990, up almost 70 percent over 1989. This trade gap is forecast to grow by another 50 percent, to more than $15 billion, in 1991. While relatively small in the United States' total trade deficit account, the China surplus is the fastest growing portion.[15] Moreover, there are allegations of Chinese dumping, cheating on and evasion of textile quotas, and failures to protect intellectual property according to international standards (a new Chinese copyright law is scheduled to come into effect at the end of June 1991, but the draft has been kept secret, raising fears that the law will severely disadvantage non-Chinese parties). "Super 301" action is a possibility; administration softening over the maintenance of China's MFN status is also possible.

One wonders if Beijing's America-watchers subscribe to the *Economist.* If they do, they might ponder the caption (and implied advice) on the cover of the 2 February 1991 issue. Bannered over a somber picture of President Bush and Secretary of State Baker, it reads, "They'll remember their friends."

NOTES

1. For "Pixie" shoes, see Marilyn Berger, "China Notebook," *Washington Post,* 20 February 1973, p. A-18. For the "slave labor" advertisement, see the *San Francisco Chronicle,* 14 August 1990, p. A-9.
2. See "Focus — China 1990: Back to the Future," *Far Eastern Economic Review* 147, 32 (23 August 1990), pp. 29–48, for an excellent review of these trends.
3. See, for instance, the statement by Richard H. Solomon, assistant secretary of state for East Asian and Pacific affairs, "China and MFN: Engagement, Not Isolation Is Catalyst for Change," *Current Policy* No. 1282 (Washington, DC: U.S. Department of State, June 1990).
4. The sources for these and subsequent figures on trade are the official United States and PRC statistics listed in the *Direction of Trade Year Book 1989* (Washington, DC: International Monetary Fund, 1989); official United States and Chinese statistics quoted in Central Intelligence Agency, Directorate of Intelligence, *The Chinese Economy in 1989 and 1990: Trying to Revive Growth While Maintaining Stability* (Washington, DC: 1990), and Central Intelligence Agency, Directorate of Intelligence, *The Chinese Economy in 1988 and 1989: Reforms on Hold, Economic Problems Mount* (Washington, DC: 1989). See also official Chinese trade statistics listed in *Business China* 16, No. 8 (April 1990), pp. 60–61; and "Report on Social and Economic Growth in 1989," *China Daily,* 26 February 1990, p. 6.

   There are significant problems with all of these data which should be brought to the reader's attention. First, they count only merchandise trade and do not include trade in services or gains or losses from the "invisible empire" of global foreign exchange operations. Second, they may omit economically significant but politically sensitive items of trade (such as arms and other national security goods). Third, exports are valued on a f.o.b. ("free on board") basis (that is, the price ex-factory, delivered to the nearest shipping point), while imports are valued on a c.i.f. ("cost, insurance, and freight") basis (that is, the price ex-factory plus shipping and insurance costs); in other words, for the same item, the f.o.b. figure will always be lower than the c.i.f. figure for an imported product, automatically creating a current imbalance. In addition there are problems with converting RMB to U.S. dollars — the exchange rate has changed several times, and because the RMB is not convertible and China is a non-market economy, establishing real costs and prices is not feasible. Finally, the data give current, not constant, values. Because of differing inflation and changing exchange rates it really is not practical to calculate constant prices — the only real basis for comparing trade over time. If all this were not enough, the United States and China count bilateral trade differently: the United States includes Chinese goods that transit Japan and Hong Kong (a significant amount); the Chinese include those goods in their Japan and Hong Kong accounts. Accordingly, we should be cautious in using these numbers and should avoid the delusion of spurious precision. They give us a general idea and trends, but we should not subject them to too great an analytical stress.

5. Most of the substance of these arguments comes from Solomon, "China and MFN," and U.S.-China Business Council Position Paper, "The Cost of Removing MFN from China," (Washington, DC: UCBC, 23 April 1990).
6. For instance, the now banned reformist 1988 television film "River Elegy" found the reason for China's backwardness in "feudalism" — a term used in this instance as a code word for Marxism-Leninism — and saw Westernization and democracy as a way for China's older, humanistic traditions to reemerge. Fang Lizhi, the noted scientist and critic who was forced to seek asylum in the American embassy in June 1989, and other reformers wrote in their "Declaration to Support Democratic Reform in Mainland China" (reprinted in World Affairs 152, No. 3 [Winter 1989–90], pp. 135–37) that "Chinese have been people who are diligent, wise, old, honest, and filled with a sense of justice." But they fell into an abyss of suffering, poverty, backwardness, and "ignorance" and despite their best efforts to change this "shameful situation," the Chinese people have continued to fall behind because of the "weakness of the state system" — that is, Chinese political impotence and corruption. The solution, Fang writes, is democracy, but the implication is that democracy is a tool that will restore China's great traditions of wisdom and justice, rather than a system that creates a responsible civic culture.
7. See the very stimulating exchanges of view in Zhang Jialin, "Protectionism: A Curse for Both China and the United States," and Nai-Ruenn Chen, "Comments," pp. 84–97; Wu Jixian and Tang Shayun, "China's Open Door Policy and Trade Problems with the United States," pp. 119–30; Nai-Ruenn Chen, "Issues in U.S.-PRC Trade: An American Perspective"; and Wang Xi and Chen Yawen, "Issues in Sino-U.S. Trade: A Chinese Perspective," pp. 133–72," in Richard H. Holton and Wang Xi, eds., *U.S.-China Economic Relations: Present and Future* (Berkeley: Institute of East Asian Studies, University of California, 1989).
8. The Chinese trade writer in question is Zhang Jialin of the Shanghai

Institute of International Studies. See Holton and Xi, *U.S.-China Economic Relations,* p. 172.

9. See Bureau of Public Affairs, *U.S. Export Controls and China,* (Washington, DC: U.S. Department of State, March 1989). Also see Chen, "Issues in U.S.-PRC Trade," in Holton and Xi, *U.S.-China Economic Relations,* passim.
10. Unclassified State Department cable, SecState 101618 300257Z Mar 90, from which the following discussion is drawn.
11. Author's private interview, with a senior member of a Chinese law firm specializing in foreign trade matters run by the Beijing city government. The firm represents a number of foreign companies; the lawyer spoke on a background basis.
12. For a sample of these studies, see John Frankenstein, "Doing Business in China," *Global Business Management in the 1990s,* ed. Robert Moran (Washington, DC: Beacham Publishing, 1990), pp. 245–57. Besides Holton and Xi, *U.S.-China Economic Relations,* see also E.K. Lawson, ed., *U.S.-China Trade: Problems and Prospects* (New York: Praeger, 1988); Nigel Campbell, *China Strategies: The Inside Story* (Hong Kong and Manchester: University of Manchester Press/University of Hong Kong Press, 1986); William Davidson, "Creating and Managing Joint Ventures in China," *California Management Review* 29, No. 4 (Summer 1987), pp. 77–94; S. Hendryx, "The China Trade: Making the Deal Work," *Harvard Business Review* 86, No. 4 (July–August 1986), pp. 75, 81–84; and Lucian Pye's classic study, *Chinese Commercial Negotiating Style* (Boston: Oelgeschlager, Gunn & Hain, 1983), plus numerous articles and continuing coverage in *China Business Review.*
13. John Frankenstein, "The Chinese Foreign Trade Environment: The Beijing Wind Revisited," *International Studies of Management and Organization* 20, no. 1–2 (Spring–Summer 1990), pp. 135–48; and Frankenstein, "Trends in Chinese Business Practices: Changes in the Beijing Wind," *California Management Review* 29, No. 1 (Fall 1986), pp. 148–60.
14. Robert Delfs, "Focus — China 1990," *Far Eastern Economic Review* 147, No. 32 (23 August 1990), p. 29.
15. See G. Crothall, "U.S. Team in Bid to Mend Trade Links," *South China Morning Post,* 23 February 1991, Business Section, p. 1; and D. Yumoi, "Trade Surplus Could Cause Loss of Status," *Hong Kong Standard,* 15 March 1991, Business Section, p. 1.

SIX

Minimizing Maximum Regrets:

American Interests in Science and Technology Relations with China

Richard P. Suttmeier

As the post-Mao era dawned in China in the late 1970s the new Chinese leadership, headed by Deng Xiaoping, committed the country to the national development program known as the Four Modernizations. Central to China's development strategy was the enhancement of national capabilities in science and technology (S&T).

American responses to the new leadership in China at the time were calculated to improve Sino-American relations by appealing to geopolitical interests shared by the two countries and to Chinese needs for expanded economic, technological, and scientific interactions with the West. As part of its response, the United States initiated what was at the time a bold experiment in the use of science and technology as instruments of foreign policy. This response, in its scope and complexity, reflected the fact that Sino-American S&T relations were a central part of both American and Chinese strategy in the overall improvement of bilateral relations.

In the decade that followed, many of the political and economic assumptions shaping behavior of the two sides in the late 1970s required modification or abandonment. Many others proved viable. By holding to the latter and creatively altering the former, the two sides were able to convert thirty years of mutual isolation and hostility into a reasonably normal, functioning bilateral relationship. The early assumptions about the importance of science and technology, while requiring modifications, nevertheless served the two sides well. Thus, in the course of a decade, a complex, multifaceted "thick" bilateral S&T relationship — involving commercial technology transfers, government-run cooperative programs, and extensive academic and scholarly exchange — came into being.

In addition to and, in some respects, derived from the bilateral S&T relationship, China emerged as a full participant in a whole range of international scientific and technical organizations and regimes such as the World Meteorological Organization, the International Atomic Energy Agency, and the International Council of Scientific Unions. The experiment in using S&T as an instrument of foreign policy was apparently working.

Progress in the development of the bilateral relationship, however, came to a halt with the forceful suppression of mass political demonstrations in China in June 1989. Since the relationship had come to involve both official governmental elements and private parties in the United States, American reactions to the events in Tiananmen Square have involved both official condemnations and sanctions and the erosion of private incentives for cooperation with China as good feelings towards Beijing were replaced by moral repugnance.[1]

High-level governmental contacts with China were forbidden by the Bush administration, programs to encourage commercial activities (and technology transfer) — such as the Trade and Development Project (TDP) and the Overseas Private Investment Corporation (OPIC) — were frozen, and American export controls against China were tightened. In the private sector, programs of scholarly exchange were suspended (that of the National Academy of Sciences being perhaps the most prominent), and commercial interest in new trade and investment opportunities in China plummeted. With the passage of time, many of these responses to the Tiananmen crackdown are being reversed, but it is likely to be some time before the relationship is restored to its pre-June 1989 levels of quality and quantity.[2]

The New Context

Should anyone care about where Sino-American S&T relations are going? If so, why? To begin to answer these questions, it will be helpful to examine the conditions which would have threatened the progress of the relationship whether the Tiananmen political suppression had occurred or not. We must also recognize that the context for the Sino-American relationship has changed enormously since the days—just ten years ago—when rapprochement began.

While the Tiananmen incident has been the proximate cause of disrupted S&T ties, we should not forget that a number of other problems in the relationship made reassessments by both sides both inevitable and desirable. On the American side, a number of considerations were on the agenda. From a commercial perspective, the problems of doing business in China remained. Technology transfer is best thought of as part of commercial transactions; disincentives for the latter thus become disincentives for the former. While both China and the United States worked seriously throughout the 1980s to improve the business climate in China, by the end of the decade China's relative appeal as a destination for foreign investment, compared to many of its Asian neighbors, had not improved noticeably.

Science and technology relations with China also became closely linked with evolving United States trade policy and with concerns for the protection of intellectual property as an important source of American foreign trade anxieties. In the face of a deteriorating trade picture, continued opportunities for S&T cooperation with the United States were made contingent, by both executive order and legislation, on foreign nations' adopting intellectual property rights (IPR) regimes acceptable to Washington. In the Sino-American case, the Agreement for Cooperation in Science and Technology, which provided the framework for cooperation throughout the 1980s, expired in early 1989. While the Tiananmen Square events have certainly influenced the context for renewal of the agreement, substantive disagreements over IPR provisions must first be reconciled if the agreement is to be reactivated.

From a security perspective, the gradual relaxation of United States export controls during the 1980s was reassessed in 1988 because of Chinese strategic exports to the Middle East. The thorny issue of China as an international supplier of sophisticated weapons cast a dark shadow over the progress in scientific cooperation and liberalized export controls.

On the Chinese side, continuing financial difficulties stemming from macroeconomic problems were working against the deepening of science and technology ties with the United States. With countries such as Japan, Germany, and France offering "package deals" for trade, technology transfer, and S&T cooperation on terms which the United States would not — or could not — meet, China on the eve of the Tiananmen crackdown was prepared to shift a greater share of its science and technology cooperation energies away from the Americans to others.

The financial incentives for doing so reinforced other reasons. By the late 1980s, China's policies for the development of high-level technical manpower were beginning to show serious internal contradictions. Many in the leadership feared that the possible non-return of students sent to the United States for graduate study was looming as a policy failure. In the eyes of some in China, policies for sending students abroad were out of line with policies for domestic higher education. Underlying contradictions between the objectives of realizing short-term practical benefits from technical education and of establishing a tradition of quality education and research for the long term were becoming increasingly "antagonistic." The nature of China's relationship with the United States, and the appeal and porosity of the American university system, complicated the management of what, in essence, was a Chinese domestic problem of managing its own institutions of higher S&T education.

Thus, quite apart from the incident in Tiananmen, there were a number of events affecting the S&T relationship by the late 1980s. These must be kept in mind as we assess where the Sino-American relationship might go in the 1990s. In addition to this legacy of unresolved problems, our thinking about the future must also address the radically new environment in which the resumption of a vigorous relationship would occur.

The American Decline

When the Sino-American S&T relationship was established in 1978–79, many of the elements of American power were still unquestioned. Trade imbalances had not yet reached crisis proportions, American superiority in most areas of technology was not seriously questioned, and the American system of higher education was the envy of the world. The "American system" for supporting science and technology as well as advanced education was taken as the main reference case for other nations in assessing their own research and innovation policies and institutions.

These conditions no longer apply. United States trade deficits are now chronic and are intermixed in complex ways with macroeconomic problems. International trade competitiveness has been closely linked with technological capabilities; but the United States seems to be unable to adapt the "American system" to the meeting of new competitive challenges. This is, at least in part, because the macroeconomic climate does not permit the full exploitation of the technical capabilities which the United States continues to possess.

Meanwhile, weaknesses in the American higher education system are more obvious. Research support in higher education has become more unpredictable and is now, in the eyes of some, inadequate. Science and technology have become ever more unappealing subjects for American students, and American excellence in S&T is more and more dependent on foreign-born professors and graduate students, including many Chinese. Institutions of higher education are beginning to come under increasing public scrutiny, a process which is likely to continue for a few years.

In short, even without mention of the drugs and AIDS crises, it is clear that American society and culture are considerably more frayed than they were in the late 1970s, a fact which has eroded the capabilities of American society. In turn, the United States' relations with the rest of the world are changing to much higher levels of dependency for such critical items as money and trained technical manpower.

Chinese S&T Capabilities

The backward condition of the Chinese S&T system of the late 1970s was one of the more important reasons for Beijing's initiation of the new "open" policy of the last decade. In spite of substantial investments in S&T development over the previous thirty years, the policies and practices of the Mao era had left an incapacitating legacy. The Chinese system of higher education had been disrupted by the Cultural Revolution, technical talent was squandered by the capricious operation of an irrational job assignment system, national defense claimed a disproportionate share of human and material resources for science, and the organization of research and economic activities ensured that the former's contributions to the latter would be minimal.

While the Chinese S&T system continues to have serious problems, progress in solving many of the old problems has been quite remarkable. The education system is again functioning, having graduated some 1,767,200 students in all fields in the period 1979–85, a large percentage of whom were in science and engineering. A small but significant cadre of scientists and engineers have now had research and training experiences abroad and have returned to assume leadership positions in the Chinese research system. Significant changes have occurred in the management and funding of research, and progress has been made in linking research to production. Much of the talent which had been segregated in the defense system has been released to serve the civilian economy. Serious programs have been initiated to prepare China to participate profitably in the emerging international high-technology community. In short, the past decade has seen a significant mobilization of human and organizational resources for S&T development, which makes the Chinese S&T scene of the early 1990s a far cry from that of the 1970s. China's potential to contribute to international S&T cooperation is thus considerably enhanced.

Problems of Chinese Politics

Lest the progress described above suggest that China's S&T development is on a simple upward trajectory, we should recall that Chinese society is a deeply troubled one, and there is no way to make S&T immune from the general malaise. China's ability to realize its aspirations for scientific and technological development is closely related to the deepening of its international S&T relations and to the successful implementation of economic and S&T system reforms. Progress in these two areas, however, is now slowed by conservative elements in the political elite who rightly fear that reform and internationalization threaten the Communist party's monopoly on power. Whereas the Sino-American science and technology relationship began at a time when there was considerable optimism in China about the prospects for political stability, reform, and orderly succession, the climate today is one of political gloom brought on in no small part by the high degree of uncertainty surrounding the political succession.

The uncertainties and apparent immobility of Chinese politics thus contribute to a climate which is inhospitable to the implementation of those policies most likely to move science and technology forward, and thus most likely to make China an attractive partner in cooperation internationally. However, the relationships between Chinese politics and Chinese S&T may be more complex than this.

The boundaries of the Chinese political elite and the technical community have come to be more overlapping than is commonly realized. In the first instance, the Chinese state structure in its upper middle ranks has become more "technicized" over the past decade as younger, technically trained individuals come to occupy important positions as state cadres. Secondly, generational change in the military is also bringing to the fore a new cohort of officers with keener appreciation of the importance of S&T for Chinese defense. In those parts of the military which have been responsible for strategic weapons programs, there is much shared experience with the leaders of the scientific community who emerged in the 1980s. Most importantly, many of the children of the senior leadership have career interests in S&T development, either as scientists or engineers themselves or, in recent years, as officers of the new technology-driven corporations spun off from the military-industrial complex.

On the assumption that China's political future will be settled less on the streets of China's cities than by the curtained machinations of elite family networks, the interests of the children of high-level cadres (*gaogan zidi*) are likely to figure prominently in the political deals cut to assure a stable succession. To the extent that those interests are linked to advanced technology industries and the research system, the "S&T factor" in the succession may not be insignificant.

The point of this digression into Chinese succession politics is to again highlight the important changes which exist in the context of the S&T relationship. Succession was an issue in the late 1970s as well. Arguably, the cooperation extended to Deng Xiaoping by the United States and other countries bolstered Deng and his reformist coalition. The succession politics of the early 1990s, however, are considerably more complex; seemingly, the polity is no more institutionalized than it was a decade ago, and no single individual with Deng's experience and political skills has appeared on the scene. Succession, therefore, is likely to be the result of behind-the-scenes maneuvering of elite families, many of which have members with a stake in the country's technological future.

"Greater China"?

The concept of a "Greater China" — nations and territories tied together by Chinese cultural and ethnic commonalities and increasingly close economic interests — was far from being a reality in the late 1970s. Today, after a decade of change on the mainland, on Taiwan, and in Asia more generally, and in spite of the Tiananmen events, a more integrated Greater China has begun to appear.

For the United States, a higher degree of integration among China, Taiwan, and Hong Kong is on balance probably a plus, at least in the short run. It helps to diffuse the Taiwan issue in Sino-American relations, it brings Taiwan's and Hong Kong's capital and managerial skills to bear on the problems of Chinese modernization, and it could be a force for moderation of Chinese politics. Integration with China also offers an alternative to Japanese economic hegemony as an organizing force for the Asian regional economy.

Realizing the potential benefits of a Greater China for the United States will require that the latter — in the governmental, commercial, and academic areas — make adjustments in its strategies and programs for science and technology cooperation both to induce new forms of intra-Greater China cooperation and to exploit the synergies which such cooperation can produce.

The Changing Eastern Bloc

The implications of the changes in Eastern Europe and the Soviet Union also set the 1990s apart from the late 1970s. The geopolitical rationale of S&T relations with China noted at the outset is no longer credible. A fair amount of official United States foreign policy attention, and private-sector commercial attention as well, once given to cooperation with China have been shifted to Eastern Europe and the Soviet Union. Whether China can regain that attention will depend on the availability of attractive commercial opportunities and the quality of research China offers, and not on China's strategic importance to the United States. At the same time, China's S&T relations with the Soviet Union have become more intimate in the 1990s than they were in the period of initial Sino-American rapprochement, a factor which should add a new element of complexity to the development of United States export controls.

Globalization and the Continuing Technological Revolution

The pace of change toward the globalization of industry and technology accelerated during the 1980s, with the result that the requirements for global operations look much larger in the calculations of business firms than was the case in the late 1970s. Arguably, national governments and institutions of higher education have been slower to react to globalization than have private corporations.

Rapid technological change is related in complex ways to globalization; it facilitates global operations and at the same time alters the rationales for international business decisions. Sharp reductions in the labor component of manufacturing costs, for instance, have in some industries reduced the appeal of low-labor cost in off-shore manufacturing sites. On the other hand, having access to foreign communities of technical manpower takes on greater importance as innovation becomes more central to competitiveness, and as market-specific research and engineering becomes a key to the successful implementation of global strategies.

China has yet to find its place in this new world of globalization. Its comparative advantage seemingly would still lie with its abundant low-cost labor and its large community of scientists and engineers (whose services are also available at relatively low costs). This suggests the possibility of the Chinese economy's fitting into the rapidly evolving international division of labor in new ways. Whether it be software production, technical services (including the provision of satellite launch services), or the development of niche technologies (such as high-powered magnets and customized optical crystals), China is not without S&T assets to bring to the world of global commercial strategies.

The Rise of Japan

Whereas Japan was on its way to becoming an economic and technological superpower in the late 1970s, today it has arrived. Japanese achievements are a cause for unease in both China and the United States (as well as in other countries of Asia), but there are few signs of any type of coordinated response. Instead, China continues to try to keep from becoming dependent on Japan, and the United States and Japan continue down a course characterized by deepening S&T cooperation, unending trade friction, and deteriorating political relations.

The role of Japan in Sino-American S&T relations is clearly conditioned by some of the other environmental factors noted above — globalization, the changes in Europe, the emergence of Greater China — as well as the economic and technological dynamics of the East and Southeast Asian region as a whole. The result is a highly fluid, dynamic, little-understood system which is beyond the control of any one player. That the United States' economic and technological influence in the Asian region has declined markedly over the past year is clear. That Japan has restructured, or will ever be able to restructure, the regional system is less certain. A more likely scenario is the continuation of the trend towards a system of multi-level, shifting bilateral and multilateral forms of commercial interactions and S&T cooperation.

In such a context, China is likely to become a much more important player in the 1990s than it has been. China will continue to seek science and technology from abroad — from the United States, Japan, and Europe — but it is also likely to become a more visible supplier of science and technology to the system as well. For countries such as the United States and Japan, China can offer research, engineering, and other technical services for some industries at low costs, as noted above. For the Newly Industrialized Economies (NIEs) and neo-NIEs, whose technical communities are dwarfed by China's, China offers a rich pool of technical talent to be exploited in mutually advantageous ways. Cases of NIE firms entering into joint ventures with Chinese research institutions, which began to happen in the late 1980s, can be expected to multiply.

The Fate of the Earth

A final factor conditioning Sino-American science and technology relations today is the increasing concern felt internationally for global environmental dangers. Many of these considerations lay behind the establishment of S&T relations with China in the late 1970s, but they have now taken on greater urgency.

China's enormous population, its great land mass, and its geographical characteristics make it especially important for the future of the global commons. Having access to China is important for understanding such global issues as world weather patterns, ocean currents, and biological diversity. How China manages its energy, transportation, food, and pollution problems is of major interest to the United States and to the international community.

Conclusion

The discussion above illustrates how very changed the context for Sino-American science and technology relations has become from the heady days of a decade ago when relations were first established. Implicitly, it has also addressed the "Should we care?" question raised at the outset. Explicitly, yes, we should care about our S&T relations with China. We would like China's political succession to be resolved in ways which do not harm our interests, and S&T may be a factor in that outcome; we would like to prevent the inevitable enhancement of China's technological capabilities from being directed towards destabilizing arms exports; we would like Chinese S&T to be an accessible resource in the shifting patterns of Asian economic and technological cooperation and competition; and we would like the full cooperation of the Chinese technical community in international efforts to avert global environmental crises.

But while a case can be made that the United States should

care, *how* it cares must be seen in the context of the shifting ground of foreign policy assumptions which have been forced on it by international change. Central to these is the growing importance of economic factors in national security calculations, the Gulf war to the contrary notwithstanding. Again, the world has changed since the late 1970s, when Soviet-American military and political competition was a driving force behind Sino-American rapprochement.

The growing importance of economic factors in national security is clearly conditioned by national economic competitiveness in world trade. As competitiveness has come to be linked to national capabilities for technological innovation, and as the latter has come to depend on national scientific resources, so science and technology have become increasingly intermixed with trade policy. A strong S&T base is essential for the production of competitive goods, but in addition, S&T can be used as an asset in trade expansion and market access and development.

Under current circumstances, the complex issues surrounding Western export control policy have become more confusing than ever. Efforts to streamline and rationalize national and multilateral export control machinery continue, but the enthusiasm for maintaining such controls is uneven, and its rationale is considerably less clear. The inherent tensions between export control objectives and technology-driven trade expansion have become even more acute.

In the final analysis, how the United States relates to China in S&T is contingent upon how it relates to a rapidly changing Asia more generally. While Washington continues to assert its interest in and commitment to Asian security, its economic and technological position in the region increasingly seems out of phase with its military position. While not surprising, it appears that this fact is not fully recognized. It may be that the elements of a coherent new Asian strategy are inherently elusive; there is just too much change and uncertainty for the confident setting of directions.[3]

If so, the best strategy may be one of minimizing maximum regret. While the appeals of S&T cooperation with China are less compelling to many today than they were a decade ago, the context of the relationship today is also markedly different than it was, and markedly more uncertain. Chinese S&T has changed and Asian regional interactions have changed. It is important that the United States not be surprised by the new synergies which will result East Asian socioeconomic dynamicism, and remaining engaged with China in areas of S&T is one way to stay "ahead of the curve." Thus, a "minimax" orientation does not imply passivity. On the contrary, it implies activism in preparing for, and seizing upon, targets of opportunity for economic, technological, scientific, and political gains as they come along while avoiding costly long-term entanglements. For the reasons given above, a minimax approach to S&T cooperation with China commends itself.

NOTES

1. For a review of reactions, see Genevieve K. Knezo, "Status Report on U.S.-Chinese Science and Technology Relationships," *CRS Report for Congress* (Washington, DC: Congressional Research Service, 16 April 1990).
2. Ibid. Also see Mary Brown Bullock, "The Effects of Tiananmen on China's International Scientific and Educational Cooperation," in U.S. Congress, Joint Economic Committee, *China's Dilemmas in the 1990s: The Problems of Reforms, Modernization, and Interdependence* (forthcoming).
3. Cf., Pierre M. Perrolle, "After Tiananmen: Science Relations with China," *International Science and Technology Insight* 2, No. 2 (Spring 1990), pp. 41–44.

SEVEN

The Role of Chinese Students at Home and Abroad as a Factor in Sino-American Relations

Stanley Rosen

FOLLOWING THE MILITARY CRACKDOWN of June 4, 1989, the hardline Chinese government sought explanations for the anti-regime activities of the broad masses of its urban constituency. Restored to influence, conservative elders who had been eased out of power by Deng Xiaoping pointedly noted how the side-effects of China's reform program had contributed to a social order in which material values dominated spiritual concerns, and where political consciousness had become appallingly low. Perhaps most alarming to the elders, this erosion of regime-sponsored values was particularly serious among those who were expected to inherit the revolutionary goals of their predecessors, that is, China's youth.

In apportioning the blame for this ideological backsliding, Chinese leaders singled out Western countries, particularly the United States, and accused them of deliberately attempting to impede and corrupt the Chinese revolution. American policy toward China was seen as part of a consistent, grand strategy to promote the "peaceful evolution" (*heping yanbian*) of socialist systems to capitalism. By opening the country to reform and the outside world in an effort to import the expertise, technology, and capital required for their ambitious modernization program, Chinese leaders could not prevent the entry of undesirable Western political and philosophical theories, which spread widely on university campuses in the 1980s. With thousands of visiting lecturers and foreign teachers and students passing through Chinese campuses, and with tens of thousands travelling in the opposite direction, it was impossible to limit the exchange of heterodox ideas.

Moreover, the more than 50,000 Chinese students in the West — particularly the largest number, who were in the United States — were seen as especially vulnerable. Beyond the immediate control of the Chinese government, these students were referred to in internal documents after June 4 as "hostages" whose return to China was a "card" the Americans might play to induce the Chinese government to follow Eastern Europe and abandon its socialist political system.

This paper will examine the role of Chinese students as a factor in Sino-American relations. It will be argued that by the late 1980s the regime's instruments for political socialization had broken down both organizationally and ideologically, leaving students searching for new ideals. Even more striking was the open debate within the leadership over the most fundamental principles of the Chinese revolution. Thus, the ideological and organizational failures in the Communist party's youth policy were mirrored at the elite level as well, with articles in the open, official press questioning the proper role for both Marxism and the CCP as China modernized and became part of the global community. The loss of authority over Chinese youth, combined with the open skepticism over core values at the elite level, created a fertile environment for the introduction of Western values into China, primarily through the United States.

At the same time, the overseas study policy seemed to suggest a tacit, even sometimes as explicit admission that China was unable to succeed on its own through the kind of self-reliance which Mao Zedong had consistently stressed. Moreover, it implied that those youth not chosen to study abroad were less able, and that their education in China was lacking by world standards. Thus, both youth who studied abroad and those who remained at home came to acknowledge the superior achievements of the West and Japan and felt that advanced training abroad was a sine qua non for China's modernization and their own upward mobility. The acknowledgment of China's backwardness in relation to the outside world inevitably led to a search for the reasons for China's unhealthy condition. Was capitalism superior to socialism? Should China adopt a more democratic structure, even a multiparty system? Was there something about Chinese culture that hampered modernization? Was Marxism-Leninism-Mao Zedong Thought an ideology ill-suited to economic growth? Having unlocked Pandora's box with the reform and the open door policy, the regime has been unable to import Western learning on a selective basis while preventing an assault on the core values that justify the party's continued monopoly on power.

In the aftermath of June 4, the contradictions between state and society have been exacerbated, with state policies themselves often internally inconsistent. Thus, on the one hand, the government is attempting to attract back to China the tens of thousands of overseas students and scholars crucial for modernization. But those studying abroad, given their tenure in ideologically hostile territory, must be viewed warily, must even be "reeducated," if and when they return. In like manner, facing a serious legitimacy problem after June 4 and recognizing the inroads of Western philosophical and political thought in China, the regime has begun to embrace traditional Chinese culture and nostalgia for the certainties of the Mao era. These are viewed as bulwarks against the encroachments of "Westernization," to be chosen unequivocally for stability at any cost, despite the likely negative effects this will have on the reform program.

This chapter has two main sections, focusing on Chinese students at home and abroad, respectively. The first section depicts an uncertain China on the eve of the 1989 demonstrations, as students within China devoured a wide variety of Western philosophies in their search for an appropriate value system to give meaning to their lives. Closely linked to this quest was the desire to study abroad, which reached a crescendo following the Tiananmen events, as students became more and more dispirited over China's future.

While Western influence on students in China has remained relatively indirect and has operated primarily at the level of ideas, for Chinese students in the United States, particularly after June 4, American policy has become crucial both for their individual futures and for the Sino-American relationship. The temporary legal protection offered by the Bush administration will have to be renegotiated prior to 1994. It is suggested here that "the student question" will reemerge as a salient issue affecting Sino-American relations, though it is currently on the back burner.

Linking these two sections is the interpretation of American intentions offered by China's post-Tiananmen leadership. In the long-term strategy for transforming China they impute to the

United States, Chinese authorities see the students, as future leaders and opinion-makers in their fields, playing a key role. The battle for the future of China, as they see it, will be fought in the minds of the students.

The Turmoil before the "Turmoil": China on the Eve of the 1989 Demonstrations

The student demonstrations, which began following the death of former CCP General Secretary Hu Yaobang on April 15, 1989, occurred at a time of heightened political contention within the party and, even more relevant for our purposes, intense ideological uncertainty within society. In contrast with standard operating procedure throughout most of post-1949 China, the Chinese press openly reflected this uncertainty, providing access in the most authoritative newspapers and journals to those who would be accused after the June 4 crackdown of disseminating "bourgeois liberalism" and promoting the "Western-inspired peaceful evolution" of China. In effect, questions were raised concerning the continuing relevance of all of the Four Basic Principles (adherence to socialism, the dictatorship of the proletariat, rule by the CCP, and subscribing to Marxism-Leninism-Mao Zedong Thought).

Influential economists argued that the essential nature of capitalism had changed, that Marx's theory of capitalist exploitation had become outdated, and that a developing economy benefited everyone, including both capitalists and workers.[1] Many commentators argued that advanced capitalism and developing socialism would eventually "converge," although the nature of that final convergence was a subject for debate.[2]

Party journals held forums on the proper role of the CCP under the reforms, with some advocating a reduced role suggesting that "the party should mind its own business."[3] Indeed, the lack of clarity regarding the purpose of ideological and political work — the raison d'etre of a vanguard party under socialism — made it difficult even to delineate "the party's business" from other business. Thus, the very future of political work was being openly questioned, and the failures of past and current ideo-political work were unabashedly acknowledged.[4] As a result, the scope of political work was systematically narrowed, with some critics, writing in authoritative party organs, demanding that ideological workers not interfere with an individual's "private affairs" and, simultaneously, that party leaders not interfere in academic or social science debates and thus politicize them.[5]

The meaning and function of Marxism in the modern world was likewise a source of contention. For example, most of the first-year graduate students specializing in philosophy at Shanghai's Fudan University readily agreed that "a so-called crisis actually exists in Marxist philosophy," even before the major convulsions in Eastern Europe and the Soviet Union.[6] Respected political theorists such as Li Honglin argued that Marxism needed to evolve to remain relevant, and that the history of post-1949 China was marked by an adherence to "different kinds of Marxism at different times," often at great cost to the country. Critical of the borrowed nature of much of Chinese Marxism, Li pointed out inadequacies and outright mistakes in the writings of Marx, Engels, Lenin, and Stalin and noted hopefully that "beliefs that stand in the way of modernization, whether in writing or uttered by an authority, have indeed been abolished [in China]." He concluded that "practice is the only thing that counts . . . . Anything that does not conform to reality should not be upheld." Interestingly, Li rejected the notion that the state should demand that everyone uphold Marxism, suggesting rather that "it was a citizen's right to choose what ideology to believe in." Even within the CCP, where Marxism by definition should be upheld, Li noted that only a few people had a genuine mastery of the theory.[7]

In a similar fashion, political theorists even questioned the continuing relevance of the "uncompromising struggle" between socialist and bourgeois ideologies. Writing in the party's premier ideological journal, Sun Huichang suggested that Lenin's classic assessment that there could be no neutrality or "third stream" in ideology was out of date.[8] Liberally citing American and other Western social scientists such as Daniel Bell on the end of ideology and the nature of post-industrial society, Sun saw issues of global interest — for example, environmental concerns — as transcending ideology. Moreover, he cited approvingly from Soviet and Eastern European leaders who had argued that socialist countries should not practice "ideological dictatorship," but rather should encourage "diversification."

The suggestion that there should be a well-defined sphere of individual rights, including privacy and the freedom to choose one's belief system, was being echoed by many other writers who called for a transformation of moral concepts in China. The propagation of "model personages" or "selfless individuals" to provide a moral compass for the rest of society — a consistent feature of governmental propaganda efforts from traditional China down through the communist period — came in for particularly harsh criticism. The moral examples presented by the most familiar heroic icons of post-1949 China — peasant Li Shunda; worker Wang Jinxi; soldier Lei Feng; cadre Jiao Yulu; intellectual Hou Juan — were seen as inadequate, if not irrelevant in managing and motivating a modern society. As one critic noted, such fine examples cannot substitute for "perfect institutions, strict and impartial laws, and a sound legal system."[9] Other critics went further, seeing selfless behavior as potentially counterproductive in the new commodity society being created. An individual who emulates Lei Feng, for example, and offers to repair broken items for free is actually wasting social resources, since often the repaired item is of low value. According to this view, the problem stems from "an incomplete understanding of morality which regards individual sacrifice in service to others as beneficial to society."[10]

As Leo Lee has noted, a new mentality had developed. For individuals, life began to center on the self. Society was seen apart from, even in opposition to, the party-state. Increasingly visible, the development of a nascent civil society could be detected. Even the Chinese nation was no longer easily identifiable with the political authorities. Rather, it was perceived as something greater, more closely associated with the generic pursuit of modernization common to all systems.[11]

Given its opening to the outside world, China could not isolate itself from the main currents of global culture, in which ideas and the intellectuals who produced them travelled freely across national boundaries. While Chinese graduate students in the United States contributed articles to influential mainland journals on democracy, feminism, and postmodernism, Chinese universities and research institutions, remarkably free from political interference over culture and intellectual exchanges under Zhao Ziyang's enlightened leadership, sought out and invited foreign scholars as diverse as Milton Friedman and Jacques Derrida.[12] The frenzied search for new ideas strongly suggested that the old ideas and the old values had no market.

The Effects on Ideological Uncertainty: Student Attitudes and Behavior in the Late 1980s

The rapid introduction of such a wide variety of new thinking had a major impact on Chinese students. Concurrent with the relative openness of the Chinese media, which permitted the publication of views questioning longstanding officially sanctioned values, was the recognition that college students had also become confused. Widely circulated publications referred to students in Guangzhou, who were "perplexed, confused, vexed and helpless;" to a Qinghua University student who confided that the destruction of the old values without their replacement by new beliefs had left him "at a loss as to what to do"; to a Beijing University student who no longer knew why he was studying, since "things that were relatively clear have now become unclear."[13] At an April 1988 forum of university students from a number of campuses in the city of Hangzhou, "four symptoms" were diagnosed as afflicting college students: a feeling of being purposeless, a doubt about knowledge, a lack of drive, and lethargy.[14]

Survey research uncovered an even deeper crisis of values among students than was revealed by more impressionistic data.[15] For example, a survey of 2,000 university students in Hangzhou found that 76 percent agreed that ideals were necessary. When asked their own ideals, however, 66 percent said they did not know what they were; another 20 percent answered that it was impossible to formulate such ideals; and only 14 percent responded that they actually had ideals.[16] Nor was the malaise restricted to the university level. A survey of 1,079 junior and senior high school students from rural and urban schools around Jinzhou city, Liaoning province, found that 40 percent of the students either had no belief system, or did not know what they believed; only 30 percent gave the "correct" answer of Marxism-Leninism-Mao Zedong Thought and the Communist party.[17] Other surveys showed that, when offered a limited number of specific choices, students overwhelmingly opted for concrete values such as honesty or freedom of choice over the regime's more abstract core political values like "Communism" or "The Four Basic Principles." Interestingly, in one such survey of high school students in Shanghai, members of the Communist Youth League and graduating seniors were less likely to choose core political values than other students.[18]

The Influence of the United States and the West on Student Attitudes

Having become openly skeptical of some of the core collectivist values of the regime, many students began to look to the West as a source of new moral, philosophical, and political concepts. As noted earlier, articles in the official press broadly sympathetic to the concepts of privacy, academic freedom, and even ideological diversity and pluralism encouraged the students to experiment with new theories and legitimized their quest for a viable belief system. Indeed, the search for new ideas and the interest in Western concepts seem not to have been limited to youth, but were rather a society-wide phenomenon. Table 1 is from a national survey of Chinese political culture conducted in 1987 by an independent group of young and middle-aged Beijing political scientists. In one sense, this study can be seen as an example of the influence of the West on young Chinese social scientists, since the researchers explicitly reject "the philosophically-oriented discussion of political questions" common in China in favor of "behavioral and post-behavioral methods," citing the work of such American behaviorists as Gabriel Almond, Sidney Verba, Lucian Pye, and Heinz Eulau. Some questions are modeled on well-known political science texts such as Nye, Verba and Petrocik's *The Changing American Voter.*[19] Among the revealing results, it is not surprising to find support for Western ideas strong among the highly educated and urbanized segment of the population, or among those forty-five years old and younger. What is striking, however, is the overwhelming support by party and youth league members, as well as cadres in general.

The political culture study cited above is unusual, since the authors display a surprising knowledge of the behaviorist revolution in American political science. The majority of college students were unaware of such literature, but were devouring more standard works of Western philosophy. Given the task of determining the impact this philosophical literature was having on students, the regime's ideological-political workers conducted their

Table 1
Should We Allow Western Thought to Have an Impacrt on China Now?

	% Yes	% No	Sample
Total Sample	75.49	9.26	1365
Occupation			
Worker	73.49	15.26	246
Self-employed	62.81	10.74	122
Intellectual	85.52	3.42	361
Cadre	86.74	3.94	290
Peasant	58.80	15.95	317
Age			
25 and under	74.09	10.12	494
26–35	79.33	5.67	353
36–45	76.29	11.64	232
46–55	70.71	11.62	198
56–65	66.67	15.28	62
66 and over	50.00	18.25	16
Education			
Illiterate	47.72	27.27	44
Primary school	43.51	18.32	131
Junior high	72.50	13.33	460
Senior high or secondary technical school	77.17	9.45	381
College and above	86.86	2.35	426
Political Status			
Communist party member	80.26	9.21	380
Communist youth league member	89.02	6.27	383
Democratic party member	70.29	14.71	34
Influential figure	33.33	25.00	12
Ordinary citizen	68.17	10.94	512

Table 1 (Continued)
Should We Allow Western Thought to Have an Impacrt on China Now?

	% Yes	% No	Sample
Residence			
Large city	82.09	6.54	413
District central city	84.49	6.53	245
Suburban	79.31	7.76	116
County town	72.85	10.34	232
Village	61.11	13.19	288
Border and poor areas	47.05	31.37	51

Source: Min Qi, *Zhongguo zhengzhi wenhua: minzhu zhengzhi nanchande shehui xinli yinsu* [Chinese political culture: the social psychological elements that make it difficult to produce democratic politics] (Kunming: Yunnan Renmin Chubanshe, February 1989), pp. 128–29.

own attitudinal and behavioral surveys linking the introduction of Western beliefs to Chinese domestic developments, and noting the consequences of such beliefs for student life.

One extensive survey, for example, traced the "Sartre mania" (1979–82) to the "first crisis of faith" over Marxism, in the aftermath of the leftist policies of the Cultural Revolution. This was followed by the "Freud mania" (1982–84), which was marked by a lack of interest in studies and a fascination with sexual matters. Next came the "Nietzsche mania" (1984–86). While all three of these "manias" were seen as promoting individual interests at the expense of societal interests and inducing pessimism about the country's future, the Nietzsche mania was viewed as particularly dangerous, since it spoke more directly to economic, political, and cultural values. Chinese authorities blamed it for a variety of subsequent ills associated with the student demonstrations of 1986 and 1989, including the negation of traditional culture, the distrust of all authority, the desire of students and intellectuals to enhance their power directly, and so forth. In the context of the

1989 demonstrations, the Nietzsche mania was seen as the source of the "elite political theory" on which the movement was based.[20]

With the Nietzsche mania as the entering wedge, new trends in thinking from 1986 to 1989 became much more specific in suggesting solutions for China's economic and political problems. Influential Western imports noted and analyzed by Chinese authorities included Democratic Socialism (1985), Political Pluralism (1986), Economic Liberalism (1986–88), Neoauthoritarianism (1987), Maslow's Self-Actualization Theory (1987–89), and Privatization (1988–89), among others.[21]

Given the number of new theories filtering in from the West, there were frequent attempts by the authorities to determine which ones had actual staying power and which were short-term fads. Tables 2 and 3 are drawn from one such survey. Several points are worthy of note. First, Francis Bacon was popular with students because he argued that "knowledge is power" and because his book, *On Life,* provided a guide to living that students found useful. Second, researchers found males more interested in Western philosophy than females; the latter preferred romantic novels. Third, the majority of the students thought that Marxist and non-Marxist philosophy should be treated equally in academic debate, so that in the contention between them truth would emerge. Fourth, a majority of the students had learned about Western philosophy through articles (50.76 percent); a smaller number had read relevant books on the subject (35.51 percent); some had been introduced to such material in political theory courses (16.92 percent), through contact with friends (19.53 percent), lectures by famous people (7.90 percent), or party and youth leagues activities (2.17 percent). As the surveyors ruefully noted, there was a great deal of spontaneity in the process of learning. If some theory suddenly became fashionable, no one wanted to be left out.[22]

Another survey from Lanzhou, Gansu province, found that in some schools over 80 percent of the students had read one or two books on Western philosophy. Those who had not read anything nevertheless found it necessary to at least keep such books on their shelves, to show that they were au courant (*shidai chaoliu*).[23] Indeed, the general atmosphere on the campuses by the mid- to late 1980s made it difficult for the regime's political instructors to have

Table 2
Which Western Scholars Have Had a Comparatively Great Influence on You?

N=780

Western Scholar	%
Bacon	27.69
Freud	22.17
Nietzsche	17.17
Hegel	13.20
Sartre	12.43
Rousseau	10.12
Feuerbach	7.30
Kant	6.66
Toffler	2.82
Fromm	1.79
Others[†]	13.46

Source: Cheng Changchun, *"Xifang zhexue sichao dui daxueshengde yingxiang"* [The influence of Western philosophical thought trends on university students], *Qingnian yanjiu* No. 3, March 1990, p. 19.

[†]Of the 789 respondents, 105 added additional responses in a column marked "others." The responses included Schopenhauer, Marx, Carnegie, Einstein, Hitler, Maslow, Jung, Socrates, Plato, and so forth.

much effect, as the following story, reportedly circulating at Beijing University suggests:

> When a doctoral student used a quote from Nietzsche to explain a problem, he incorrectly cited Engels as the source, so some listeners immediately began hissing all around. Then the student realized his error. When he explained that it was actually Nietzsche's viewpoint, the former opponents promptly tried to find an out, indicating their understanding and praise for this view.[24]

Table 3
Which Academic Thought Trends Have Had a Comparatively Great Influence on You?

N=780

Thought Trend	%
Pragmatism	40.89
Existentialism	32.69
Freudianism	27.69
"Individual Personality-ism" (*renge zhuyi*)	15.64
"Individual Will-ism" (associated with Nietzsche) (*yizhi zhuyi*)	12.56
Positivism	10.25
Neo-Hegelianism	7.87
Historicism	7.82
Structuralism	7.82
Neo-Thomism	6.15
Critical Rationalism	5.76
Phenomenology	5.38
Neo-Kantianism	4.35
Logical atomism; logical positivism	3.97
"Mach-ism"	3.20
Bergsonianism	3.20
Others†	6.92

Source: Cheng Changchun, *"Xifang zhexue sichao dui daxueshengde yingxiang"* [The influence of Western philosophical thought trends on university students], *Qingnian yanjiu* No. 3, March 1990, p. 19.

†Respondents could opt for more than one choice, so the percentage exceeds 100 percent. In the "Others" column, 54 students listed such choices as Marxism, Behaviorism, the Frankfurt School, Schopenhauer-ism, and so forth.

Nor were political instructors even trained to debate the relevant merits of Engels and Nietzsche. A survey of 225 political workers at seven campuses in the north China city of Taiyuan showed how little preparation such officials had received.[25] For example, 72.9 percent had received no prior training, 16.4 percent had had a short training course, and only 11.1 percent had received an extensive theoretical training in their specialty. As many as 48.4 percent seldom read newspapers and magazines, 59.1 percent seldom read books related to their work, and 67.2 percent seldom consulted reference books in their field. Nor were they generally treated as well as other college teachers. In terms of housing and welfare, only 1.3 percent were treated better than their counterparts in other disciplines; another 32.9 percent got equal treatment, and 62.2 percent received fewer benefits.

By their own admission, political workers were facing insurmountable obstacles in trying to stem the influence of Western philosophy on the campuses. Western humanism had convinced many students that since both traditional Chinese morality and the collectivist values of socialism restricted the development of the individual, both were essentially tied to China's feudal past. Political workers not only had little knowledge of Western theories, but also had an unsophisticated view of Marxism and its twentieth-century evolution. They were no match for China's "elite" intellectuals, a considerable number of whom had travelled to the West and introduced much of this new literature, either through commentaries or in the form of translations.[26]

The influence of these elite intellectuals is apparent from a wide variety of surveys published before and after June 4, which revealed student admiration for Western democracy, even praise for capitalism, in the period leading up to the turmoil.[27] But many students, confronted with a bewildering variety of suggested solutions to China's economic and political transition, seemed less concerned with "isms," and more concerned with results. A successful country was one which was rich and powerful, according to the results from one survey of Guangzhou youth; social equality, common belief systems, even individual rights and freedoms were less highly valued.[28]

The impact of Western ideas on Chinese students within China was undeniable and a source of great frustration for those responsible for imparting proper political, social, and cultural values.

Such "spiritual pollution" might have been contained, however, had Chinese students not had the opportunity, and therefore the aspiration, to study abroad, to see and compare for themselves the advantages and disadvantages of "bourgeois democracies." Moreover, given China's fascination with importing state-of-the-art knowledge, residence abroad became almost a sine qua non for students, particularly in scientific and technical fields, to be taken seriously and to achieve rapid promotion. For those in thc social sciences and humanities as well, overseas study brought intellectual rewards as well as enhanced status.

Beginning in 1985–86, noting the serious side-effects the overseas study policy was producing back home, Chinese authorities gradually moved to regain greater control over the outflow of students. By then, however, the numbers of students abroad, particularly in the United States, had become enormous and constituted an emerging issue in United States–China relations. The overseas students, especially those not dependent on Chinese financing, were in many ways independent of government control. But it was only in the aftermath of June 4, when Chinese students in the United States were protected — at least temporarily — by United States law from the obligation to return to China, that the issue became crucial to the long-term Sino-American relationship. The remainder of this chapter therefore addresses the impact of the overseas study policy on this relationship, with particular emphasis on the lingering effects of June 4.

Sending Students Abroad: A Double-Edged Sword

A key plank in China's program of modernization has been the policy of sending large numbers of students and scholars abroad.[29] Indeed, despite new regulations from the Chinese government that limit overseas study, the largest number of foreign students studying in American universities in the 1989–90 academic year came from China. Moreover, the 33,390 Chinese students represented an increase of 15 percent over 1988–89.[30] The dispatch of Chinese students to foreign countries to obtain and return with advanced knowledge is not new; between 1847 and 1949, more than 40,000 Chinese studied abroad.[31] Between 1949 and 1966, China sent 8,424 students to the Soviet Union (only 206 after 1960), and 1,109 students to Eastern Europe.[32] But the recent, concentrated effort to send so many students abroad in so short a time is unprecedented in Chinese history. Not surprisingly, the policy has been a source of contention within the Chinese leadership, primarily because of fears of a "brain drain," since many students have delayed their return to China and because students who do return may have become infected by "bourgeois liberalization" while in the West.[33] These concerns have, of course, been heightened following the June 4 events.

Despite the continuing internal controversy and a series of readjustments which have sought to diminish the loss of talent by exercising tighter control over who may leave and where they go, the overseas study policy has virtually taken on a life of its own, with important ramifications for China's educational and employment systems. It has become almost a cliche to say that everyone wants to leave China to study abroad. While clearly an exaggeration, there is ample evidence to document the dissatisfaction with opportunities in China and the desire to leave, at least until such time as conditions in China improve.

This problem is revealed most clearly in both government and "unofficial" surveys conducted after June 4. Tables 4 and 5 are drawn from a survey conducted in May 1990 without official approval by the Beijing University Graduate Student Association. As table 4 shows, 56.5 percent of respondents felt that the motivation to go abroad was based on pessimism about the future in China. Not surprisingly, as table 5 indicates, the new restrictions on the eligibility of self-supported students to go abroad imposed in February 1990 (see note 30), were viewed as unreasonable or extremely unreasonable by over 80 percent of the students.[34]

But the official surveys, intended primarily for internal circulation, yielded rather similar results and suggested that the government's reeducation program had been ineffective. For example, a joint State Education Commission/Beijing Municipal Party Committee survey conducted at eight universities in Beijing discovered that 40 percent of the interviewees resolutely opposed the February 1990 measures, while another 25 percent "disagreed" with them.[35] One-third of the students said they "would make every effort to leave the country as soon as possible," another 29 percent would wait for a change in the policy, and only 10 percent "did not plan to leave the country at all." There were also indications that

Table 4
What Is Your View of the Now Common Practice of Going Abroad?

Responses	N=453† %
After finishing your study, you can return and render service to the country	18.7
It represents a desire for life in the West	15.8
It is an attempt to catch up with the tide	9.0
Since there is no future in China, it is the only alternative	56.5

Source: Beijing University Graduate Student Association, "Beijing daxue xuesheng sixiang diaocha baogao" [A survey of the thinking of Beijing University students], May 1990, mimeo.

†Questionnaires were distributed to 250 graduate students and 350 undergraduates; 453 questionnaires were returned.

"bourgeois liberalization" continued unchecked; 42 percent of the students still thought that "the main trend of the times" was the gradual convergence of socialism and capitalism, while only 7.1 percent felt it was "the triumph of socialism over capitalism." While 25.4 percent felt that the problems encountered by the reform program could be solved by "political pluralism and a larger extent of democracy and freedom," only 8.8 percent felt that the solution was "to depend on the CCP's leadership and all the people's efforts in tiding over difficulties."

Student orientation toward the outside world and their pessimism over China's future come through in another survey of 2,000 students at sixteen Beijing colleges, conducted in November 1989 by the Beijing Institute of Social Psychology.[36] There was an extreme interest in the impact of changes in Eastern Europe and the Soviet Union on the future of socialism, and in the relation-

Table 5
What Is Your Attitude about the Current Policy of Sending Students Abroad?

Responses	N=453 %
It's reasonable	5.4
I don't care one way or the other	14.4
It's unreasonable	36.1
It is extremely unreasonable	44.1

Source: Beijing University Graduate Student Association, "Beijing daxue xuesheng sixiang diaocha baogao" [A survey of the thinking of Beijing University students], May 1990, mimeo.

ship of the Romanian events to conditions in China. "Significantly increased" listening to the Voice of America was perhaps one indication of dissatisfaction with the sparse and unreliable reporting of these developments by official sources. "At least half" the students were "dissatisfied with" and "did not trust" the government. More than 70 percent supported a multi-party system and separation of powers "should the government system change orientation."

The importance of studying overseas likewise comes through in surveys conducted prior to June 4. Particularly striking are those which asked university students in various large Chinese cities to rank twelve "professions" by social and economic status, and then to rank in order their actual choice of profession. Table 6 is from a survey conducted at several universities in Xian, while table 7 is drawn from a survey of juniors and seniors at seven universities in Beijing, Shanghai, Nanjing, Jinan, and Qingdao. In each of the surveys, "student studying overseas" ranked first in actual choice, despite lower rankings in terms of economic and social status. Other professions ranked near the top were closely tied to China's foreign economic policy. Interestingly, being a graduate student

Table 6
Choice of Future Profession by College Students in Xian

N=445 Male=77.6% Female=22.4%

	Economic Profession	Social Status	Actual Choice of Student
Scientific or technical researcher	8	3	5
Graduate student in China	11	9	9
Cadre in party, government or mass organization	6	1	8
Administrative cadre in enterprise or institution	5	2	3
Engineer or technician	7	7	7
University teacher	10	10	10
Staff member in an industrial or commercial company	4	8	6
Military personnel	12	11	11
Self-employed in individual economy	1	12	12
Student studying overseas	9	4	1
Staff member in a foreign trade, import-export company	3	5	2
Staff member in enterprise or company with foreign capital	2	6	4

SOURCE: Zhao Ying, "Dangdai daxuesheng zhiyeguande biange" [The changes in contemporary university students' views of professions], *Gaodeng jiaoyu yanjiu,* No. 2, December 1989, p. 93.

Note: Numbers represent aggregated rankings of the 12 professions.

or a university teacher *within* China was ranked both low in status and in actual choice in the two surveys. As the surveyors note, this represents a shift in student perceptions. When optimism about the future of reform ran high, the "ideal" track had been "university student-graduate student-job assignment to a scientific research unit." But as the Xian survey discovered, fewer than 10 percent of the students wanted to take the examination for graduate school.[37] For those already in graduate school, the lure of going abroad is equally strong. In a survey conducted among more than 200 graduate students at Xian's elite Jiaotong University at the end of 1988, 55 percent of the students thought of going abroad before even thinking about taking up a profession in China, while another 18 percent wanted a job in a joint-venture enterprise.[38]

But the interest in going abroad is even more pervasive than such limited data might indicate. Statistics from nine of China's largest cities revealed that from 1988 to June 1990, almost 170,000 people applied to study at their own expense.[39] In Beijing, the numbers of those taking the Test of English as a Foreign Language (TOEFL) examination have increased each year. In 1981, the first year it was offered, 285 people took the exam. By 1983, the figure had risen to 2,500; by 1985 it was 5,000; in 1986, it was 18,000; and by 1988, the exam had to be offered three times to accommodate more than 26,000 examinees.[40]

Moreover, the desire to study abroad appears to be widespread at all educational levels. For example, according to restricted-circulation official sources, at Shanghai's prestigious Jiaotong University, 30 to 40 percent of the young teachers have already left, while the number desiring to leave is at least 80 percent. At Fudan University, in the physics department and the life sciences institute, the number of undergraduates who have taken the TOEFL and GRE examinations has reached 40 percent, but among young teachers and graduate students the number exceeds 85 percent.[41] Among the more than 5,300 master's degree students at the Chinese Academy of Sciences, 65 percent have already made contact with overseas institutions.[42] At several Shanghai secondary schools, 600 students were asked in a sample survey whether they were thinking of studying abroad. Over 83 percent said they were. One can easily see the impetus behind the recent regulations to stem the flow of students leaving China.

Table 7
Evaluation and Choice of Professions by University Students

N=197 Male=76.2% Female=23.8%

	Economic Profession	Social Status	Actual Choice of Student
Self-employed in individual economy	1	12	11
Staff member in enterprise or company with foreign capital	2	8	3
Staff member in a foreign economic or trade company	3	5	2
Staff member of non-state supported (*minban*) enterprise or company	4	11	10
Cadre in party or government	5	1	6
Enterprise management cadre	6	2	4
Scientific researcher	7	4	5
Engineer or technician	8	6	7
University teacher	9	9	9
Student studying overseas	10	3	1
Graduate student in China	11	7	8
Secondary school teacher	12	10	12

Source: Teng Yucheng and Yin Qing, "Daxuesheng qiu zhi ze ye diaocha yanjiu" [An investigation of the choices of professions by university students], *Shandong gongye daxue xuebao* 3, No. 4 (1988), p. 55.

Popular Chinese journals have acknowledged the "nearly insane 'upsurge in going abroad,'" particularly after June 4, although it is often seen as an emotional response which will pass in time.[43] Colorful accounts described the atmosphere at elite universities:

> The October 1989 TOEFL registration at Qinghua University set a national record: People were standing in line nine days before the actual time of registration. Everyone who was registered had to return each day to reregister. It was extremely exhausting. It is said that it got to the point that, since a (take-a-number) ticket was needed to obtain a registration form, the tickets themselves were selling for over 100 yuan![44]

To educational officials, this "ferocity . . . to get out of the country" was worrisome, with some critics hoping that appeals to patriotism, nationalism, and socialism would lead students back to the ideal of serving their country.[45]

The most frenzied period — fall 1989 — can now be seen in some perspective.[46] Following Tiananmen, rumors that China would eliminate its study abroad policy and thus suspend TOEFL examinations were rife. Everyone wanted to catch the last train. In the year immediately following Tiananmen, the number of TOEFL registrations grew to 65,000, from the previous year's 39,000. Nor are we likely to see a decline in the demand to study abroad over the next five years. The Educational Testing Service has estimated 55,000 TOEFL tests from July 1990 to June 1991, with a 20 percent increase to 66,000 the following year. Moreover, as Glenn Shive notes, when the Tiananmen college generation completes the new five-year work requirement — necessary for those college graduates without overseas relatives to study abroad — the "pent-up demand" could produce another surge by the mid-1990s.

The Aftermath of June 4: The Implications of Government and Student Responses for Sino-American Relations

After June 4, China's leaders were confronted with a difficult dilemma. Success in their modernization program depends substantially on their ability to create a domestic environment which will be conducive to enticing significant numbers of students currently abroad to return home. At the same time, expanded mobility opportunities must be created for those who do not — or cannot — pursue overseas study. But those abroad have witnessed the events of spring–summer 1989 from the perspective of Western broadcast and print journalism, as well as the critical overseas Chinese media. The large majority appear to have rejected the government's account of these events and are not sanguine about the prospects for a favorable policy shift in the near future. Students within China have likewise been demoralized by government policies of the last two years. Since the government has accused the United States of deliberately seeking to use Chinese students to overthrow the communist system, government-student relations have become indirectly linked to the Sino-American relationship.

China's Case against the United States

In assessing the background and immediate causes of the spring 1989 demonstrations, Chinese authorities singled out the United States as pursuing a long-term policy goal to transform China from a socialist to a capitalist country through a process of "peaceful evolution." While this charge has been levelled openly, the most detailed accounts of reputed American intentions and activities have appeared in internal publications. The material presented below, unless otherwise indicated, is drawn from the most widely circulated of these internally issued books; as of the fourth printing in August 1989, around two million copies had already been circulated in China.[47]

A key plank in the American strategy, according to this account, has been the use of cultural and educational exchange programs. These programs are said to have both general and specific targets.

First, broad ideological and cultural penetration have been achieved through the use of the Fulbright faculty exchange program and the Voice of America (VOA) broadcasts. Since the establishment of diplomatic relations in 1979, 162 American professors have been sent to twenty-four key Chinese universities; since 1983, around 20 "roving scholars" (*xunhui xuezhe*) each year have travelled around lecturing at a variety of colleges and research institutes. The aim, say the Chinese, quoting American government cables, is to use the transmission of American culture to "democratize" China, and to spread "pragmatism." Moreover, listeners are warned not to be misled by the shift to "news," "facts," music, and English language programs by the VOA starting in the 1980s. American aims remain the same as they were when the VOA used the cruder tactic of "psychological warfare" from 1949 through the end of the 1970s.

Second, the United States is said to be concerned that many current Chinese officials studied in the Soviet Union, while none studied in America. It is therefore necessary to cultivate individuals who can understand and appreciate American policies, who will become "America hands" (*Meiguo tong*). This costly endeavor not only includes the presentation of library materials and the establishment of American studies institutes on college campuses, but also requires that current and future Chinese opinion-makers be invited to visit the United States.

In this scenario, America's key resource becomes the Chinese students abroad. As evidence, former President Ronald Reagan is alleged to have said privately that "accepting students from China is a strategic investment." In 1982, when China had 6,500 students and visiting scholars in the United States, Reagan reportedly noted that "65,000 would be even better; this is a long-term investment."

American strategy toward Chinese students, the internal report goes on, singles out children of high-level officials and those most gifted academically for special cultivation. When they return to China, it is hoped that their rise to influential positions will benefit the United States. At the same time, measures are taken to introduce American democratic freedoms and material civilization in the best possible light to the overseas students, so that upon their return they can serve as a bridge to the rest of society in promoting a transition to capitalism. The role of the American FBI in encouraging talented foreign students to defect is also scored in the report.

Additional charges, of less direct relevance to this chapter, accuse American government officials of direct interference in Chinese organizations, notably such units as the Chinese Economic System Reform Research Institute and the Research Institute of the Rural Development Center, which have been dismantled because of their activities before and during the 1989 demonstrations. American programs, such as those in Dalian, Nanjing, Beijing, and Guangzhou set up "to train future leaders," are likewise singled out for criticism.

If hardline Chinese authorities had interpreted American policy since 1949 as consistently aimed at the peaceful evolution of their country toward capitalism, American actions during the 1989 "turmoil" were seen in even starker terms. The United States was accused of seizing the opportunity to intervene more directly in events in China, of seeking to overthrow socialism quickly, thus avoiding the long process of gradual transformation. American interests, it was claimed, were now being pursued in coordination with Chinese students at elite institutions such as MIT, Harvard, the University of California, and Stanford, who were given access to free telephone and telex lines, allowing them to gather information and influence events in more than twenty Chinese cities.

The American government was also blamed for the actions of the Chinese Alliance for Democracy (*Zhongguo minlian*), an organization made up primarily of students and scholars from China seeking to transform the Chinese political system.

American Policy after June 4: Chinese Government and Student Responses

Even before the "June 4 incident," some Chinese authorities were disturbed by the relatively large number of students not returning from overseas study.[48] After June 4, according to both official and unofficial sources, a far smaller percentage have gone back.[49] One Hong Kong source, citing internal data from the Ministry of Public Security and the State Education Commission on all Chinese students abroad, suggested that only 200-odd state-sponsored students of the more than 10,000 that had completed their studies or projects by the end of 1989 had gone back after June 4 (a total of 670 went back in 1989). Of the 8,000 additional state-sponsored students whose work had been completed by July 1990, only 520 (6.6 percent) had returned to their work units by August. Of self-supported students, they reported that 6,000 had concluded their studies, but only 12 had returned in 1989, while another 8 had returned by June 1990, making a rate of return of one in 300.[50]

The role of the American government in providing a safe

haven for Chinese students has of course been crucial in allowing state-supported students to delay their departures. An executive order signed by President Bush on April 11, 1990, directed the attorney general to defer until January 1, 1994, the enforced departure of nationals of the PRC and their dependents who were in the United States. In addition to "irrevocably" waiving the two-year home-country residence requirement until that time for students on J-1 visas, the order also made Chinese nationals and their dependents eligible for employment, and allowed them to maintain lawful status for the purpose of changing non-immigrant status or adjusting to permanent residency. The requirement that PRC nationals hold a valid passport was likewise waived until January 1, 1994.[51]

President Bush's decision has eased the most immediate concerns of Chinese students, but the issue may resurface as an irritant to Sino-American relations as 1994 draws closer. Already, legal advisers for Chinese student associations have noted that the greatest long-term protection — the right to apply for lawful permanent residence status — may not be possible for most students under current American law.[52] Since only a relatively small number have close United States-citizen relatives who could petition for them, the majority will have to find employers willing to sponsor them. For some, this would mean leaving school early and finding a job with such an employer. However, under American immigration laws, no more than 4,000 persons per year may immigrate to the United States from any one country through job offers. In the unlikely event that all the 40,000 to 50,000 PRC students and scholars were to apply for permanent residence, it would take ten years for all to be accommodated, during which time many students would cease to be protected by Bush's executive order. Without legal status, they will not be able to hold jobs and, theoretically, could even face deportation.

Clearly, the American government will be faced with another decision on the Chinese student issue before the end of 1993. Recognizing this, Chinese authorities in their public statements have sought to convince the students, and foreigners as well, that the atmosphere in China is highly favorable to those who return. They have appealed to the students at several levels. Materially, they have been told that they will receive preferential treatment in job placement and the allocation of research funds, and that they will be able to travel abroad again or accept appointments in joint venture projects or international organizations.

The appeal to patriotism and the possibility of taking part in the building of an independent and strong China, one which is no longer exploited by outside forces, is another frequent emphasis. In this regard, those who participated in demonstrations while in foreign countries are told that such behavior will be forgiven. Even those who joined "reactionary" organizations are welcomed back if they repent, while those who have completed their education but "cannot return to China for the time being," are told that they can still serve the country by providing "intelligence-inflow," through such avenues as lecturing or counseling.

As further evidence that the students should feel free to return, the Chinese press repeatedly stresses the continuation of the policy of sending students abroad, reports on high-profile meetings of returned-student groups with leading Chinese officials, and publishes regular reports by students still abroad.[53]

Despite the upbeat nature of articles in the widely circulated official press, a far more revealing indication of official views toward overseas study policy and its effects on Sino-American relations can be seen in internal party documents, which provide detailed guidelines for embassy and consular officials in dealing with Chinese students overseas. At a conference of Education Attaches (consuls) from PRC Embassies and Consulates convened by the State Education Commission in March 1990, the effort to bring Chinese students home was addressed in terms reminiscent of pre-1949 guerrilla warfare.[54] Thus, the "competition for talented personnel" was viewed as a "protracted struggle," in part against the United States, which was perceived as "holding our overseas students as hostages," and in part against the organizations set up by disaffected students and scholars, namely the Independent Federation of Chinese Students and Scholars, the Front for a Democratic China, and the Chinese Alliance for Democracy.

Unlike the sanitized Chinese press, the internal documents display few illusions regarding the ideological views of the overseas students. Although they are seen as generally patriotic, it is acknowledged that "there is little love for socialism." The nurturing of such patriotism, therefore, is the key to China's long-term strategy to convince the overseas students to return, particularly since only "a core of less than five percent . . . have a high degree of political and ideological consciousness and strong patriotic feelings." The documents note that just over 100 of the students have become key anti-government figures, while about 10 percent "took an active part in anti-PRC government activities." The struggle will primarily involve the remaining "70 to 80 percent" of those studying at Chinese public expense in the United States and Canada. It is admitted that "they will not return home in the immediate future, will be detained for a long time, or will immigrate."

The protracted struggle is described in classic united-front terminology. The students are divided into five categories ranging from those who can be relied upon to those who must be "ruthlessly exposed and cracked down upon," with the majority in categories two and three (patriotic but wavering elements; those deeply affected by Western values, politically dissident, unlikely to return home but not involved in anti-PRC government activities) to be won over by persuasion and education. Those who have been active in anti-government activities (category four) are to be divided and demoralized.

The analysis of Sino-American relations starts from the premise that little real improvement is to be expected in the immediate future, given the few "cards" held by the Chinese side. Indeed, the overseas student issue is called "a heavy bomb [the U.S. is using] to pressure us." To prevent further "plunder" of Chinese personnel, the documents note that overseas students should no longer be sent to the United States and Canada at public expense to pursue graduate degrees.[55] Visiting scholars should be sent in smaller numbers and "must be politically mature and reliable" and "have plenty of actual work experience."

When one examines the available data on the attitudes of Chinese students currently in the United States, the Chinese government strategy described above, marked as it is by a mix of patience and persuasion, would seem to be the only viable alternative. For example, "The Political Science Society of the Overseas Chinese Students and Scholars Studying in the United States" sent out questionnaires to over 1,000 students at twenty-one American universities; their analysis was based on the 360 valid returned responses.[56] They found that the largest number — 46.2 percent — intended to return to China only in the medium long term (ten to fifteen years). Another 31.7 percent intended to return in the midterm (five to six years). Only 2.6 percent intended to return home immediately, while 14.5 percent declared they would never return.

The results suggested that the main "pulling" forces in the United States were a stable democratic political system and a free academic environment, while the major "pushing" forces were China's lack of political democracy and political stability, no guarantee of freedom to leave the country, a low-quality academic environment with little freedom, and the Tiananmen massacre. Congruent with the analysis of Chinese authorities, the surveyors found that a great many students were patriotic, but that "their patriotism is directed toward the Chinese culture and not China's 'socialist' political economic system." This suggested that a failure to improve academic and political conditions in China could convince the majority to stay in the United States and exercise their patriotism through participation in traditional cultural rituals, even through such simple activities as going to Chinatown to eat. Since those not intending to return for ten to fifteen years have been seeking suitable employment, purchasing homes, and having children, their ties to China may, over time, become weaker. If the 31.7 percent who expect to return to China within five to six years see no improvement at home, they too could delay their departure, dependent of course on future American government policy.

Conclusion: Students and the Sino-American Future

By early 1991, China had completed its third and last round of political trials for those accused of fomenting the 1989 "turmoil." With outside observers generally viewing the majority of the sentences as "lenient by Chinese standards," human rights issues seemed to recede once more into the background. The vast majority of the 40,000-plus Chinese students in the United States were quietly going about their studies, thoroughly disillusioned by the factionalism and ineffectiveness of the overseas dissident movement.[57] Basic economic conflicts, such as the ballooning American trade deficit and China's continuing piracy of software and other intellectual property, had begun to dominate the news.[58] It appeared that, at least until 1993, the issue of Chinese students would not be an important factor in Sino-American relations.

Discussion of the United States in the Chinese press, however, was unabated, as Chinese authorities adopted a long-term view of the dangers the image of America posed to Chinese students. It was acknowledged privately that many, if not most, of those already abroad might be lost; the focus was placed instead on the socialization of those still in China, particularly at the secondary school level and below. Intensive propaganda on the "true nature" of American democracy and imperialism permeated the Chinese press. Reminiscent of the early 1950s, primary and high school students were issued a booklet entitled "Historical Examples of American Imperialism's Invasion of China."[59] Authorities who had written positively of American democracy and its lessons for China, such as Hu Jiwei, were openly criticized, while lurid stories of panic-stricken New Yorkers combined with the latest murder statistics from the New York Police Department to convince readers that "other than a few people who are infatuated with the bourgeois way of life, the majority of well-meaning people do not show any interest in such a society."[60]

Appeals to avoid the seductiveness of Western blandishments were couched in the rhetoric of cultural conservatism. China's positive traditional moral culture, not very carefully distinguished from its negative legacy of feudalism, was highly praised as a sound basis for socialist modernization, in contrast to "Westernization," a perverted form of modernization which could only be achieved by a third world country at the cost of "national nihilism."[61] In this context, overseas dissidents were repeatedly ridiculed as "self-claimed Westernized intellectuals" who are "slaves of a foreign master."[62] Harsh restrictions were placed on the use of satellite dishes nationwide in an effort to deflect foreign broadcasts deemed to be subversive.[63]

Despite the propaganda onslaught, it is difficult to see how what in effect remain half-measures can reverse the impact that the decade-long reform program has had on Chinese youth, or how they can restore the government's greatly diminished legitimacy. Indeed, the ambivalent nature of China's relationship with the West constantly reveals itself, even in articles devoted to combatting "peaceful evolution." Thus, in the same paragraph,

Chinese citizens are told to maintain a high degree of vigilance against the schemes of the "imperialist forces," whose advanced technology and capital are nonetheless deemed essential "to accelerate China's social modernization."[64]

If the Chinese government finds America's wealth and technology crucial for the achievement of developed socialism, China's young people likewise are inexorably drawn to the United States. Retelling the story of America's role in subjugating China during the Opium War 150 years ago, or even recounting the glories of the Chinese revolution and the birth of the PRC, now over forty years in the past, has little practical significance for those born during the Cultural Revolution. The wealth of the United States is portrayed on Chinese television by shows like "Hunter" and "Falcon Crest," dubbed in Chinese. The freedom and independence of American youth comes across in such movies as "Breakdance," which helped set off a break-dancing fad among high school youth when it was shown in China.[65]

After ten years of "opening up," Chinese youth no longer have a China-centered view of the world. Appeals to the glories of Chinese history and traditional moral culture cannot serve as prime motivating factors for this generation. Unlike their predecessors, they were not shipped off to the countryside and exposed to the backwardness and poverty of a still-traditional China while having little information about the world outside. Such discontinuity in life experiences has created a generation gap which is palpable. As one youth told a foreign reporter, "I can discuss the songs of Pink Floyd with my classmates, but if I ask my professor what he thinks of them, he won't have any idea what I'm talking about. I have never been to America, but I have more in common with young people over there than with my own professors."[66]

This strong attraction to explore American culture, and the concomitant desire to study in the United States, has already shown signs of limiting the ability of the state to carry out and enforce the desired restrictive policies on overseas study. For example, the new regulations on studying abroad have made things more difficult for university graduates, but the policy has produced some unanticipated consequences. Now that there are restrictions on the number of graduates and undergraduates from each university going abroad, and those graduating must complete a service period of five years before applying to leave, one finds an increasing number of middle school students in large cities refusing to sit for the university entrance examinations. They take the TOEFL examination while in senior high and apply directly to foreign universities, raising the possibility, if this trend continues, that some of China's best students may forgo domestic university training. In Shanghai, for example, more than 5,000 qualified senior high graduates (one-sixth of all qualified graduates) did not register for the university examinations in 1990.[67] In response, China has recently announced that "the state will draft a set of stricter regulations" for the TOEFL examination, although there are as yet no details on what, if any, restrictions will be introduced.[68]

With far fewer students applying to graduate schools as well, discontent with the restrictive policies has grown. American citizens the Chinese authorities respect highly, such as Nobel Prize winner Yang Zhenning, have urged a more tolerant and flexible policy toward overseas study.[69] One State Education Commission official told a foreign reporter privately that "graduate applications are dropping now because no one wants to delay going abroad for another one or two years," predicting that some of the government's stringent policies would "definitely change soon, but not immediately, because any sudden reversal would be seen as an embarrassing failure."[70]

The discontent revealed through internal sources is even more direct. One Shanghai publication summed up the current cynicism, noting that: "Teachers and Students at not just a few schools had many things to say about the children of cadres who had been able to go abroad. They asked: Which central leader doesn't have a child abroad? . . . At the end of last year, when another large group of children of cadres caught the last train out, the newspapers said that the overseas study policy would not change. We were cheated."[71] Significantly, in an indication of just how much influence the disaffected students feel the West exercises over Chinese policy in this area, they also claimed that "CCP policy often changes, so this regulation will definitely have a short life. Once the foreigners oppose it, the policy will be rescinded."[72]

Although the West clearly does not have such power to alter Chinese decisions, the roots of policymaking are often strange. A recent secret internal memorandum outlined the Western strategy of peaceful evolution, suggesting that the original plan was to "change Eastern Europe in two to three years, change the Soviet Union in five years, and change China five years after that." Unnamed senior Chinese party leaders were then quoted as saying that the only way China can avoid the fate of Eastern Europe and defeat this Western strategy is to solve China's economic problems and develop a strong economy.[73] This new emphasis on economics at the expense of ideology has been a major theme in the Chinese press in the first part of 1991 and can be interpreted as a clear loss, at least temporarily, for more conservative elements who had insisted that ideological work, especially combatting "bourgeois liberalization," is as important as economic work. It is thus possible, ironically, that the so-called "peaceful evolution" strategy spearheaded by the United States will turn out to be the major goad to keeping China's reform and open policy on track.

NOTES

1. Zhuge Lin, "Has the Essential Nature of Capitalism Changed? — Commenting on Several of Comrade Tong Dalin's Ideas on the Question of the Essence of Contemporary Capitalism," *Qiushi,* 16 October 1990, translated in Joint Publications Research Service, *China* (hereafter JPRS-CAR) -90-087, 27 November 1990, pp. 26–33.
2. Xin Xiangyang, "Reform and Social Convergence," *Guangming ribao,* 27 February 1989, translated in Foreign Broadcast Information Service Daily Report, *China* (hereafter FBIS) -CHI-89-051, 17 March 1989, pp. 24–26; Liu Fangyu, "The Confusion Caused by the 'Theory of Convergence' Must be Cleared Up," *Renmin ribao,* 26 November 1990, translated in FBIS-CHI, 13 December 1990, pp. 29–32.
3. "Does 'The Party Should Attend to Its Own Work' Mean 'The Party Should Mind Its Own Business?' — A Collection of Letters to the Editor," *Sixiang zhengzhi gongzuo yanjiu,* August 1988, translated in JPRS-CAR-88-077, 30 November 1988, pp. 9–11.
4. See, inter alia, Zhou Baohua and Zhao Chuangming, "The Focus Should Be on Reform — An Inquiry into Enterprise Ideological and Political Education Efforts," *Sixiang zhengzhi gongzuo yanjiu,* November 1988, translated in JPRS-CAR-89-015, 23 February 1989, pp. 13–18, and Pen Wenyang, "A Problem in Current Ideological and Political Work: Several Considerations on 'Adverse Psychology,'" *Shehui kexue,* May 1988, translated in JPRS-CAR-88-064, 12 October 1988, pp. 7–11.
5. Zhu Ming, "Please Close One Eye — On Respecting an Individual's Private Affairs When Doing Ideological and Political Work," *Banyuetan,* 10 January 1989, translated in JPRS-CAR-89-028, 31 March 1989, pp. 8–9; Deng Weizhi, "Raise the Coefficient of Political Security for Theorists," *Jiefang ribao,* 8 June 1988, translated in JPRS-CAR-88-056, 19 September 1988, pp. 18–19.
6. Li Ling, "The Question of Crisis in Marxist Philosophy," *Wenhui bao,* (Shanghai), 7 June 1988, translated in JPRS-CAR-88-056, 19 September 1988, p. 18.
7. Li Honglin, "The Evolution of Marxism in China," *Makesi zhuyi yanjiu,* No. 1, 20 March 1989, translated in JPRS-CAR-89-066, 27 June 1989, pp. 7–11.
8. Song Huichang, "The Basic Characteristics of the Evolution of Ideological Theories in the Contemporary World," *Qiushi,* No. 11, 1 June 1989, translated in JPRS-CAR-89-076, 21 July 1989, pp. 20–24.
9. Gao Wen, "The Limitations of Fine Examples," *Guangming ribao,* 24 February 1988, translated in JPRS-CAR-88-029, 13 June 1988, pp. 1–2.
10. Mao Yushi, "From Negation to Affirmation," *Shijie jingji daobao,* 29

February 1988, translated in JPRS-CAR-88-024, 23 May 1988, pp. 36–38.

11. Leo Ou-fan Lee, "The Crisis of Culture," in Anthony Kane, ed., *China Briefing 1990* (Boulder: Westview Press, 1990), pp. 83–105.
12. Ibid.
13. For example, see Song Bin, "What Are Today's University Students of China Thinking About?," *Liaowang* (Overseas Edition), No. 36, 5 September 1988, translated in FBIS-CHI, 14 September 1988, pp. 30–33.
14. Ibid.
15. These and other surveys are discussed in more detail in Stanley Rosen, "Students and the State in China: The Crisis in Ideology and Organization," in Arthur Rosenbaum, ed., *State and Society in China, 1978–1990* (Boulder: Westview Press, forthcoming).
16. Ying Hang, "On the Establishment of Ideals by Contemporary University Students," *Zhejiang daxue jiaoyu yanjiu,* No. 1, March 1990, pp. 17–21.
17. Wang Shuzhi, "Secondary School Students' Beliefs and Marxist-Leninist Education," *Xiandai zhongxiaoxue jiaoyu,* No. 2, 1990, pp. 24–25.
18. Investigation Group of the Educational Information Research Office of the Educational Research Institute of Shanghai Municipality, "An Investigation of the Values of Some Secondary School Students in Shanghai," *Shanghai jiaoyu keyan* No. 6, November 1989, pp. 36–38.
19. Min Qi, *Zhongguo zhengzhi wenhua: minzhu zhengzhi nanchande shehui xinli yinsu* [Chinese political culture: the social psychological elements that make it difficult to produce democratic politics] (Kunming: Yunnan Renmin Chubanshe, February 1989). The authors reprint a table from *The Changing American Voter* showing the sharp decline from 1958–1973 in the American voter's sense that their political system operates fairly, suggesting that similar longitudinal studies should be undertaken in China.
20. See, for example, the compilation by many teachers at the Beijing Chemical Engineering Institute, "The Passive Influence of the Tide of Western Philosophy on University Students," *Xuanchuan shouce,* No. 1, 1990, pp. 25–30, reprinted in *People's University Photocopied Materials: Ideological-Political Education,* No. 4, April 1990, pp. 85–88.
21. Ibid.
22. Cheng Changchun, "The Influence of Western Philosophical Thought Trends on University Students," *Qingnian yanjiu,* No. 3, March 1990, pp. 19–24.

23. Li Yizeng, "The Assault of Western Humanism on Ideological Education in Universities," *Sixiang jiaoyu yanjiu,* No. 2, 1990, pp. 39–40.
24. Jin Wenju, "University Campus Maladies," *Daxuesheng,* No. 4, April 1990, translated in JPRS-CAR-90-046, 26 June 1990, pp. 87–89.
25. Shu Chengchang, Wu Shijun and Li Haixing, "Some Relevant Statistics about Full-Time Political Workers," *Sixiang jiaoyu yanjiu,* No. 2, 1990, p. 39.
26. See *Xuanchuan shouce,* n. 20.
27. For details, see Rosen, "Students and the State," n. 15.
28. Wang Zhixiong, Liang Feng, Wu Xiaoping and Zhang Bin, "An Inquiry into the Special Characteristics of the Political Culture of Guangzhou Youth," *Qingnian tansuo,* No. 6, 1989, pp. 15–16, 12.
29. Among many useful studies on the subject, see Leo A. Orleans, *Chinese Students in America: Policies, Issues and Numbers* (Washington, DC: National Academy Press, 1988); David M. Lampton et al., *A Relationship Restored: Trends in U.S.-China Educational Exchanges, 1978–1984* (Washington, DC: National Academy Press, 1986); Joyce K. Kallgren and Denis Fred Simon, eds., *Educational Exchanges: Essays on the Sino-American Experience* (Berkeley: Institute of East Asian Studies, 1987); Ruth Hayhoe, *China's Universities and the Open Door* (Armonk, NY: M.E. Sharpe, 1989); Ruth Hayhoe and Zhan Ruiling, eds., "Educational Exchanges and the Open Door," *Chinese Education* 21, No. 1 (Spring 1988); the articles by Ruth Hayhoe and Leo Orleans in *China Exchange News* 17, Nos. 3–4 (September and December 1989); Glenn Shive, "Policy Debates and Rumor Mills: China Considers Restrictions on Study Abroad," *China Exchange News* 18, No. 1 (March 1990), pp. 3–7; and Glenn Shive, "Where Has the Dust Settled on U.S. China Educational Exchange?," *Institute of International Education* (Hong Kong office), 5 March 1991. *China Exchange News,* published quarterly by the Committee on Scholarly Communication with the People's Republic of China, and the *Chronicle of Higher Education* remain among the best sources on an ongoing basis.
30. Robin Wilson, "Foreign Students in U.S. Reach a Record 386,000," *Chronicle of Higher Education* 37, No. 13 (28 November 1990), pp. A1, 36. It should be noted, however, that the new restrictive regulations only went into effect on February 1, 1990. For self-supported students the main thrust is to require a five-year period of work in China for all graduates from Chinese universities who do not have overseas Chinese in their immediate families. Students with other, more distant relatives overseas may pay a fee in lieu of the five years' work based on the years of education they have received in China. State-sponsored students face restrictions on entering degree programs

overseas, with the government's emphasis shifting to support for senior and mid-career academics engaged in shorter research and training programs. On these measures, see Glenn Shive, "New Rules on PRC Students Studying Abroad: Who Can Leave, Who Cannot and Why," *Institute of International Education* (Hong Kong office), 23 March 1990. Moreover, the burgeoning numbers are now being inflated by those who have not returned to China as a result of the June 4, 1989, military crackdown. As a result of the effort to leave before the rumored new restrictive regulations appeared, the number of self-supported students increased from 4,771 in 1988 to 7,386 in 1989. Of those, 5,702 arrived after the June 4 crackdown. See *Chronicle of Higher Education,* 23 May 1990, p. A35. On the other hand, the number of state-sponsored students has dropped. As Glenn Shive notes, "In the peak months of June, July and August of 1988, the U.S. consulates issued about 3,500 J-1 visas [used by state-sponsored students]. In the troubled summer of 1989, J-1 visas dropped by a third to about 2,400. By 1990, the first summer of the new rules, the three month count of J-1 visas fell another 50% to about 1,200. Comparing the summers of 1988 and 1990, about 2,000 more F visas [for self-sponsored students] were granted whereas about 2,300 fewer J visas were issued." See Shive, "Where Has the Dust Settled," p. 3.

31. Yao Chun and Shen Gang, "Why Not Come Home, Chinese Students Abroad? — A Survey of the Situation of Shanghai Students Trained Abroad between 1978 and 1985," *Shijie jingji daobao,* 7 April 1986, translated in Stanley Rosen, ed., *Chinese Education* 23, No. 2 (Summer 1990), pp. 56–62.
32. Huang Shiqi, "Contemporary Educational Relations with the Industrialized World: A Chinese View," in Ruth Hayhoe and Marianne Bastid, eds., *China's Education and the Industrialized World* (Armonk, NY: M.E. Sharpe, 1987), pp. 225–26.
33. On the brain drain issue, see Leo A. Orleans, *Chinese Students,* pp. 36–56. For the "liberal" Chinese view on what it would take to entice more overseas students home, see Stanley Rosen, ed., "Selections on Education from the *World Economic Herald,*" *Chinese Education,* Summer 1990, especially pp. 56–92.
34. For details on these restrictions see Shive, "New Rules on PRC Students." For restrictions even before the new regulations, see Wu Yung-chao, "Probing Into the Chinese Communist Policy of Reducing the Number of Students Studying Abroad," *Zhonggong yanjiu* (Taiwan) 24, No. 3 (15 March 1990), pp. 54–60.
35. *Ming bao* (Hong Kong), 10 June 1990, p. 18.
36. Hsu Hsin-you, "An Investigative Report on Political Attitudes of Cur-

rent University Students in Beijing," *Ching Pao* (Hong Kong), July 1990, translated in JPRS-CAR-90-081, 31 October 1990, pp. 37–39.

37. There was a 38 percent drop in applicants for master's degrees in 1989 compared to 1988, with the drop around 50 percent in Shanghai, Beijing, and Guangzhou. Although there are a variety of reasons for the declining interest in doing graduate work, one important factor is the delay it presents for those who desire to study abroad. See Xiong Yuesheng, "Analyzing the Reasons; Seeking Countermeasures: Discussing the Decline in Applicants for the 1989 Master's Examinations," *Xuewei yu yanjiusheng jiaoyu,* No. 6, 1989, pp. 22–24. An important change in 1990 eliminated the unified national examination for graduate school, with recommendations now playing a crucial part. Moreover, only around 10,000 of the expected 25,000 new students to be enrolled in master's degree programs in 1990 were to come directly from universities and colleges. See Radio Beijing, 3 November 1989, translated in FBIS-CHI, 8 November 1989, pp. 28–29.
38. Gu Limin, "An Investigation and Analysis of the Ideology of Graduate Students," *Gaodeng jiaoyu yanjiu* (Xian Jiaotong University), No. 1, 1990, pp. 39–42.
39. Chen Ming, "Studies Abroad are Places of No Return," *Cheng Ming,* No. 157, November 1990, translated in JPRS-CAR-90-089, 30 November 1990, pp. 45–46.
40. Xiao Qinfu, *Wuci langchao* [Five tides] (Beijing: Zhongguo Renmin Daxue Chubanshe, November 1989), p. 141.
41. Chen Hao, "'Hot Topics' among Teachers and Students at Shanghai's Universities after the Start of Classes," *Gaoxiao xinxi yu tansuo,* No. 5, 15 March 1990, pp. 1–2.
42. *Wuci langchao,* p. 146.
43. Gao Yan, "Cast Aside Arrogance, Break Away from Dejection," *Daxuesheng,* February 1990, translated in JPRS-CAR-90-040, 29 May 1990, pp. 20–22.
44. Wang Chuanchen, "TOEFL Craze Sweeps Qinghua University," *Daxuesheng,* May 1990, translated in JPRS-CAR-90-046, 26 June 1990, pp. 89–91.
45. Ibid. Also, Zhang Yihua and Wang Huihua, "Perspectives on 'the Craze to Go Abroad' among University Students," *Rencai kaifa,* No. 4, 1990, pp. 10–11.
46. Data in this paragraph is drawn from Shive, "Where Has the Dust Settled."
47. See the Social Science and Art and Literature Education Section of the State Education Commission, the Ideological and Political Work Section of the State Education Commission, and the Higher Educa-

tion Work Committee of the Beijing Municipal Party Committee, joint editors, *Wushitiande huigu yu fansi* [Looking back and reflecting upon the fifty days] (Beijing: Gaodeng Jiaoyu Chubanshe, 1989), especially pp. 72–82.

48. Figures published in official Chinese sources for the number of students and scholars sent abroad and returnees are inconsistent. On the discrepancies, see Leo A. Orleans, "China's Changing Attitude toward the Brain Drain and Policy toward Returning Students," *China Exchange News* 17, No. 2 (June 1989), pp. 2–5, and Orleans, "Chinese in America: The Numbers Game," *China Exchange News* 17, No. 3 (September 1989), pp. 9–10. In 1988–89, before June 4, Chinese figures for students and scholars going abroad since 1978 ranged from 40,000 to 64,000, with the number of returnees listed as between 20,000 and 22,000, depending in part, it appears, on whether self-sponsored students are included. More recently, the figures have been updated. For much of 1990, figures of from 30,000 to 33,000 returnees were common. For example, see Xinhua reports in English for 20 January, 5 July, and 21 September 1990 in JPRS-CAR-90-010, 7 February 1990, p. 73; FBIS-CHI, 19 July 1990, p. 20; and FBIS-CHI, 25 September 1990, p. 24, respectively. By the end of 1990, the number climbed to 40,000. This would presumably include those going for short stays and perhaps those who have gone back and forth several times. The number of scholars reportedly returning from the United States was given as 12,500, or 29.8 percent of those sent. This represented a higher percentage than any other country. See *Beijing Review* 34, No. 4 (28 January, 3 February 1991), p. 32 and FBIS-CHI, 25 September 1990, p. 24. On the other hand, Leo Orleans had estimated the number of returnees from the United States between 1978 and January 1988 at 19,500, which would include virtually all the state-sponsored students and scholars. See *Chinese Students in America,* p. 22.
49. Chen Ming, "Studies Abroad."
50. Ibid. These statistics are as much as 50 percent lower than the few officially released figures that are available. For example, Premier Li Peng noted in January 1990 that more than 700 Chinese students had returned since June 1989. See *Xinhua* English, 20 January 1990, in JPRS-CAR-90-010, 7 February 1990, p. 73. It should be noted that even official figures show only 1,000 self-supported students had returned to China since 1949, so the current low rate is not surprising.
51. For Executive Order 12711 of 11 April 1990, see *Federal Register* 55, No. 72 (13 April 1990). For further information, see *National Association for Foreign Student Affairs* handout at 42nd Annual Conference, Portland, Oregon, 15–18 May 1990. President Bush first announced

a directive to protect Chinese students on November 30, 1989, after vetoing congressional legislation on the same subject. The formal April 1990 Executive Order was issued after congressional concern was expressed that the November announcement had not been sufficiently "official." Unlike the earlier directive, which covered only Chinese students who had come to the United States by 5 June 1989, the new order covered those who were in the United States as of 11 April 1990.

52. This paragraph draws from Carl Shusterman, "Amnesty for Chinese Students in the U.S.," *Christian Science Monitor,* 7 June 1990, p. 19.
53. For example, the Overseas Edition of *Renmin ribao* on 18 July 1990 began to devote a special page to stories by Chinese students overseas. For a sampling of the articles referred to above, see *Liaowang* (Overseas Edition), No. 5, 4 February 1991, translated in FBIS-CHI, 12 February 1991, pp. 23–25; *Renmin ribao,* 5 June 1990, translated in FBIS-CHI, 13 June 1990, p. 19; *Renmin ribao* (Overseas Edition), 18 July 1990, translated in FBIS-CHI, 26 July 1990, p. 20; *Xinhua* English, 18 July 1990, in FBIS-CHI, 19 July 1990, pp. 19–20.
54. The key document and additional directives can be found in *Pai Hsing* (Hong Kong), 16 May 1990, translated in JPRS-CAR-90-067, 31 August 1990, pp. 17–23.
55. An important distinction is made between the United States, which "hopes that our overseas students will return home to bring their roles into full play," and Canada, which "wants them to immigrate" and is more directly accused of "plundering our talented personnel."
56. *Pai Hsing,* 1 September 1990, translated in JPRS-CAR-90-081, 31 October 1990, pp. 39-43.
57. Edward A. Gargan, "China's Dissidents All Alone," *Los Angeles Times,* 17 March 1991, pp. M1, 6. On the divided dissident movement, see Yan Nanfei, "The Open Fight among the Factions of Chinese Students Studying in the United States," Pai Hsing, 16 August 1990, pp. 54–57, and Qin Liyan, "The Princeton School and the Chicago School," *Kaifang zazhi* (Hong Kong), October 1990, pp. 50–51.
58. George White, "China-U.S.: A Bulging Trade Gap," *Los Angeles Times,* 11 March 1991, pp. D1, 4.
59. Li Yu, "Openly Seeking Friendship, Secretly Hostile," *Nanbeiji Monthly* (Hong Kong), No. 247, December 1990, pp. 54–57.
60. Li Hong, "Discovery in 'Democracy' — Criticizing Hu Jiwei," *Renmin ribao,* 27 December 1990, translated in FBIS-CHI, 31 December 1990, pp. 32–33; Zhang Haitao, "The Nature of U.S. Democracy Viewed from History and Reality," *Qiushi,* November 1990, translated in JPRS-CAR-90-093, 27 December 1990, pp. 17–21.
61. Luo Guoji, "Several Theoretical Questions on Moral Principles,"

Renmin ribao, 19 October 1990, translated in FBIS-CHI, 2 November 1990, pp. 22–25.

62. He Sicheng, "Desperate Renegade 'Elite' in Exile," *Renmin ribao,* 3 May 1990, translated in FBIS-CHI, 7 May 1990, pp. 30–34.
63. James L. Tyson, "Satellite Dishes Get Static from Beijing," *Christian Science Monitor,* 6 November 1990, p. 5.
64. Qiao Wanjun and Wang Chunsheng, "Bolster Class Consciousness to Prevent Peaceful Evolution," *Qunzhong,* August 1990, translated in JPRS-CAR-90-079, 25 October 1990, pp. 19–20.
65. David Holley, "Drawn to a Dream," *Los Angeles Times,* 23 October 1990, p. H5. Soon after the Tiananmen crackdown, the government limited foreign-produced television shows to 15 percent of total air time, but this has now been eased.
66. Takashi Oka, "Between the Bicycle and the Fax, China Shapes Its Identity," *Christian Science Monitor,* 14 December 1990, p. 19.
67. Although additional reasons could be found, the desire to go abroad appears to be the most important one. Se Xi Cheng, "A New Tendency in University Recruitment in the Mainland," *Chiushih nientai,* October 1990, p. 10; Ta Wei, "Upsurge in Going Abroad on Mainland," *Chiushih nientai,* May 1990, translated in JPRS-CAR-90-065, 22 August 1990, pp. 88–90.
68. "China to Improve TOEFL Supervision," *Beijing Review* 34, No. 10 (17 March 1991), p. 9.
69. Yang Zhenning, "China Should Alter Its Conception of Sending Students Abroad," *Gaojiao wenzhai,* No. 7, July 1990, p. 10.
70. Sarah Lubman, "Facing Widespread Discontent, China May Relax Rules Limiting Graduate Education and Overseas Study," *Chronicle of Higher Education,* 12 September 1990, pp. A37, 40.
71. Chen Hao, "'Hot Topics,'" *Gaojiao xinxi yu tansuo,* pp. 1–4.
72. Ibid.
73. *Far Eastern Economic Review* 151, No. 9 (7 March 1991), p. 6. Other Hong Kong sources closely associate this position with Deng Xiaoping.

EIGHT

Military Relations: Sanctions or Rapprochement?

June Dreyer

THE BUSH ADMINISTRATION'S POLICY on military relations with the PRC since Tiananmen may be characterized as the opposite of President Theodore Roosevelt's advice to "speak softly and carry a big stick." President Bush has spoken forcefully in public while exercising quiet diplomacy that seemed to undercut the thrust of his public remarks. The issue of whether it would be preferable to punish China by imposing curbs on military sales and exchanges (the hard-line approach) or continue to do business as usual (the soft-line approach) is not a simple one, with both sides able to present convincing arguments for the course of the action they support. Moreover, the outcomes of any course of action are uncertain, given, first, the differences of opinion within the Chinese elite at present; second, the growing cleavage between that elite and the people in whose name it governs; and, third, the rapid changes in international power configurations that have been occurring in months since the events at Tiananmen. This paper will discuss the implications of different policy options that the United States might pursue and the possible consequences thereof.

United States Policy since the Tiananmen Incident

The Chinese People's Liberation Army's brutal suppression of unarmed civilian demonstrators at Tiananmen Square on the night of June 3–4, 1989, caused shock and horror around the world. Chinese communism had long been regarded as a more benign variant of its Russian model, and it had been considered still more humane under the de facto rule of Deng Xiaoping. A correspondent for the *New York Times* referred to the "cuddly communism" of the 1980s,[1] and indeed gifts of adorable baby pandas to carefully selected foreign zoos and the sale of expensive gold medallions bearing their likeness was part of the People's Republic of China's turn toward the capitalist West.

Most Western observers had assumed that this turn toward capitalism would entail increased personal freedoms for the Chinese, including the right to express grievances peacefully. After the Tiananmen Square events, the comparison that came to mind was with the Bloody Sunday of 1904 Russia: czarist troops firing on unarmed peasants as they sought to bring their grievances to the throne. Reflecting feelings of being deceived as well as disappointed, 1989 public opinion demanded that something be done. The question for American policymakers was what, and against whom in particular. There was consensus that the PRC does not formulate its policies with world opinion in mind and that it was unlikely to change its position in response to it. Most analysts agreed that the top leadership itself could not be punished by external forces, apart from verbal chastisement. They also pointed out that sanctions should not be of the sort that would hurt average Chinese citizens or students, who constituted the prime force demanding more democratic freedoms.

Since the military had carried out the suppression, it was a logical target of sanctions. After several hours of heated discussion with his advisers, President Bush announced the suspension of high-ranking visits, including military visits, with the PRC, and also banned military sales to China of all items controlled by the State Department and cited on the department's Munitions Control List, until such time as China could amend its human rights behavior. Congress went further, introducing legislation suspending military sales, nuclear cooperation, and the export of American-made satellites for launching by Chinese rockets. It also halted further liberalization of export controls for American products with potential military application going to China.

While the president and Congress had concentrated on responding to public opinion, another domestic constituency, with very different concerns, began to make its views known. This was the American business community, and particularly those defense contractors who had agreements with the PRC or who hoped to have them in the future. In an article attempting to assess the impact of these sanctions, the prestigious *Jane's Defence Weekly* noted that the administration's suspension order appeared to apply only to items contracted for under the U.S. Foreign Military Sales (FMS) rules. Since China has shown a consistent preference for conducting straight commercial transactions rather than going through the FMS procedures, a number of projects would be excluded from the ban. Among these were a contract for the Grumman Corporation involving the upgrade of China's F-7M fighters for export and a $100 million agreement with the Boeing Corporation for the purchase of the Sikorsky corporation's CH-47 Chinook cargo helicopters.[2]

As it happened, the sale of Chinooks was held up, the license for the contract having not yet been granted at the time of suspension. Sikorsky also voluntarily stopped supplying spare parts for the twenty-four C70C helicopters it had sold to the PLA several years before. By far the largest project affected by the order was the so-called "Peace Pearl" program for upgrading China's Shenyang F-8 air defense interceptor. The $550 million project had the Grumman Corporation as its prime contractor, with Westinghouse also involved for a substantial sum, $41.4 million, for fire-control radars.

Other projects suspended were an $8 million U.S. Navy contract to supply the Chinese navy with four Honeywell Mark 46 anti-submarine torpedoes, and a General Motors–Hughes $60 million contract for four ANTPQ-37 anti-artillery radars, two of which had already been delivered. Co-production ventures involving manufacture of proximity fuses with Ferranti International Signal and the development of improved tank engines with the Textron subsidiary Cadillac Gage were also halted.[3]

In terms of military exchanges, the visit to China of General Carl Vuono, the U.S. Army chief of staff, was canceled, as well as that of PLA Navy Commander Admiral Zhang Lianzhong to the United States.[4] No other high-ranking visits were publicly reported.

On the other hand, what was going on secretly or with minimal publicity tended to vitiate the impact of sanctions. A few weeks after the Tiananmen crackdown, President Bush sent a delegation headed by National Security Adviser General Brent Scowcroft on a secret mission to Beijing. He made a second, public, visit in December, during which American television showed the American officials clinking champagne glasses and exchanging compliments with the Chinese leaders. Trying to deal with outraged critics, Under Secretary of State Lawrence Eagleburger defended the trips: frank exchanges of views had preceded the champagne toasts, and the July visit in particular had been "neither easy nor pleasant."[5] They had, he said, told the Chinese leadership precisely what it needed to do in order to improve relations with the United States. President Bush, who had served in Beijing during the 1970s as head of the U.S. Liaison Office, later to become the United States embassy, argued that he had come to know China well during his time there and knew how best to proceed.

Critics, including many prominent Republicans as well as Democrats, charged that the visits had simply confirmed the Chinese leadership in its belief that the decision to shrug off outside reaction to repressive actions against its population had been correct: the United States had spoken loudly, but almost immediately began crawling back to Beijing seeking to improve Sino-American relations. Critics were also skeptical of Bush's contention that his service as head of the Liaison Office had given him an understanding of China and its leaders. Some pointed out that Bush had been in Beijing during a period when China had been so secretive that reporters and diplomats complained that they had to go to Hong Kong to find out what was happening. They also noted that Bush's understanding of the Chinese language was minimal. Others complained that Bush had overpersonalized diplomacy: that the substance of policy had been subordinated to the maintenance of good personal relationships with particular foreign leaders. Moreover, the Chinese leadership was not sentimental on the matter of friendship: it would never occur to them to temper a policy on purely personal grounds.[6] Yet another group of critics argued that, while Bush might indeed understand a few elderly members of the elite group, his actions put him squarely in opposition to hundreds of millions of Chinese citizens who wanted to change the system under which they lived. At some point in the none-too-distant future, the repressive octogenarian group led by Deng would be ousted by the forces of liberalism and democracy, and China's new leaders would neither forget nor forgive the United States for supporting those who had oppressed them.

During the months after the second Scowcroft mission, Chinese leaders freed some of the protestors who had been arrested in the wake of the Tiananmen demonstrations. A year after leading dissident Fang Lizhi had taken refuge in the American embassy in Beijing, the PRC allowed him to leave the country. Supporters of the administration argued that this proved the correctness of Bush's policy; detractors pointed out that the number of people released was a small proportion of the total incarcerated and that a general atmosphere inimical to the expression of dissent continued to exist. Indeed, the intervening year had seen a large number of personnel changes within the military, seemingly designed to replace those officers who had objected to using force against the demonstrators. And expressions of dissent in literature and art were more vigilantly monitored than they had been in the period preceding the demonstrations.

The Bush administration, while not formally ending its ban on military sales, did not seem at pains to enforce it. In October 1989, Beijing radio announced that forty-two Chinese engineers and technicians participating in the Peace Pearl project who had been asked to leave in June had returned to their posts. It quoted reports in the *Washington Post* and *Los Angeles Times* to the effect that the administration had secretly dropped the ban in early October.[7] In early April 1990, President Bush waived sanctions so that an American-made satellite could be launched by a Chinese Long March Rocket.[8] Other waivers allowed the Boeing Corporation to deliver four 757s to China. Although the aircraft were for civilian use, their inertial reference systems were on the Munitions Control List.[9]

An apparent exception to this lenient interpretation of the ban was Bush's February 1990 decision to void the sale of an aircraft parts manufacturing firm, Mamco, the previous October. However, it is interesting to note that there was no mention of the existence of a ban, or of the Tiananmen events, in the decision-making process. President Bush's announcement was made after a unanimous vote by members of an eight-agency board, in accordance with the provisions of the Exon-Florio Act of 1988. This act permits the United States government to review purchases of American companies by foreign investors and to nullify those which it deems likely to have adverse effects on United States security. The interagency board's decision was said to have been based on classified information involving past activities of the

Chinese purchasing agency CATIC (China National Aero Technology Import and Export Corporation). It is believed that the classified information indicates that CATIC illegally appropriated metallurgical technology from two General Electric CFM-56 aircraft engines it purchased in 1984.[10] Presumably, therefore, the board's decision would have been the same had the Tiananmen incident never occurred.

CATIC's response was prompt and irate. The United States would be held responsible for economic loss to CATIC and damage to its reputation. The decision would, it continued, have "negative impact on future cooperation between the aviation industries of the two countries."[11]

In May 1990, the PRC made the decision not to proceed to the development stage of its Peace Pearl contract with the United States government. The Chinese embassy in Washington refused comment on the reasons behind the decision, as did the U.S. Department of Defense.[12] There was speculation that it had been made in retaliation to the American action on Mamco. Other analysts interpreted the cancellation as the PRC's response to foot-dragging in the Department of Defense. The Pentagon had allowed production of the hardware to proceed while cautioning that delivery might be held up until Bush's suspension order was formally lifted. Yet others argued that it was likely that China would have terminated the program anyway, given the PRC's post-Tiananmen austerity program to dampen inflation and the sharp cuts it was making in other sectors. To make matters worse, rising development costs had added an extra 30 or 40 percent, or up to $200 million, to the program.[13] Whatever China's reason or reasons, the cancellation came at a bad time for Grumman. The company had already ordered layoffs due to the decline in American defense spending; 180 employees had been assigned to the Chinese project.[14]

The discontinuities between the Bush administration's words and its actions on post-Tiananmen military relationships with the PRC reflect more than the hypocrisy apparent on the surface. Rather, they reflect deep concerns about the reasons for beginning a military exchange program with China in the first place, about the alternative suppliers that China might approach, and about the effects on American business.

Until the latter part of the 1970s, China and the Soviet Union were placed in the same, restrictive, category with regard to the sale of weapons. The USSR's move into Afghanistan in December 1979, coming shortly after Deng Xiaoping announced seemingly capitalist reforms and an "open door" to the West, induced the Carter administration to tilt toward China. The PRC was moved out of the category with the Soviet Union, and placed in its own group of one. This desire to win China over to the side of the United States in any confrontation with the Soviet Union continued into the Reagan administration, which saw several further easings of restrictions on military and dual civilian-military use items. Although the PRC's military modernization program was succeeding in upgrading the PLA's capabilities, improvements in fact came more slowly than those in the Soviet military: cultivating military relationships with China, and selling military technology to it, was seen as a way to keep the gap between the military capabilities of the two countries from widening further.

Yet another rationale for wanting the Chinese to adopt American weapons was that it would give the United States some leverage over the Chinese. A China equipped with American weapons, it was argued, would be more likely to side with the United States on geostrategic and commercial issues. Moreover, training Chinese officers in American academies would presumably give them a better understanding of America and its values. It would also facilitate the formation of personal friendships among service personnel of the two countries. Democratic values are best taught by example, and here was a chance to allow some Chinese to personally observe them in action. Additionally, forging military relationships with China would be good for American suppliers. Were the United States to deny China the right to purchase weapons, the PRC could simply go elsewhere: to Britain, France, or perhaps even the Soviet Union, with concomitant gains in those countries' influence over developments in China.

Since the Soviet Union had withdrawn from Afghanistan and appeared progressively less threatening to global peace by mid-1989, the initial rationale for military sales to China was not a major factor in continuing such a relationship. The other arguments, however, remained valid and were used by supporters of the administration's soft line on military sanctions.

Policy Outcomes

An analysis of how well these theories have been borne out by events since the Tiananmen crackdown yields mixed results. There is no evidence whatsoever that continued military sales to China have influenced the PRC leadership to side with the United States on geostrategic issues, or that it has had positive spinoffs in terms of domestic liberalization. Three specific instances come to mind: the PRC's sale of missiles in the Middle East, its refusal to cease supplying the Khmer Rouge, and its willingness to discuss sales of poison gas chemicals to Libya.

With regard to the first item, missiles, during the Scowcroft visit to China in December PRC officials offered general assurances that they would not sell medium-range missiles to Middle East countries. They also stated that they would not sell M-9 missiles to Syria. Hailed at the time as an indication of the success of the Bush administration's policy, the situation appeared quite different only three months later. Among other difficulties, the Chinese had never defined what they meant by medium-range missiles and were unwilling to agree to the international standard defining them as those able to carry a 1,000-pound payload more than 160 miles. Unconfirmed reports indicated that China was considering the sale of M-9 missiles to Syria by routing them through South America. In addition, there were intelligence reports that the PRC had agreed to provide Iran with at least fifty short-range surface-to-surface 8610 missiles, with a range of about eighty miles. Other intelligence reports cited links between China and artillery technology transferred to Libya, as well as the possible transfer of Chinese missile technology to Pakistan. In March, Rear Admiral Thomas Brooks, director of naval intelligence, noted in congressional testimony that China's marketing efforts might lead to arms sales to Syria, Libya, Iran, and Pakistan.[15] China also sold CSS-2 missiles to Saudi Arabia.

The second matter, the PRC's supplying of arms to the Khmer Rouge, had also been an item discussed by the Scowcroft mission during its visits to China. In April, administration officials admitted that, in defiance of numerous requests from the United States, China continued to send large shipments of weapons to their Khmer Rouge clients. These included mortars, rifles, rocket-propelled grenades, anti-aircraft machine guns, rocket launchers,

122-millimeter howitzers, 130-millimeter field guns, and other heavy artillery.

Since the Khmer Rouge's barbarous, genocidal campaign against the Cambodian people had been well publicized by a highly acclaimed film as well as by the print media, this revelation caused considerable discomfort for the Bush administration. The *New York Times* cited a confidential April 1990 State Department report on China to the effect that there had been no discernible decrease in Chinese arms deliveries to the Khmer Rouge over the preceding six months. It also quoted an unnamed administration official as saying that the Chinese appeared to be "thumbing their nose" at the United States on Cambodia, as well as on a wide range of other issues.[16]

The third matter concerned the Chinese sale to Libya of chemicals that could be used to make poison gas. In June 1990, an American official revealed after sharp congressional questioning that talks were under way between Beijing and Tripoli for the delivery of such chemicals, and that American concerns "had been expressed to them at a very high level." He refused on grounds of national security to reveal any other details, including the Chinese response.[17] The Chinese immediately denied that they were helping Libya or any other country to develop chemical weapons, though a careful reading of the statement indicates that it contains no denial of a sale to Libya of chemicals that are ingredients of chemical weapons.[18]

This is no mere semantic quibble. The instance given above of the failure of the Scowcroft mission to obtain China's acceptance of the international definition of a medium-range ballistic missile and its repercussions for the sale of Chinese M-9 missiles in the Middle East is a case in point. One must add that Chinese behavior in international arms sales in the past has been less than forthright. After repeated denials that China had sold missiles to Iran, even after being shown satellite photographs of the same missiles in China and later in Iran, the PRC eventually stated that it had lost track of the missiles after they had left Chinese territory and that it could not be held responsible for the vagaries of the international arms market.

News of the Beijing-Tripoli negotiations, coming within days of the administration's decision to extend the PRC's most-favored-nation status, angered critics of Bush's China policy. Senator

Joseph Biden, a Democrat, questioned whether China was being responsive to concerns over the spread of missiles, poison gas, and nuclear weapons and described the administration's policy as a failure.[19]

The PRC did side with the United States on United Nations Security Council Resolution 660 condemning Iraq; it also did not condemn the sending of American forces to Saudi Arabia to defend against an Iraqi invasion of that country. The PRC chose to abstain from the Security Council vote authorizing the UN's use of force to settle the Iraq-Kuwait crisis. There is no evidence, however, that China was doing so out of gratitude for America's conciliatory policy toward it. High-ranking PRC officials, including Premier Li Peng and Foreign Minister Qian Qichen, noted that their country had always opposed the armed invasion of one country by another. They also stated that, while China was in general not in favor of the superpowers' stationing their troops in other countries, it could hardly object to Saudi Arabia's requesting the presence of American troops for defensive purposes.[20]

More is likely to have been behind the Chinese support for Saudi Arabia's decision than appears in these statements. Only a few days before the Iraqi invasion of Kuwait, the PRC and Saudi Arabia formally established diplomatic relations. The process involved a protracted, and highly secret, period of negotiations. While no details of the process are presently known, it is quite likely that the conservative Saudi leadership entertained some misgivings that had to be soothed. Chinese objections to the Saudi decision to request American help could only have reinforced these misgivings and would have made the future relationship between the two more difficult.

In addition, the PRC has received substantial loans from Kuwait. China first began to court the wealthy, conservative regimes of the Middle East in its efforts to slow the spread of Soviet expansion in that strategically crucial region. The post-Mao PRC leaders came to value affluent Muslim states even more as sources of investment to help develop the PRC's economy. China's own Muslims were enlisted to aid in obtaining loans. Hence, China's support for the United States position in the Kuwait-Iraq crisis is likely to have been made in consideration of China's interests in the Middle East rather than in consideration of a desire to support the United States.

China has also maintained close ties with Iraq in recent years, with the military relationship between the two being of paramount importance. The PRC supplied large numbers of weapons to Iraq during that country's decade-long war with Iran. A Hong Kong magazine recently estimated that one-fourth of Iraq's arms are Chinese in origin, and their sale has been a source of billions of dollars of foreign exchange for the PRC. It should also be noted that the PRC supplied Iran militarily as well, and officially remained neutral in the war. Arms deliveries to the latter were routed through North Korea. Those destined for Baghdad were first transported, in disassembled form, to Jordan by sea. From there, they were transferred to Saudi Arabia, where the weapons were assembled and shipped over land to Iraq.[21]

The PRC's past record raises questions about whether it will abide by the UN Security Council's resolution and not sell arms to Iraq. The prospect of large sales would be tempting in any case, but must be particularly so given the PRC's current economic difficulties. And, assuming that other suppliers like the United States, the Soviet Union, and France abide by their embargo, there are enormous profits to be made. Some sources consider an increase in Chinese arms sales to Iraq "likely."[22] In late August there were rumors in Hong Kong that the PRC was transporting munitions and small arms to Baghdad by plane.[23] However, there is no hard evidence on the matter. The PRC appears to want to present the image of a responsible member of the world community; to transport any substantial quantity of arms into Iraq would mean risking exposure by running the naval blockade. The amount of arms that could be transported in by plane would be quite limited.

Quite clearly, the short-term geostrategic human rights goals that the Bush administration hoped for in adopting a conciliatory policy toward China have not been achieved. That the PRC leadership has acted in accordance with its perception of China's best interests should have surprised no one; it has been a consistent feature of the Chinese foreign policy for the past several decades. To expect that a conciliatory American policy could change this pattern is so naive that it raises doubts about the competence of those in charge of the United States' Asia policy. The administration's longer-term goals of encouraging friendly ties with individuals in the Chinese military and interactions between the defense forces of the two countries are certainly more feasible, and may yet occur. A year and a half is not very long in terms of diplomatic accomplishments, and one cannot ignore the possibility that those goals will be accomplished in the future.

The argument that China will eventually be able to find other countries to satisfy its military procurement needs is certainly true. One country that was considerably more vehement in its denunciations of China's human rights abuses after the Tiananmen incident was France. In August 1989, it was announced that the French state-owned company Aerospatiale would proceed with its military programs with China. Aerospatiale had already licensed production of at least fifty SA 365-B Dauphin 2 helicopters for the PLA air force and naval air arm under the designation of Z-9a. France also cooperated with development of the SA 321 Super Frelon helicopter and sold Super Puma battlefield helicopters to the PLA.[24]

A Hong Kong magazine took note of the fact that a modernization program for China's submarines was continuing, and that the boats were being fitted with a new French sonar system and Italian torpedoes.[25]

In June 1990, the first Soviet military delegation in thirty years visited China for what was described as "a seven-day formal friendly visit." A Beijing publication reported that the two parties would discuss expanding contacts and cooperation.[26] Shortly thereafter, a Chinese delegation led by powerful Central Military Commission Vice-Chairman Liu Huaqing and including the head of the PRC's Ministry of Aerospace Industries, visited the USSR. *Jane's Defence Weekly* and a respected Hong Kong newspaper stated that a major topic of negotiations was combat aircraft. China was reportedly seeking to obtain licenses to build the MiG-29 fighter and the Su-24 ground attack planes. Both sources specifically linked China's interest in the two Soviet planes to the cancellation of the PRC's contract with the United States.[27]

Only two agreements with the PRC on items with possible military applications are known to have been canceled by foreign contractors, neither directly related to the events of June 4. The first involved the reversal, in October 1989, of a tentative Thai decision to purchase a number of Chinese F-7M fighters at bargain prices. Newly appointed Thai Air Force Commander-in-Chief Kaset Rochananin explained that his decision had been made in light of problems with the plane's weapons, engine, and logistical systems.[28] The purchase had been controversial in Thailand long before the spring of 1989, when demonstrations began in the PRC. Many Thais felt that buying inferior technology, even at low prices, was not a wise decision. Others felt that expanding the combat capability of the Thai air force would give the country's major enemy, Vietnam, an excuse to extract a larger number of higher-quality planes from its Soviet ally. Meanwhile, the less-than-successful Thai-Chinese joint tank repair venture continues to limp along.[29]

The second canceled agreement involves the November 1989 withdrawal of Australia's government-owned Aerospace Technologies (ASTA) from a joint venture to build a new generation of light helicopters with France and China. An ASTA spokesman said his company's change of mind was "purely a business decision," taken after weighing the pros and cons of participation, though he would not comment on its relationship to the Tiananmen incident.[30]

It is true also that certain American arms suppliers have been hurt by the sanctions, though it is necessary to qualify this statement in two ways. First, Chinese arms purchases have historically not involved large amounts of money. There are several mutually reinforcing reasons for the modest size of these purchases, and they are not likely to change in the foreseeable future. These may be summarized as nationalism, bitter past experience, domestic vested interests, and pinched budgets.

Let us first briefly consider the motive of nationalism. An important reason for the growth and eventual success of the communist movement in China was its leadership's deeply felt and often-reiterated desire to end the humiliation of their country by foreign powers. The PRC elite's strong commitment to having China accepted as at least equal, if not superior to, foreign powers has included the desire to be independent in terms of military production. The PRC mass media announce weapons breakthroughs with great pride, generally accompanying the description of the item with a phrase such as "it reaches advanced world standards," and even, on occasion, offering a list of the other countries in the world that possess the particular capability.

As for bitter past experience, the PRC had developed a rather close military relationship with the Soviet Union during the early 1950s. As Sino-Soviet relations cooled, so did the level of cooperation. In 1960, Soviet advisers in all fields, including the military, abruptly left the PRC, carrying away as many of their plans and blueprints as they could. China claimed that the USSR had reneged on several weapons systems that had been promised, and the PRC's military modernization program was undoubtedly set back. The lesson that policymakers derived from this experience was that, while one might not be able to become completely self-sufficient in weapons production, one must not allow oneself to rely too heavily on a single supplier. PRC weapons purchases are, therefore, typically preceded by lengthy international shopping expeditions and intense negotiations. They do not tend to make a great deal of money for whatever company finally concludes the deal.

Another factor limiting Chinese arms purchases is the existence of a domestic research and development sector. Design bureaus, their bureaucrats, and associated scientists and engineers have a vested interest in limiting foreign suppliers that take funds and attention away from their own efforts. They emphasize reliance on indigenous technology and are often successful in their quest for self-reliance.

Finally, the PRC budget has little money available for arms upgrades. Given an exceptionally peaceful regional environment and faced with environmental pollution, a burgeoning population, and rising expectations for better living standards, the government has very sensibly decided that military modernization should not be given a high priority.

In consideration of the above factors, it cannot be said that even rigidly applied military sanctions in themselves could have done major damage to arms suppliers in the United States. A second qualifier to the statement that American arms suppliers have been hurt by the sanctions is that any damage may be short-term only. The PRC leadership holds American military technology in high esteem and prefers to make its modest arms purchases where it feels they will do the most good. Still, the announcement of military sanctions against the PRC came at a bad time for defense contractors, given the dramatic decreases in government spending mandated by the Gramm-Rudman-Hollings Act and strongly reinforced by developments in the Soviet Union and Eastern Europe.

Conclusion

A year and a half after the Tiananmen incident, results of the Bush administration's conciliatory policy toward the PRC are minimal. Some dissidents, including the prominent Fang Lizhi, have been released from prison or allowed to leave the country. However, the human rights climate in China continues to be repressive, and it is not clear that American pleas for liberalization have had any effect. In the military sector, China has not acceded to American wishes with regard to the sale of medium-range missiles in the Middle East or ceased its arms deliveries to the Khmer Rouge; it has held talks with Libya on the sale of items used in the manufacture of chemical weapons. The PRC has supported the American-backed United Nations Security Council decision condemning Iraq's invasion of Kuwait while abstaining on a subsequent resolution to authorize the use of force against Baghdad. However, it is likely that other considerations besides a desire to coordinate its own strategic policies with those of the United States were paramount in the Chinese leadership's decision to support, or at least acquiesce to, these UN Security Council initiatives. While China is currently pursuing a low-key military and arms sales posture in the Persian Gulf and other third world areas at present, it remains unclear to what extent Beijing will continue to do so over the longer term.

On balance, arguments appear to be valid that American arms manufacturers who have assisted in building China's military capabilities or aspire to do so for profit have been or will be hurt more than will China by the Bush administration's military sanctions levied against Beijing. Alternative suppliers exist in abundance, and no other country appears to have canceled or postponed making contracts with the PRC because of the Tiananmen incident. However, the overall dollar amounts involved are not great, since the PRC wishes to minimize its foreign military purchases.

It is not clear that any other policy would have achieved better results for the United States than Bush's policy has delivered. On the other hand, to have publicly announced a rather firm policy and then almost immediately to have quietly begun to undercut its effects, presents the image of the United States as vacillating and irresolute to the Chinese leadership. This is likely to make the PRC more difficult for the United States to deal with in the future. Clearly, the administration acted almost immediately to assure the Chinese leadership that it did not mean what it said. China has always acted on its own best interests, and will presumably continue to do so. The lack of understanding of this at the highest levels of American policymaking is astonishing and, in its implications for future decisionmaking, profoundly upsetting.

NOTES

1. Nicholas D. Kristof, "Suddenly, China Looks Smaller in the World," *New York Times,* 27 March 1990, p. 5.
2. "China: Paying the Price of a 'Bloody Crackdown,'" *Jane's Defence Weekly* 10, No. 24 (17 June 1989), pp. 1210–11.
3. Richard E. Gillespie and Kelly Ho Shea, "The Military Sales Ban," *China Business Review* 16, No. 5 (September–October 1989), pp. 32–33.
4. Andrew B. Brick, "Rebuilding U.S.-China Relations," Asian Studies Center, Heritage Foundation, *Backgrounder* No. 98, Washington, DC, 25 January 1990.
5. See Eagleburger's statement to the Senate Foreign Relations Committee, 7 February 1990, reprinted in U.S. Department of State, Bureau of Public Affairs, *Current Policy* No. 1247, Washington, DC, February 1990, p. 3.
6. This view is exemplified by Elliot Abrams, a former assistant secretary of state in the Reagan administration, in "Bush's Unrealpolitik," *New York Times,* 30 April 1990, p. A-11.
7. A Beijing Radio report (untitled), 29 October 1989; translated and reprinted in *Foreign Broadcast Information Service, China* (hereafter cited as FBIS-CHI), 30 October 1989, p. 9.
8. Andrew Rosenthal, "Bush, Citing Security Law, Voids Sale of Aviation Concern to China," *New York Times,* 7 April 1990, pp. A-1, A/7.
9. Gillespie and Kelly Ho Shea, "Military Sales Ban," p. 34.
10. Rosenthal, "Bush, Citing Security Law."
11. "CATIC Statement on Mamco Issue," *Xinhua,* Beijing, 19 February 1990, in FBIS-CHI, 20 February 1990, p. 3.
12. Charles W. Stevens, "China Cancels Plan to Use Grumman Systems in Its Jets," *Asian Wall Street Journal Weekly,* 21 May 1990, p. 2.
13. "China Seeking Soviet Fighters," *Jane's Defence Weekly* 14, No. 3 (21 July 1990), p. 70.
14. Ibid.
15. Michael R. Gordon, "Beijing Avoids Giving U.S. New Assurance on Missile Sales," *New York Times,* 30 March 1990, p. A-4.
16. Robert Pear, "China Is Said to Send Arms to Khmer Rouge," *New York Times,* 1 May 1990, p. A-6.
17. Michael R. Gordon, "Chinese Reported to Weigh Sale of Poison Gas Chemicals to Libya," *New York Times,* 7 June 1990, p. A-8.
18. The Chinese response may be found in "Ministry Denies Helping Libya with Chemicals," *Agence France Presse* (Hong Kong), 11 June 1990, and reproduced in FBIS-CHI, 11 June 1990, p. 1.
19. Gordon, "Chinese Reported to Weigh Sale."

20. See, e.g., "Li Peng Holds Airport Press Conference: Criticizes Iraqi Invasion," *Kyodo* (Tokyo), 6 August 1990; reprinted in FBIS-CHI, 6 August 1990, p. 17; and "Li Peng Holds News Confrence in Jakarta," Beijing Radio, 8 August 1990; translated and reprinted in FBIS-CHI, 8 August 1990, p. 10.
21. Li Ming-Chiang, "One-Fourth of Iraq's Arms Are Supplied by China," *Tang tai* (Hong Kong), 18 August 1990, pp. 13–14; translated and reprinted in FBIS-CHI, 23 August 1990, pp. 11–12.
22. Seth Faison and Willy Wo-Lap Lam, "Increased Arms Sales to Iraq Likely," *South China Morning Post* (Hong Kong), 4 August 1990, p. 1.
23. Michael Chugani, *South China Morning Post,* personal communication, 29 August 1990.
24. "Aerospatiale Chinese Ventures Continue," *Jane's Defence Weekly* 10, No. 30 (29 July 1989), p. 181.
25. Ling Yu, "The Actual Strength of the Submarine Units of Communist China," *Kuang chiao ching* (Hong Kong), 16 October 1989, pp. 18–21; translated and reprinted in FBIS-CHI, 26 October 1989, p. 9.
26. Li Wei, "Chief of External Relations Directorate under Soviet Ministry of Defense Arrives in Beijing," *Zhongguo xinwen she* (Beijing), 1 June 1990; translated and reprinted in FBIS-CHI, 4 June 1990, p. 9.
27. *Jane's Defence Weekly* 11, No. 2 (21 July 1990), p. 70; and the *South China Morning Post,* 12 August 1990, p. 14.
28. "Air Force Said Undecided on PRC Jet Fighters," *Bangkok Post* (Bangkok), 21 April 1989; translated in *Foreign Broadcast Information Service, East Asia* (hereafter cited as FBIS-EAS) 19 April 1989, p. 64.
29. "PRC Tank Manufacture Joint Project," *The Nation* (Bangkok), 23 April 1989; translated and reprinted in FBIS-EAS, 28 April 1989, p. 75.
30. *Agence France Presse* (Hong Kong), 17 November 1989, in FBIS-EAS, 17 November 1989, p. 75.

Part Three

Sino-American Relations in the New International Order

NINE

Domestic Responses to Retreat and Setbacks in the Soviet Union and China

Thomas P. Bernstein

WHAT DO SOVIET AND CHINESE FOREIGN POLICY have in common that would warrant comparison between them? At first glance, very little. Though both countries are Marxist-Leninist states, the Soviets have been discarding their ideological dogma, whereas the Chinese have reasserted ideological orthodoxy since the Tiananmen massacre. Internationally, the Soviet Union seems to be giving up as a superpower; the Chinese are still striving towards superpower status. The Soviets have made extraordinary concessions on Germany and Eastern Europe, which not so long ago were defined as vital interests that could not possibly be compromised. A Chinese counterpart of similarly historic proportions might be willingness to accommodate to Tibet's or Taiwan's independence, but of course there is no trace of this.

At the same time, the Soviets and the Chinese do share a commonality, in that both have recently faced major new problems of adaptation to the international environment. The Soviets have had to adapt to the consequences of drastic retreat from Afghanistan, and while they themselves were the initiators of their involvement, questions of support and consent of relevant elites and publics arose. For their part, the Chinese had to adapt to a less favorable international environment in the wake of the Tiananmen incident and the collapse of communism in Europe, as well as to the loss of leverage resulting from the unprecedented Soviet-American reconciliation. In both cases, the new situations caused debate and contention among the decisionmaking elites. In the Soviet Union, debate was open and included unofficial public opinion. In China, differences over the orientation of foreign policy existed within the elite, but the extent of the differences were only dimly discernible.

In both cases, the issues included how to respond and whether the new situations should be accepted, a question of particular importance to the Soviet military. On a deeper level, retreat and setbacks raised questions about the fundamental stance which each nation ought to adopt in respect to the outside world. Should there be an attitude of withdrawal and isolation, or should there be a high degree of involvement with the outside world? Both countries had intellectual currents that justified withdrawal and isolation and, conversely, traditions that justified involvement and learning from the West. In pre-1917 Russia, these were the Slavophile and Westernizing currents, which dated back to the nineteenth century. In China, currents of xenophobic nativism had also contended since the nineteenth century with currents that sought limited Westernization — symbolized by the term *tiyong* or "Chinese essence and Western learning" — and others that pursued all-out Westernization. These currents came to the fore in varying degrees in China after the Tiananmen crackdown and in the Soviet Union during the later Gorbachev era. In the USSR, the dominant leadership under Gorbachev aligned itself with the Westernizing tradition, believing that the country's salvation required wide-ranging and vastly increased Western involvement. In China, the dominant leadership under Deng Xiaoping defended *kaifang*, the opening to the outside world, but sought at the same time to ward off the subversive impact of foreign ideas.

Retreats and Setbacks in Soviet and Chinese Foreign Policy

In the last few years, the Soviets withdrew from Afghanistan and from other third world bastions like Angola. They acquiesced in a noncommunist Eastern Europe from which Soviet troops would be withdrawn and agreed to a united Germany free to remain in NATO. Gorbachev removed troops from the Mongolian People's Republic (MPR) and adopted a conciliatory approach to troop reductions on the Chinese border as well as to the border issues. The USSR adopted a more forthcoming attitude on various arms control issues.

Domestic Responses

The decision by Gorbachev to withdraw from positions held stubbornly since 1945 arose from the growing danger of domestic economic collapse and the concomitant inability to sustain international commitments. The customarily high levels of defense and related expenditures could no longer be sustained. The country had not been able to keep up with the latest American technological advances, such as the Strategic Defense Initiative (SDI) and the Stealth bomber. Revitalization of the Soviet economy, moreover, required greatly stepped-up foreign participation, and for this reason, too, the old militant, confrontational foreign policy stance had to be scrapped.

The retreat was legitimized by an extraordinary outpouring of criticism of Soviet foreign policy, including its history — the Nazi-Soviet Pact, the Hungarian and Czechoslovakian interventions, and Brezhnev's third world adventures. Much of the critique showed that Soviet foreign policy had been based on self-fulfilling prophecies that aroused increased American hostility to the "evil empire." Ideology was held responsible. Gorbachev's predecessors had regarded peaceful coexistence as amounting only to suspension of hostilities, resulting in little progress. According to Foreign Minister Eduard Shevardnadze, it was the inflexible Soviet attitude toward talks on missile reductions that led to "14 years of idling negotiations," and it was the "enemy image" of the United States which "drastically limited possibilities for rational and controlled action." Soviet dogmatism, missionary zeal, and ideological tunnel vision led to an unrealistic view of less developed countries (LDCs) as naturally anti-capitalist and Soviet allies, causing immense waste of resources in Afghanistan and elsewhere. The a priori Soviet image of Washington as the world communist movement's primary enemy was a main source of tension between the superpowers.[1]

Gorbachev and his colleagues proposed a new approach to international cooperation which smacked of Wilsonian idealism. Speaking at the Twenty-eighth Congress of the Communist Party of the Soviet Union (CPSU) in July 1990, Gorbachev defined his regime's "new thinking" as meaning that the only security worth having was security for all. Security could no longer be in zero-sum terms. Defense had to be limited to reasonable sufficiency. Peoples ought freely to be able to choose their governments, a point essential to the new world order. Adversary concepts such as international class struggle would have to be discarded and replaced by interdependence and the pursuit of common human values. Isolationism could not result in a prosperous, free, democratic society. "The inclusion of our national economy in the world economy is necessary," he said, not only for modernization of the Soviet Union but also from the global point of view:

> Thanks to restructuring and the new thinking, a turnaround has taken place in relations between the USSR and the US from confrontation and competition in the arms race to mutual understanding and, on a number of questions, even to partnership. This has changed the entire world situation for the better and initiated movement toward an unprecedented peaceful period in the life of mankind.[2]

In China, three major setbacks diminished the Chinese role in the world. The first was the industrial world's reaction to the Tiananmen crackdown. Sanctions were imposed by the United States and its Western allies, with Japan tagging along somewhat reluctantly. Sanctions reflected a fundamental decline in China's prestige. Not so long ago, China's bold reforms had aroused much excitement around the world. There was substantial confidence in China's stability, leading to international willingness to invest. After the Tiananmen Square events, China's political stability became publicly and starkly an open question. The transformation of China's international status was best symbolized by Deng Xiaoping, who as a great reformer not long before had graced the cover of *Time* as "Man of the Year" but who now was called the "butcher of Beijing."

China's diminished prestige could not be blamed only on the Tiananmen incident. China's capacity for imaginative reform and dynamic economic performance had eroded long before the events of May and June 1989. Moreover, even without the political crackdown, the dramatic changes in Eastern Europe in 1989–90, where the effort to reform Marxism-Leninism turned into the abolition of communism, necessarily diminished China's stature as an innovator by comparison. Undoubtedly, however, it was the Tiananmen incident that most directly destroyed China's image of purposeful movement towards the rule of law, towards predictability, and towards the embrace of Western values.

The second setback was the collapse of communism in Eastern

Europe and its increasing erosion in the Soviet Union. The contrast was profound as China reasserted Marxist-Leninist orthodoxy in the wake of demonstrations at Tiananmen Square, the cornerstone of which was the effort to restore the unquestioned authority of the Chinese Communist party's monopoly power. The fact that popular upheaval resulted in the overthrow of party rule in an entire set of countries necessarily conjured up the specter of a similar catastrophe in China, all the more so since China's party elders had defined the Tiananmen strife as a "we versus they" struggle against counterrevolutionaries. The apparent ease with which Communist party rule had ended in Eastern Europe reinforced the Chinese leaders' sense of vulnerability. The fact that an old friend, Romania's Nicolai Ceausescu, could be violently overthrown and then executed was especially painful to contemplate. Ceausescu and the German Democratic Republic's Erich Honeker were the only Eastern European leaders who had supported the June 4 crackdown. "It was not groundless," lamented the Chinese press, "that some veteran comrades did not feel like eating or could not sleep after hearing the news."[3]

The collapse of communism in Eastern Europe was a major blow to the Chinese world view. Chinese leaders had continued to believe that a socialist world existed. Only a few years earlier, Chinese reformers had eagerly studied the Yugoslav and Hungarian "models" of reform. Conservative Chinese leaders might have had doubts about the liberalizing policies pursued by some European communist states prior to 1989, but liberalization was still pursued within the Marxist-Leninist framework. Now the Chinese had to come to grips with the disappearance altogether of Marxist-Leninist rule, at a time when they were trying to reinstill in their populace the message that Marxist socialism must be viewed as the wave of the future. An even greater shock was that the party of Lenin, the CPSU, formally proclaimed the end of the party monopoly at its February 1990 plenum. All this meant that China was ideologically more isolated than at any time since the Cultural Revolution. Kindred ideological states existed, notably North Korea, Vietnam, and Cuba, but the latter two were hardly close to China.

Third, China's position on one side of the global strategic triangle lost importance as reconciliation between the United States and Soviet Union proceeded apace. For two decades, China had enjoyed influence disproportionate to its actual status as a regional power because of the role it was able to play as a sought-after counterweight to Soviet hegemonism. China's heyday in this role was in the 1970s and early 1980s. Its position eroded as Soviet-American relations improved from the mid-1980s on. But with the fundamental turn in relations between Washington and Moscow for the better, the United States' need for China sharply declined, and so did China's leverage outside of Asia. Journalists wrote of a sense of "helpless hurt" among China's officials and that "China's leaders are painfully discovering that the Middle Kingdom matters less on the international stage than it did not long ago."[4]

Chinese comment on Soviet-American relations contained hints of regret that the Soviets were not more strongly resisting Washington's advances. *Liaowang,* in an article on the May 1990 Bush-Gorbachev summit, emphasized difficulties between the two superpowers: European issues had not been resolved, it pointed out, especially that of Germany in NATO. American insistence on NATO membership for a united Germany sought to strengthen the alliance's military, economic, and political power, "so that the scales will be tipped in favor of the West. This is precisely what the Soviet Union firmly opposes." The Soviet people would find it emotionally difficult to accept a unified Germany in NATO, which had "been an enemy of the Soviet Union for more than 40 years." Soviet domestic difficulties put the USSR into an unfavorable position, making it easier for the Americans to get their way. The Soviet Union was willing to compromise, the United States was not. Washington was "covertly applying pressure on the Soviet Union" by tying most-favored-nation status to the Lithuania issue, which will be a "long-term hidden obstacle" in Soviet-American relations.[5]

The extent of the loss of Chinese influence should not be exaggerated, since China is, after all, Asia's only overt nuclear power, and its potential military reach extends beyond the region as the country gradually acquires a missile capacity sufficient to reach the American homeland. As a permanent member of the United Nations Security Council, China plays an important role in such matters as the recent Iraq crisis. It can, as by selling missiles to Middle East customers, influence events outside the Asian-Pacific region. The Soviet decline itself may also have caused

China's relative power position to rise. Still, China's foreign policy gains, for example in relations with the Soviet Union, did not come from China's capacity to play the triangular game but from the unilateral Soviet retreat and increased Soviet-American amity.

Soviet Responses

The staggering scope of Soviet retreats from the world stage should have been accompanied by an outburst of protest. After all, pride in the country's great military accomplishments, especially the victory in World War II, and in the country's global stature and power had been the core of the Soviet regime's legitimacy. Seweryn Bialer defined Soviet nationalism as the world's last imperial nationalism. "It is a nationalism of leaders who worked so hard, waited so long, and hoped so fervently to achieve a dominant international position." This nationalism was shared by younger leaders, who did not have memories of past vulnerabilities and hence might well be willing to take more risks than their elders.[6] Given Soviet concessions, therefore, there should have been wounded pride, a sense of humiliation, anger, and charges of surrender, appeasement, and sellout.

Protests against surrender were voiced in the military, by members of the civilian elite, and by Russian nationalist groups. Although protest existed, it was modest in comparison to what one might have expected. The fundamental reason was the crisis in the Soviet system. The priority issue in terms of nationalism was not the preservation of the "outer empire" of the Soviet Union in Eastern Europe and the third world, but the fate of the "inner empire" of Russia and the non-Russian nationalities, many of which were struggling for autonomy or independence. The first priority of Russian nationalism was the Soviet Union. Some wanted to preserve the union, even on the basis of russification; others wanted a distinctive Russian republic to emerge from a dismantled empire; still others, such as Alexander Solzhenitsyn, wanted to unite all the Slavs and let the non-Slavs go. Only a few had an interest in the preservation of the "outer empire."[7]

Conservative leaders such as Egor Ligachev criticized the "new thinking" for discarding the principle of the primacy of the class character of international relations, attacking Foreign Minister

Eduard Shevardnadze and Gorbachev adviser A. Yakovlev on this issue. In spring 1990, Ligachev warned against the reunification of Germany, the consequent destabilization of Europe, and the "total annulment of the achievements of World War II."[8] Other hard-liners urged Gorbachev to use his new presidential powers to preserve Soviet dominance in European affairs by preventing German reunification. The conservative newspaper, *Literaturnaia Rossiia,* pleaded for continued control of Germany by the victorious World War II powers even after unification, suggesting that the Soviet commander-in-chief in Germany exercise his legal powers to curb the German threat.[9]

Senior Soviet military leaders were perhaps the single most vocal group disturbed by Gorbachev's foreign and security policy and by the disintegrating impact of *perestroika* and *glasnost* on the military. Army General Al'bert Makashov attacked Gorbachev at the Russian Party Conference on June 19, 1990, for "leaving the country vulnerable to attack." Earlier he had called unilateral disarmament a crime. The army would not accept "ideological surrender," he said. A united Germany in NATO and a powerful Japan posed real dangers. He castigated "learned peacocks," civilian defense intellectuals, who under Gorbachev were redefining security needs. He implicitly blamed Gorbachev and Shevardnadze for the fall of Eastern Europe, referring to "these troubled times, when because of the so-called victories of our diplomacy, the Soviet army is being driven without a fight out of countries that our fathers liberated from fascism."[10]

At the Twenty-eighth Congress, whose 269 military delegates had reportedly been chosen by conservatives, these attacks continued. General Ivan Mikulin, head of the Political Administration of the Southern Group of Forces, blamed the ouster of Soviet forces from Eastern Europe on the "new thinking." He told reporters that he found Gorbachev indecisive and Shevardnadze hasty. He rejected the idea of a "common European house," and charged that the Vienna talks on conventional arms control would lead to unilateral Soviet disarmament. Another officer attributed the "successes" of the country's foreign policy to "capacity to give in." Admiral Gennadi Khvatov, commander of the Pacific Fleet, said that "we have no ally in the West. We have no allies in the East. Consequently we are back where we were in 1939." According to some generals, while the Soviets were withdrawing the West was strengthening its military potential. Minister of Defense Dmitri Yazov, though a defender of Gorbachev, pointed out that the Soviets had to be able to balance American strategic power and complained about NATO's continuing policy of nuclear intimidation and direct confrontation. How could NATO be allowed to extend its reach to the Polish border? Chief of General Staff Mikhail Alekseyevich Moiseev defended Gorbachev against Mikulin's attack, pointing to the country's "reliable rocket shield." But Moiseev also charged NATO with continuing to rely on force and aiming for military superiority.[11]

Unease over the possibility of the United States taking advantage of Soviet concessions was expressed by a Soviet scholar, Henry Trofimenko, who criticized the American media, especially that on the right, for insisting that the United States had won the cold war. Their aim was to push "the Soviet Union into a corner, showing that it has no way out other than to succumb to whatever demands the United States and the West might make." Trofimenko criticized the asymmetry of the concessions each side had made: "Although the so-called Brezhnev doctrine is definitely dead, the Reagan doctrine, which is absolutely analogous to it, is not." The Panama invasion was a case in point. The fact that the Soviets could not deter the United States from invading Panama was a source of chagrin among the military as well as among some Russian nationalists, who bemoaned the incapacity of a weakened Soviet Union to restrain "the expansion of bourgeois empires."[12]

Some critics charged that the United States was benefiting from the "new thinking" and that it had sponsored conspiracies which had caused the loss of Eastern Europe. Nina Andreeva, a chemistry teacher who came to public notice several years ago as a strident defender of Stalin, spoke of "domestic and foreign reactionary forces" that profited from the failure of East European leaders to solve economic problems and managed to turn the "people's legitimate discontent in the direction of anticommunism and anti-Sovietism." According to Andreeva, American analysts acknowledged that the "pseudo-revolutions" had been "carefully prepared and synchronized." Coordinated action of "foreign political forces," including emigres, churches, concealed descendants of the old upper classes, nationalists, Zionists, and nationalist communists, were at work in bringing about the overturn. Andreeva's language, it is worth noting, was very similar to that of the Chinese press, which charged "hostile international forces" with subverting China (see below).[13]

Gorbachev, and especially Shevardnadze, vigorously defended the "new thinking." "I know," Shevardnadze told the Twenty-eighth Party Congress, "that I have been reproached, and recently, speaking plainly, have suffered much abuse [*rugat'*] for having made concessions in the sphere of security." Earlier, he compared Soviet conservatives to American witch hunters in looking for subversives responsible for the "loss" of China. "You get the impression that some of them would like a zealous investigation into those who 'lost East Europe.'"[14] The case of the defenders of the new thinking was strengthened by the July 5, 1990, NATO declaration that the two blocs had ceased to be adversaries, by the NATO invitation to Gorbachev to speak to that security organization's ministers, and by changes in NATO strategy. As Foreign Minister Gennadii Gerasimov put it, "Now we can tell those grumbling generals that they are wrong."[15] The Gorbachev line was approved at the Twenty-eighth Party Congress, though some observers detected in the country's hardened arms control line and in the opposition to Lithuanian independence an effort to propitiate the critics.

Soviet public opinion for the most part seemed to support the "new thinking" in foreign policy. One reason was the apparently extreme unpopularity of Soviet foreign aid given the extent of economic deprivation in the country. One academic charged that the country would be spending in 1990 about the same amount on various authoritarian and military adventures as would be spent on increasing the people's standard of living: 12 billion rubles versus 13.4 billion rubles. The Soviet Union spent 3 billion on Cuba, but only half a billion on subsidizing the backward Central Asian republics of Kirgizia and Tadzhikistan.[16] Revulsion against foreign adventures was so widespread that Boris Yeltsin reported that every third letter he had received dealt with Afghanistan.[17] Much of Russian nationalist opinion reportedly also favored the new course, despite Russia's historic association with imperialism. According to Nicolai Petro, "On the issue of foreign policy, Russian nationalism should be understood as a consistent force for moderation. Unanimously, Russian nationalist groups condemn external adventures, which they believe have accelerated the country's impoverishment and contributed nothing to its security. Every statement on foreign policy by Russian informal groups, including those by reactionary Pamyat, demonstrates this isolationist, nonaggressive foreign policy."[18] Russian patriots supported "the reorientation of the government toward domestic concerns." Some advocated the diversion of military and space funds to domestic needs and an across-the-board withdrawal from international commitments.[19]

While the weight of nationalist Russian opinion appeared thus to be on the side of reducing foreign commitments, it was much more vocal on the issue of Western cultural and economic influence, which Gorbachev's integrationist policies were intensively promoting. The prospect of integration into the world economy prompted one author to suggest that the hope that Western money could revive "our birchbark and bast economy," meant that "we are putting ourselves in the hands of the world's true bosses."[20] Others emphasized the threat posed by Western values. Warm applause greeted Marshal Ivan Kodzhedub at the March 1990 Congress of People's Deputies when he complained that "our young people's heroes are without conscience, as in the West. And our organs of mass information are full of amorality, raising the young in the spirit of egotism, without morals."[21]

Russian nationalists drew on the Slavophile tradition, meaning that they hoped to revive "the real Russia," her old values, customs, and culture, including the Orthodox church, with emphasis on the moral worth of Russians and on the exceptionalism and uniqueness of the Russian people. Some representatives of this current were anti-Semitic and xenophobic. The doctrine propounded by leaders of the extreme right such as the mathematician Igor Sharagevich was that the Russian people faced biological and cultural extinction at the hands of foreign and domestic enemies. Abroad, dissidents, emigres, historians such as Richard Pipes of Harvard, and others were promoting anti-Russian sentiments. Jews, who hated Russia, were the main menace, one Jewish aim being to make Russia into a Western democracy. The critic Igor Sharafevich, for example, "has some very harsh things to say," according to at least one observer, "about the Western belief in progress, and, in particular, about the United States, which exploits the rest of the world to keep up its artificially high living standards." The extreme Russian right, the observer went on to conclude, saw Gorbachev as a puppet of international finance and Zionism.[22] The support which far-right views received should not be exaggerated. In elections in Moscow and Leningrad, anti-Semitic right-wingers lost. As Soviet domestic turmoil increases, however, support for extremist views could well increase. Whether this will include greater emphasis on the revival of the country's international role remains to be seen.

China's Dualism: Normal Diplomatic Relations and Fear of Foreign Subversion

Chinese leaders reacted to events in Eastern Europe and the Soviet Union with fear and anger, worrying about the domestic effects on their country, yet determined to carry on normal state-to-state relations, thereby avoiding the mistake of the 1960s. The same determination essentially applied to the United States and other Western countries after the events in Tiananmen Square.

In contrast to their American problem, Chinese leaders did not fear deliberate subversion by the Soviets and Eastern Europeans. What they did fear was the subversive effect of the overthrow of communism in Europe on "bourgeois liberals" within China, who would be encouraged by East European events. This theme was not new. Mao Zedong warned in 1957 against the inspirational effects of the Hungarian Revolution and the Polish October of 1956. In 1980, the rise of the Polish trade union Solidarity frightened Chinese leaders into shelving reform proposals to permit a greater measure of pluralism. In 1989–90, China's leaders reacted in an even more drastically defensive manner. To them, changes in Eastern Europe represented the successful plotting of "peaceful evolution" by the international bourgeoisie. The question was, could this happen in China?

In the Chinese diagnosis, Eastern European leaders had made many mistakes — mismanaging the economy, failing to cope with corruption, and failing to ameliorate mass dissatisfaction. Most important, the ruling parties had tolerated the "mischief of bourgeois liberalization for a long time." They had failed to take preventive measures. Hence, when a major change in the international climate occurred, they had no defense. And they had relied too heavily on the Soviet Union. When the Soviets became shaky, so did they. Deng Xiaoping had warned Eastern European leaders repeatedly in recent years of the peril they faced, but they had failed to pay attention. He had sent Yao Yilin to East Germany in 1989 to help forestall peaceful evolution. Yao advised Honecker that he must not retreat. But he had retreated, and retreat had led to rout: "Once they retreated, they were utterly routed." Eastern Europe's leading cadres had not been firm ideologically, and had lacked preparation for the struggle against bourgeois liberalization.[23]

A top-level meeting on December 11–17, 1989, discussed the impact on China of the Eastern European events, concluding that preventive steps were essential. According to Deng, events in Eastern Europe showed that "our guiding principle of quelling the [Tiananmen] rebellion was completely correct."[24] Imperialist and hostile foreign forces had never ceased to subvert and undermine socialist states. "But some comrades inside the party simply turn a deaf ear to it, saying that we are talking nonsense. Now everything is clear. . . . We must oppose bourgeois liberalization and never show mercy to it." The plots of international hostile forces to foment peaceful evolution must be foiled; there could be no retreat.[25]

Specifically, control over the army had to be strengthened. When Romania exploded, Chinese leaders concluded that military rebellion had to led Ceausescu's overthrow. Hence, ideological-political work in the People's Liberation Army had to be intensified so as to teach resistance to bourgeois liberalization. Those who had advocated that the army ought to be separate from the party and become a politically neutral organ of the state had to be silenced. The party had to continue to exercise absolute leadership over the PLA.[26]

Chinese leaders sought to determine just how China differed from Eastern Europe and the Soviet Union, hoping to find solace in China's immunity. They reportedly concluded that China had unique characteristics which made counterrevolution less likely. Students of comparative communism have long distinguished between imposed and authentic communist revolutions; Chinese leaders seized upon this difference to enhance their confidence that Chinese communism would be less prone to collapse. They also took comfort in Mao Zedong Thought, which had integrated Marxism-Leninism with China's unique features. China had never been subjected to social democratic influence. China also had never yielded to any foreign country, and the majority of her neighbors were friendly, whereas Eastern Europe was encircled by capitalist states. China could avoid the fate of European communists because it differed from them.

But these distinctions left open the problem of how to explain the apostasy of the Soviet Communist party, which had voluntarily renounced its monopoly at the February 1990 Plenum, an event that greatly disturbed the Chinese. Like the Chinese Communist party, the CPSU had gained victory with an army under party leadership. Nor did the Soviet Union suffer from the dependent status of the Eastern Europeans. Chinese leaders concluded, however, that there were important differences between themselves and the Soviets. China had a system of multiparty cooperation and political consultation, whereas in the Soviet Union there was only one party, implying that China had political structures able to absorb pressures for broadening participation within the traditional Marxist-Leninist framework. Also, China did not have a Soviet-style nationalities problem.[27]

More broadly, Chinese leaders sought to assess the implications of the fall of communism in Eastern Europe for the fate of socialism in China and elsewhere. Reportedly, Deng and his colleagues adopted a long-term perspective. Socialism had not failed. Since October 1917, great achievements had been made, but so had major mistakes. Socialism was developing and perfecting itself through reform. In the long run it would prevail. After all, the French bourgeoisie required eighty years from 1789 to the establishment of the Third Republic in 1875 to fully establish itself. The English revolutionary process, which began in 1640, was also very long.[28] There was hope for socialism so long as at least China, with its one billion people, remained socialist.

Beijing's Diplomatic Response

Despite their deep concern over the diplomatic implications of the upheavals in Eastern Europe, Chinese leaders sought to maintain normal diplomatic ties with the outside world. Its bifurcated reaction was remarkable when viewed against the recent history of the PRC. The appraisal of Gorbachev and events in Eastern Europe was quite similar to the diagnosis of revisionism in the Soviet Union made by Mao Zedong in the late 1950s and 1960s. Leaders such as General Secretary Jiang Zemin, commenting on the February 1990 Plenum, reportedly lashed out at Gorbachev as a "traitor" to communism for abandoning the CPSU's leading role.[29]

In the 1960s, ideological conflict had been carried on in public polemics, and strife spilled over into state-to-state relations. Denunciations reached hysterical heights in the Cultural Revolution, as when the *Peking Review* had carried articles labeling their adversaries "filthy revisionist Soviet swine."[30] Now, however, China's public media were not allowed to label Gorbachev a traitor. After the CPSU abolished the one-party monopoly at the February 1990 Plenum, Chinese party elders and the Politburo decided that China would not comment publicly on the Soviet changes, but that internal criticism would be intense. Party members would be thoroughly educated on Gorbachev's deviation from socialism. The public would also be informed about the capitalist nature of the Eastern European reforms, presumably through China's internal communication systems. But in public, friendly relations would be maintained even if the Soviets renounced socialism. Some leaders, notably Wang Zhen, wanted a harder line, including cancellation of the visit to Moscow by Premier Li Peng scheduled for April 1990. But Deng overrode their objections.[31]

Normal diplomatic ties and economic relations were maintained. Relations continued to progress, as in the negotiation of a border settlement and reduction of border troops and in the form of increased military contacts. China apparently pressured the Soviets not to establish ties with Taiwan, a worrisome issue for them. According to one report, Chinese leaders decided that economic ties should develop "naturally," not at excessive speed. This meant adoption of a more cautious line on economic relations and something of a change from the time after the Tiananmen crackdown, when Yao Yilin had called for the PRC to go all out in fostering economic ties with the Soviet Union so as to balance Western sanctions.[32] But the main thrust was to develop ties further. Similarly, despite the pain of seeing their stout ally Ceausescu overthrown, China recognized the new Romanian regime on the grounds that China respected the choice made by the Romanian people. Apparently, this rapid response sought to forestall embarrassing disclosures. When Politburo member Qiao Shi had visited Romania in November 1989, he had talked to Ceausescu about the Tiananmen suppression. China's reported fears that the Romanian National Salvation Front would make these talks public prompted early recognition as well as assistance to the new regime.[33]

The Chinese press was not devoid of critical comment or skeptical appraisals of Gorbachev's domestic troubles. For instance, press reportage on the February 1990 Plenum included mention of workers and party secretaries who expressed determination to struggle for the Marxist-Leninist party and its leading role. The negative side of marketization was emphasized, as in an article on Polish economic reforms which cited warnings by the Polish United Workers party that privatization would cause 400,000 workers to lose their jobs, and in warnings of excessive borrowing and dependency on the West.[34] But these criticisms were not made in polemical form.

This bifurcated reaction showed the ability of the Chinese to separate ideological considerations from normal participation in international relations. Thirty years earlier, the Maoist polemics and their spillover into state-to-state relations had signified the all-consuming importance of the Soviet heresy. Now, the Chinese decision not to denounce Gorbachev in public showed the extent to which even the conservative leaders had retreated from taking ideology as seriously as Mao had. Consequently, they were able to avoid plunging China into the isolation of the 1960s, when the break with the Soviets had come at a time when China was already excluded from much of the world by the United States.

China's Marxist-Leninist leaders also sought to avoid retreat into an isolationist club of the orthodox united by a common siege mentality. Formation of an axis of China, North Korea, Vietnam, and perhaps Cuba was an option. Deng Xiaoping apparently proposed that the three Asian socialist countries should guard the socialist banner and that China ought therefore to improve relations with Vietnam. Yet Deng also said that "some comrades" claimed "that the world revolution was shifting to the East but I do not favor this," apparently signifying unwillingness to establish a new revolutionary headquarters in Beijing. To be sure, the growth of China's ties with South Korea slowed, presumably due to the desire to support North Korea. The concealed ideological conflict with the Soviets thus had an impact, but a minor one.[35]

Domestic Responses

China's Two-sided Policy toward the United States

In the case of the Soviet Union and East Europe, the Chinese leaders viewed events unfolding throughout 1989–90 with hostility. Similarly, they regarded the bourgeois world, and particularly the United States, as a subversive threat to their own regime's survival. This latter fear became manifest after the Tiananmen demonstrations, but it was not the first campaign against "spiritual pollution" or "bourgeois liberalization." Whereas the Chinese chose to keep Soviet-East European heresy under wraps, however, they openly and vehemently denounced the United States, though at the same time seeking to maintain relations. One reason for the difference in publicity was that the impact of the United States on China had been much greater because of the close cultural contacts between Washington and Beijing and the strong appeal of Western ideals to the young. Hence, open attacks on Western values were a necessity.

The image which China conveyed after Tiananmen was of a country besieged by the threat of John Foster Dulles' strategy of "peaceful evolution." According to Jiang Zemin, international forces hostile to socialism used either military might or peaceful evolution. The latter came into play when military means turned out to be impractical and meant waging a "gunpowderless third world war." Peaceful evolution posed "a major danger" for socialist states, as demonstrated by events in Eastern Europe and the necessity for the June 4 crackdown in China itself: It revealed a viciously plotted scheme to overthrow the Chinese communist leadership and socialist system. Bourgeois liberalization created an atmosphere in which the strategy of peaceful evolution could prevail. Some bourgeois liberals "colluded with external hostile forces." They spread chaos and violence, hoping to establish a "capitalist republic appended to the West."[36]

Subversion of China was promoted by governments, including that of George Bush, despite the fact that his efforts to be conciliatory toward China had earned him much domestic criticism. Bush wanted to win without war by promoting peaceful evolution and by using capitalist ideology. His visits to Poland and Hungary were examples of this strategy. "Obviously, the 'strategy of transcending deterrence' is far more offensive and aggressive than the strategy of 'deterrence' adopted by the United States for the past 40 years." This showed that the contradiction between two social systems and ideologies could "become relatively acute and sharp even thought the international situation as a whole becomes relaxed."[37]

In February 1990, the Central Committee declared in Beijing that the Western bloc headed by the United States and other "antagonistic forces" could well increase its pressure on China by adding new sanctions, despite the strong opposition of the Chinese government and people. New mud would be slung at China for "crimes with regard to human rights in all aspects." International reactionary forces were targeting China after the socialist defeats in Europe. China had to be prepared to wage intense struggle against these forces.[38]

Western human rights pressure on China also came in for slashing attacks as "wanton interference" in China's internal affairs. Since China has signed seven international conventions on human rights, rejection of the concept as bourgeois was not possible. But human rights, in the Chinese view, could not be treated in the abstract. During the counterrevolutionary rebellion, "a very tiny number of persons" preached absolute, abstract human rights in disregard of the Chinese constitution and laws. The United States posed as a defender of human rights so as to interfere in the affairs of other states, citing, inter alia, a congressional resolution for the "establishment of a free and open political system in China which protects basic human rights." The real American purpose was subversion. In order to mobilize a democratic upsurge in communist states, Americans sought contact with "democratic elements" and supported independent publications, trade unions, and enterprises seeking to "break through" the monopoly of the ruling party and government. The goal of such American "interference" in China's affairs, using human rights as a pretext, was to force China to recognize illegal organizations, such as the College Students' Autonomous Federation and the Workers' Autonomous Federation, all in pursuit of the "sinister aim" of overthrowing the party and socialism.[39]

Nongovernmental subversion was another bourgeois tactic. In 1986, Premier Zhao Ziyang's secretary, Bao Tong, had permitted George Soros, an American businessman active in the promotion of democracy in Eastern Europe, to establish "The Fund for the

Reform and Opening of China" in Beijing and to operate independently (at least formally) from the government. After Tiananmen, Soros' fund was accused of having been manipulated by the CIA. Top leaders blamed Zhao Ziyang and Bao Tong for having permitted the fund to operate. Premier Li Peng asked for an investigation. Minister of Public Security Wang Fang charged that the fund, which consisted of about one million dollars, promoted subversive activities.[40]

At the same time, the existence of a variety of American voices allowed China to praise those Americans who were "far sighted"— that is, those who took a pro-Chinese line. When Henry Kissinger announced that he would visit China in the fall of 1989, a Chinese press report commented that during the counterrevolutionary rebellion, "certain personalities in the US ruling and opposition sectors instigated a wave of anti-Chinese uproar, while the US government also adopted so-called 'sanctions against China,'" and the "propaganda machinery of the United States and other countries came out with bucket after bucket of dirty water to pour onto China." But Kissinger praised China's unprecedented progress and insisted that "a weak and divided China will lead to turmoil in all of Asia." The open door was in the interests of both the United States and China. Kissinger's stance was in sharp contrast to the "very shortsighted and very unwise" position of "certain people in power" and in Congress. Kissinger pointed to Chinese sensitivity to interference in her affairs. "Well said! China is not the vassal of any country. Whoever tries to dictate to China will definitely meet with failure."[41]

The press integrated the current activities of "hostile international forces" into the history of China's grievance-laden nationalism. Commemorating the 150th anniversary of the Opium War, the *Army Daily* wrote of the urgent need for "European and American capitalists" to expand, plunder, and open markets. Since 1840, "Western capitalism has never stopped its aggression against China and its plundering of China." Since 1950, the American embargo, the United States' advance into North Korea during the Korean War, and the "peaceful evolution strategy" to "triumph without fighting a war" showed that nothing had changed. Western capitalism was trying to impose pluralist ideology and the "spiritual opium" of its moral standards and values. During the 1989 demonstrations, "Western hostile forces actively incited and supported the domestic reactionary forces in our country to stir up turmoil and to revolt." After June 4, the Western bourgeoisie did not resign itself to failure but imposed economic sanctions and sought to create confusion in the minds of people and to disrupt stability and unity. The *Army Daily* concluded that "the contemptible means and dirty tricks of the Western bourgeoisie fully show that the aggressive and plundering nature of the bourgeoisie has not changed."[42]

The Chinese dissident "elite" who had advocated bourgeois liberalization had betrayed the country by advocacy of "wholesale westernization." In their view, Chinese were an "inferior race," and China should be run as a colony for three hundred years in order to escape from backwardness. A "foreigner should be welcomed to serve as China's premier," thus causing loss of independence. This "scum of the nation" fled after June 4 and have been trying to subvert the people's government from abroad.[43]

Chinese, however, were "standing tall and feeling proud and elated," having smashed the "US imperialist encirclement of China," having resisted the bullying of the "big lords" of the Soviet Union in the 1960s, having always upheld its independence, and having avoided becoming the vassal of one of the superpowers. Now China has been resisting the post–June 4 "anti-China tide" whipped up by the United States and other Western countries and the gross interference in China's internal affairs by the imposition of sanctions.[44] Young people had not had the painful experience of losing independence and hence should be taught the realities of Western attempts to reduce China to the status of a dependency.[45]

Judging by these indictments, the machinations of American imperialism and other "international forces" posed a clear and present danger to China's survival. But this diagnosis did not prevent China from making efforts to carry on business as usual. "It is clear to all what attitude the United States has adopted toward China. However, China has not suspended contacts with the United States. Being neither overbearing nor servile, China readily made reasonable responses to proposals conducive to relations between the two sides, but refused to make any concessions on the practices that harm China's sovereignty. . . . In the most difficult days, China still received the special envoys of the US President on two occasions, carried out dialogue, preserved its flexibility and left room for maneuver." China complained that the United States' interference in Chinese domestic affairs was an obstacle to improved Sino-American ties. "Sooner or later, the United States will have to make a choice of pursuing US strategic interests of the state or continuing to interfere in the internal affairs of other countries."[46] Principled Chinese prose aside, the fact is that China continued to bargain with the United States. When Chinese interests were at stake, as in the case of the renewal of MFN, China proved quite willing to negotiate over the departure of the dissident Fang Lizhi, who had been blamed for the 1989 demonstrations and who had taken refuge in the United States embassy. Similarly, the Chinese did not simply reject the Western approach to human rights but engaged in a dialogue, seeking to defend the Chinese record.

Assessments and Conclusions

What is most striking in China's approaches both to the United States and to events in the Soviet Union and Eastern Europe was the sharp distinction between words and deeds. On the one hand, harsh accusations and denunciations were made — in the American case in public, in the Soviet–Eastern European case in private — while at the same time China sought to maintain normal diplomatic and economic relations with the very countries whose governments it was excoriating.

China's pursuit of normal relations was the product of a decision by Deng Xiaoping after the Tiananmen massacre to combat counterrevolution yet carry on with both internal reform and external opening up (*kaifang*). Suppression of counterrevolutionaries thought to be linked to foreign powers could easily have given rise to an isolationist response. Deng sought to nip such possibilities in the bud by putting the weight of his authority behind the continuation of *kaifang* immediately after June 4. Deng had pioneered the PRC's open door policies with the West. He believed that China had made a historic mistake when it had isolated itself in the eighteenth century, thereby excluding itself from the industrial revolution, and that China's modernization required foreign technology and knowledge.

The decision to maintain the Open Door also reflected the

new realities of China's interdependence. The reform era had brought about a revolution in Chinese foreign trade. About 25 percent of the country's gross national product depended on foreign trade in 1989 as opposed to 6 percent in 1980. The situation was totally different from that in the 1960s, when China could close the door to the Soviet Union because the PRC was far less dependent on foreign trade at that time. By the late 1980s, external markets had become a central component of China's economic life. Sanctions hurt, and it was in the Chinese interest to try to get them lifted using diplomacy rather than to take actions that might exacerbate foreign hostility to China still further.

Why, then, the diatribes against foreign plunder, aggression, and subversion? Lucian Pye would probably offer a psychological explanation, pointing to the Chinese belief in the power of words to shame their adversaries.[47] Perhaps the Chinese thought that firing "empty cannons" would not hurt their cause — that is, that their enemies could and would tolerate public abuse.[48] But it can also be suggested that the denunciations were intended to satisfy internal constituencies who came to the fore with the Tiananmen massacre, whose orientation is to hunt down subversives and revitalize orthodox Marxism-Leninism, and who were inspired by the tradition of xenophobic nativism. In suppressing the student movement and purging Zhao Ziyang, Deng had given them their current scope to maneuver, even though he evidently sought to limit their influence by proclaiming the inviolability of the opening to the outside world. The result, of course, was an unstable mix, as leaders with a strong outward orientation contended with those who preferred to erect barriers to the outside world.

Since Tiananmen, China's leaders have in fact been obsessed with the specter of domestic instability. Fear of instability has led Deng Xiaoping to add another message to the outside world, namely that chaos in China would be costly to the world and that therefore foreigners ought not to undermine Chinese stability. In talking with foreign guests, Deng fell into a pleading role. The outside world, he said, should think about the consequences of promoting instability in China. If socialism collapsed, there would be chaos. If chaos prevailed in China, the world would also be in chaos. The outflow of population could not then be stopped. Ten million would go to Thailand, a hundred million to Indonesia, half a million to Hong Kong. Maintenance of stability in China is thus in everyone's interest. "The statesmen with a sense of responsibility for the world, China, and the globe must understand us." A Chinese collapse, Deng said, would mean retrogression by decades or a century. "The next three to five years will be very difficult and also very important for our party and state."[49]

NOTES

1. Shevardnadze in *Literaturnaia Gazeta,* 18 April 1990, as translated and reprinted in Foreign Broadcast Information Service, Soviet Union (hereafter cited as FBIS-SU), 26 April 1990, pp. 5–11, and Nicolai N. Petro, "New Political Thinking and Russian Patriotism: The Dichotomy of Perestroika," Hoover Institution Working Paper in International Studies, July 1989, p. 5.
2. Gorbachev, "Keynote Speech to the Twenty-eighth Congress of the CPSU," *Pravda,* 3 July 1990, as translated and reprinted in *Current Digest of the Soviet Press* (hereafter cited as CPSU) 42, No. 27 (8 August 1990), pp. 11–12.
3. *Cheng Ming,* No. 147, 1 January 1990, pp. 6–8, as translated and reprinted in Foreign Broadcast Information Service, China (hereafter cited as FBIS-CHI) No. 250, 2 January 1990, p. 21. Virtually all of the information on elite reactions to the collapse of communism comes from Hong Kong magazines opposed to the current regime, including *Cheng ming, Tang tai,* and *Chiu shi nien tai,* whose sources appear to be reliable but which cannot be independently confirmed.
4. *New York Times,* 15 August 1990, and Robert Delfs, "Exit (World Stage Left)," *Far Eastern Economic Review* 149, No. 34 (23 August 1990), pp. 32–34.
5. See special dispatch from Washington by Wu Jin, "Many Problems Still Remain Despite the Many Agreements," *Liaowang* (Overseas Edition), 11 June 1990, as translated and reprinted in FBIS-CHI, 21 June 1990, pp. 3–5.
6. Seweryn Bialer, *The Soviet Paradox: External Expansion, Internal Decline* (New York: Alfred Knopf, 1986), p. 266.
7. See Roman Szporluk, "Dilemmas of Russian Nationalism," *Problems of Communism* 38, No. 4 (July–August 1989), pp. 15–35. See also a report on Solzhenitsyn's proposal for a Slavic state in "Solzhenitsyn Urges Slavic Nation to Replace USSR," *Los Angeles Times,* 19 September 1990, p. 12.
8. A. Rahr, "Conservative Opposition to German Reunification," Radio Liberty *Report on the USSR* 2, No. 29 (11 May 1990), pp. 15–17.
9. Ibid., p. 15.
10. Stephen Foye, "Military Hard-Liner Condemns 'New Thinking' in Security Policy," Radio Liberty, *Report on the USSR* 2, No. 28 (13 July 1990), p. 5.
11. See Stephen Foye, "Defense Issues at the Party Congress," Radio Liberty *Report on the USSR* 2, No. 30 (27 July 1990), pp. 1–5.
12. Henry Trofimenko, "The End of the Cold War, Not History," *Wash-*

ington Quarterly 13, No. 2 (Spring 1990), pp. 21–35. Also, Alexandr Prokhanov in *Literaturnaia Rossiia,* 5 January 1990, as translated and reprinted in CDSP 42, No. 4 (28 February 1990), p. 3.
13. Nina Andreevna in *Sobsednik,* No. 25, June 1990, as translated and reprinted in CDSP 42, No. 23 (11 July 1990), p. 19.
14. Shevardnadze in *Pravda,* 5 July 1990 and 26 June 1990.
15. Foye, "Defense Issues at the Party Congress," p. 2.
16. Andrei Kortunov in *Moskovskoye Novosti,* 3 December 1989, as translated and reprinted in CDSP 42, No. 2 (14 February 1990), p. 15.
17. Petro, "New Political Thinking and Russian Patriotism," pp. 11 ff.
18. Nicolai N. Petro, "Nationalism in the Soviet Bloc: Rediscovering Russia," *Orbis* 34, No. 1 (Winter 1990), p. 48.
19. Petro, "New Political Thinking and Russian Patriotism," pp. 18 ff.
20. A. Prokhanov, *Literaturnaia Rossiia,* p. 2.
21. David K. Shipler, "A Reporter-at-Large: Between Dictatorship and Anarchy," *New Yorker* 66, No. 19 (25 June 1990), p. 57.
22. See Liah Greenfeld, "The Closing of the Russian Mind," *New Republic* 202, No. 6 (5 February 1990), pp. 30 ff. Also consult Walter Laqueur, "From Russia with Hate," ibid., pp. 1–25.
23. Lo Ping, "Notes on the Northern Journey: A Convulsive Shock in Zhongnanhai — Beijing is Prepared against All Possible Emergencies Following Drastic Changes in Romania," *Cheng ming,* No. 147 (1 January 1990), pp. 6–8, as translated and reprinted in FBIS-CHI, 2 January 1990, pp. 20–21.
24. Ibid., p. 20. The article claims to be citing from Deng's "important speeches."
25. Ibid.
26. Wan Li-hsiang, "New Ploys of the CPC for Tightening Control over the Army," *Tang tai,* No. 6 (30 December 1989), p. 67; as translated and reprinted in FBIS-CHI, 3 January 1990, p. 9.
27. Chi Hsin, "The Storms in the Soviet Union and East Europe Have Shaken the Highest Leadership Stratum of the CPC," *Chiu shi nien tai,* no. 242, 1 March 1990, pp. 19–22; as translated and reprinted in FBIS-CHI, 8 March 1990, pp. 12–16, and "Report: An Important Secret Document of the CPC on the February Plenary Session of the CPSU Central Committee," *Cheng ming,* No. 151, 1 May 1990, pp. 8–10; as translated and reprinted in FBIS-CHI, 2 May 1990, pp. 19–22. Ever since 1949, China has had several small parties in addition to the CCP, and in the reform era the regime favored increased political consultation. But these differences from the Soviet model are formal rather than real. Similarly, China has a nationalities problem, especially in Tibet and in Xinjiang (Central Asia), including agitation and

uprisings for autonomy or independence. But in sharp contrast to the Soviet Union, these minority problems are peripheral rather than central to the politics of China.

28. "The Complicated and Volatile International Situation: Major Profound Changes in the World Situation," in a speech by Yao Yun, senior reporter and deputy chief editor of Xinhua News Agency, *Ban yue tan,* No. 24 (25 December 1989), as translated and reprinted in FBIS-CHI, No. 23 (Supplement), 2 February 1990, p. 1.
29. "China: Traitor (China Arraigns Gorbachev)," *Economist* 314, No. 7644 (9 March 1990), p. 31.
30. "Hit Back Hard at the Rabid Provocations of the Filthy Soviet Revisionist Swine!" *Peking Review* 10, No. 6 (3 February 1967), pp. 23–24.
31. Lo Ping, "Deng Xiaoping Tells the Fortune of the CPC," *Cheng ming,* No. 151 (1 May 1990), pp. 6–8; as translated and reprinted in FBIS-CHI, 1 May 1990, pp. 12–14.
32. *South China Morning Post,* 17 February 1990; *Asahi shimbun,* 30 March 1990, as translated and reprinted in FBIS-CHI, 2 May 1990, p. 2; and "Editorial: China's Diplomacy Becomes More Mature," *Wen wei po* (Hong Kong), 4 April 1990, p. 2; as translated and reprinted in FBIS-CHI, 6 April 1990, pp. 2–3.
33. Ho Po-shih, "The Army across the Country is on Top-Grade Alert Following Drastic Changes in Romania," *Tang tai,* No. 6, 12 December 1989, pp. 7–8; as translated in reprinted in FBIS-CHI, 3 January 1990, p. 8; and "Special Dispatch: Secret Reason for China's Aid to Romania," *Ming pao,* 1 January 1990, p. 2; as translated and reprinted in FBIS-CHI, 2 January 1990, p. 16.
34. On Soviet economic doldrums, see, e.g., "*Xinhua* Summarizes Central Committee Plenum," *Xinhua* (Beijing), 8 February 1990, as translated and reprinted in FBIS-CHI, 9 February 1990, p. 3. On the Polish situation, see Tang Deqiao, "What Changes Have Taken Place in Poland's Economic Situation?" *Liaowang* (Overseas Edition), No. 1, 1 January 1990, as translated and reprinted in FBIS-CHI, 11 January 1990, pp. 5–6.
35. Chi Hsin, "The Storms in the Soviet Union and East Europe," pp. 19–22; and Lo Ping, " Notes on a Northern Journey: Deng Xiaoping Tells the Future of the CPC," *Cheng ming,* No. 151, 1 May 1990, pp. 6–8; translated and reprinted in FBIS-CHI (1 May 1990), pp. 12–14..
36. *Nanfang ribao,* 10 January 1990, as translated and reprinted in FBIS-CHI, 21 January 1990, pp. 1–2.
37. *Ban yue tan,* No. 24, 25 December 1989, pp. 15–17, as translated and reprinted in FBIS-CHI, Supplement, 2 February 1990, pp. 1–2; and *Xuexi yu yanjiu,* No. 10, 5 October 1989, pp. 33–35, as translated and reprinted in FBIS-CHI, No. 248, 28 December 1989, pp. 5–8.

38. "Report: Important Secret Dcoument," *Cheng ming,* pp. 8–10.
39. Shi Yun, "Who Is the Real Defender of Human Rights?" *Renmin ribao,* 7 July 1989, p. 6; as translated and reprinted in FBIS-CHI, 11 July, 1989, pp. 2–4.
40. "Special Dispatch: Li Peng Accuses U.S. CIA of Controlling Fund to Stage Counterrevolutionary Activities," *Ming pao,* 9 August 1989, p. 1; as translated and reprinted in FBIS-CHI, 9 August 1989, p. 1. Also see Andrew J. Nathan, *China's Crisis: Dilemmas of Reform and Prospects for Democracy* (New York: Columbia University Press, 1990), p. 176.
41. Zhuang Hanlong, "Kissinger Is, after All, Kissinger," *Jiefangjun bao,* 15 July 1989, p. 1; as translated and reprinted in FBIS-CHI, 26 July 1989, p. 1.
42. Zhiang Zhongxian, "Carry Forward Patriotic Spirit, Keep Firm Conviction in Socialism — Commemorating 150th Anniversary of Opium War," *Jiefangjun bao,* 5 June 1990, p. 3; as translated and reprinted in FBIS-CHI, 15 June 1990, pp. 18–21.
43. Ibid.
44. *Nanfang ribao,* 10 January 1990, p. 35, as translated and reprinted in FBIS-CHI, 21 January 1990, pp. 1–2.
45. "Independence: — A Foundation for the Prosperity and Strength of the Motherland," *Ban yue tan,* 15 May 1990, pp. 19–21; as translated and reprinted in FBIS-CHI, 9 July 1990, pp. 34, 36; and *Nanfang ribao,* 10, January 1990, as translated and reprinted in FBIS-CHI, 21 January 1990, pp. 1–2.
46. "Editorial: China's Diplomacy Becomes More Mature," pp. 2–3.
47. For a recent analysis of China's situation as it relates to this point, see Lucian Pye, "China: Erratic State, Frustrated Society," *Foreign Affairs* 69, No. 4 (Fall 1990), especially p. 60.
48. In 1978, I accompanied Senator Henry Jackson to Beijing. He asked very high officials why China constantly criticized the United States. One official responded: "You mustn't mind us firing some empty cannons at you."
49. Chen Jianping, "Deng Xiaoping Comments on Two Characteristics of the Political Situation in China," *Wen wei po* (Hong Kong), 16 June 1990, p. 1; as translated and reprinted in FBIS-CHI, 18 June 1990, pp. 29–30.

TEN

Taiwan and Future Sino-American Relations

Harvey J. Feldman

The Past as Prologue

UNITED STATES RELATIONS with the Republic of China (ROC) on Taiwan have had a degree of emotional complexity not often found in relations between states. From the days of debate on "who lost China" in 1949–1950 to final diplomatic recognition of the People's Republic of China and the passage of the Taiwan Relations Act twenty years later, American policy toward the ROC has been a factor in domestic American politics. Despite this, Taiwan qua Taiwan has hardly ever been the major determinant of policy. Instead, policy has been governed primarily by the state of American relations at any point in time with the communist government on the mainland, and secondarily by the relationship between that government and the government on Taiwan. The particular needs and desires of the ROC government itself have hardly ever counted for much in the calculations of American policymakers.

Thus, on January 5, 1950, not long after the formal proclamation of the People's Republic of China on October 1, 1949, President Truman announced a policy of strict noninterference and a ban on military assistance or advice to the "Chinese forces on Formosa." This was intended primarily to signal to the newly established communist government in Beijing that the United States was prepared to negotiate diplomatic recognition, although it was also true that the Truman administration was weary of the confusions and corruptions of the Chiang Kai-shek government. For six months thereafter, the United States had only minimal contact with the Kuomintang and provided neither military nor civilian aid.

On June 25, 1950, the North Koreans invaded South Korea and President Truman, sharing with most Americans the view that this was part of an international conspiracy to seize and communize the countries of Asia, responded by ending the policy of nonintervention. The United States Seventh Fleet took up position in the Taiwan Strait to prevent a PRC invasion, and General Douglas MacArthur visited Taiwan to discuss military assistance needs with Chiang Kai-shek. In late October 1950, Chinese communist forces ambushed lead elements of the U.S. First Calvary along the Chongchun River and heavily engaged the Republic of Korea's First Division further north, near the Yalu River border with Manchuria. For the next two and a half years, the United States and the People's Republic of China were in a de facto state of war.

The view now took hold in the United States that the PRC was an implacable enemy bent on controlling much or all of Asia. It was reinforced by the two Offshore Islands crises, in 1954 and 1958, when Beijing appeared to be preparing an invasion of Nationalist-held islands near the China coast as a preliminary to an invasion of Taiwan itself. Until President Nixon's "opening to China" in 1970–71, this view of the PRC shaped American policy not only toward Taiwan but on East Asian issues generally. The United States' views on China, moreover, played a prominent role in the decision to commit American forces to South Vietnam.[1]

As views of the PRC and its intentions darkened, so relations with the ROC on Taiwan grew closer, reaching their zenith after the conclusion of the Mutual Defense Treaty of 1954 and the two Offshore Islands crises. Relations attenuated during the Nixon and Ford administrations, when the PRC was seen as a valuable makeweight in the global contest with the Soviet Union, and ended completely, at least in their formal diplomatic phase, during the Carter administration.

The idea of a special relationship with Taiwan, and of an American duty to prevent PRC conquest of the island, still commanded respect on Capitol Hill, however. Over the objections of President Carter the Congress enacted legislation — the Taiwan Relations Act of 1979 — which proclaimed American policy to "preserve and promote extensive, close and friendly, commercial, cultural and other relations between the people of the United States and the people of Taiwan" and declared that "any effort to determine the future of Taiwan by other than peaceful means, including by boycotts and embargoes, [was] a threat to the peace and security of the Western Pacific area and of grave concern to the United States."[2]

Despite 1980 campaign oratory in which he announced he "would support official relations with Taiwan," President Reagan followed the Carter administration in conducting all relations with Taiwan through the American Institute in Taiwan, the instrumentality established under the Taiwan Relations Act.[3] Indeed, he moved beyond the Carter administration in agreeing, under the terms of the joint communiqué of August 17, 1982, to limit and ultimately to end arms sales to Taiwan despite the clear language of the Taiwan Relations Act, which declared it "necessary . . . to provide Taiwan with arms of a defensive character."[4] Having gone this far to bolster relations with Beijing, however, the Reagan administration declined to go much farther and did allow technology to be transferred to the ROC to boost an indigenous defense capability.

The Bush administration largely followed in the footsteps of its Republican predecessor concerning close relations with the PRC. The president himself, having served in Beijing for some fourteen months in 1973–74, was acquainted with many of the PRC leaders and considered himself to be something of a China expert. His views seem shaped by the geostrategic considerations of the 1970s, and even the brutal crushing of the student democracy movement in June 1989 deterred him only slightly from carrying on the policy of American closeness to Beijing. He has even shown himself willing to take a stand on trade sanctions opposing the Congress, which appears far more sensitive to the repression of human rights in China. Mr. Bush has not seemed particularly active in Taiwan policy.

In fact, the general view of Taiwan in the United States has undergone a considerable change over the past forty years. The death of President Chiang Ching-kuo in January 1988 in effect cut the last link to the anti-Japanese alliance of World War II. Trade problems and a current account deficit that rose yearly during the 1980s made Taiwan seem just another Asian trade competitor rather than a friend and ally. With the distraction of other events in the Philippines, the Soviet Union, Eastern Europe, and the Middle East, by the last decade of the century the Republic of China on Taiwan, its claims and its problems, had receded quite far from public consciousness. Even the Taiwan Relations Act, debated with such energy and passion in 1979, seemed a relic of a much earlier age. Many of those who had taken a leading part in that debate were no longer in Congress by 1990. One could say that by that year the special aura of intense emotional involvement, pro or con, that had for so long largely marked the United States–Taiwan relationship had vanished.

If the feeling of a special responsibility for Taiwan vis-à-vis China was evaporating, what was there to take its place? The triangular relationship among the ROC, the PRC, and the United States was such that Taiwan could not be treated as "just another country." Given the terms under which Washington had recognized the PRC and the commitments made by three American presidents in the years since then, it would appear Taiwan could not be regarded officially as a country at all. But this condition was more notional than factual.

The reality was that although leaders in both Beijing and Washington in the Carter administration had expected that following derecognition Taiwan would wither away or consent to reunification on PRC terms, it had instead emerged as a major economic force on the international scene. Within a half-dozen years of the switch in diplomatic recognition, Taiwan had become the fifth-ranked trading partner of the United States (after Canada, Mexico, Japan, and the Federal Republic of Germany), and the thirteenth-largest trading nation in the entire world. For most of the decade of the 1980s, the United States' trade deficit with Taiwan was about equal to total United States two-way trade with the PRC. And by the end of that decade, American business had invested approximately $2 billion in Taiwan.[5] The ROC came to possess the world's second-largest foreign exchange reserves and became an important overseas investor and aid-giver in its own right.

Economic relationships on this level of complexity, involving tens of thousands of jobs and millions of dollars in corporate earnings (or losses) annually, take on political coloration. By the end of the 1980s, American decisionmakers for the first time had to pay attention to the economic policies of the Republic of China. Would there come a time when its political decisions also would bear weight?

The answer seems to be yes. The ROC under President Lee Teng-hui has moved away from the sterility of the "Three Nos" and has remade its own China policy. The second leg of the triangular relationship, that between Beijing and Taipei, is static no longer — nor is it still a game of PRC initiative and ROC passivity. Policy planners in both Washington and Beijing now need to take account of ROC decisions on trade with and investment in a mainland China that sorely needs infusions of capital and technology from Taiwan; of "flexible diplomacy" that has added to the previously dwindling number of countries according diplomatic recognition to the ROC, and of the growth in democratic institutions on the island, which is creating a real possibility that time might bring a popular decision to make de jure Taiwan's de facto status as a political entity separate from the PRC.

The Future of the Triangular Relationship

Beijing and Taipei

If, in the past, American views of and relationship with the PRC largely shaped the nature of the American relationship with the ROC, as we have seen this is less likely to be the case in the future. We therefore will begin our inquiry by looking first at the ROC-PRC leg of the triangle and at the possible types of relationship between the island and the mainland.

We can eliminate from consideration the idea of forcible incorporation of Taiwan into the PRC. The PRC lacks the necessary air- and sealift capacity for invasion; it would have to struggle hard to gain control of the air space in a conflict with Taiwan and might not be able to achieve it; and it would face a well-prepared and well-armed defender. Perhaps after six months or so of carnage, with casualties mounting to six figures, human-wave attacks could succeed. But that presumes that the rest of the world community would watch week after week and month after month of bloody struggle and take no action. Such international passivity would be most unlikely. Even aside from questions of morality and humanity, the principal industrial nations of the world are too involved with Taiwan economically to stand idly by.

For similar reasons, a PRC attempt to bring Taiwan to its knees by blockade or embargo also would not be successful. It is hard to believe the island's major trading partners would respect such a maneuver, and harder still to believe Beijing would court a confrontation by arresting or sinking an American or Japanese merchant vessel. It is well to remember the language of the Taiwan Relations Act on this point (see page 252 above), along with the fact that the United States many times in its history — including most recently in the Persian Gulf — has taken military action to protect substantial commercial interests.

For peaceful reunification to take place, integrating Taiwan into the Chinese state, one would have to imagine a combination of several unlikely events: the return to power of liberal reformers in Beijing coupled with successful stabilization of the mainland on the basis of a market economy; a change to democracy on the mainland or a reversion to autocracy on Taiwan; an end to the process within the ROC that has placed more and more decision-making power in the hands of the overwhelmingly Taiwanese electorate, or a sudden reversal in their sense of difference; a rise in Chinese living standards to something approximating the Taiwan level (currently about $8,000 per capita) or a fall in Taiwan living standards to something approximating the PRC level (currently about $400 per capita). To list the conditions necessary for reunification is enough to demonstrate how unlikely it is.

If neither conquest nor peaceful reunification are likely, continued separate existence must be the answer. In theory, at least, it could take several different forms:

- A new government on Taiwan organized around elements of the Democratic Progressive party might enact a formal declaration of Taiwan's independence of China. But unless done in the reasonable expectation of swift recognition by major regional and world powers, this would provoke Beijing without conferring any benefit on Taipei. If not coordinated well in advance with countries like the United States and Japan, it might emphasize rather than end Taiwan's status as a formally unrecognized entity.
- Far more likely would be an expanded form of the present de

facto independence, with Taiwan moving progressively back into the mainstream of organized international life, with or without Beijing's grudging concurrence.[6] Beijing and Taipei would then increasingly find themselves both represented at international meetings. Former Finance Minister Shirley Kuo's attendance at a recent meeting in Beijing of the Asian Development Bank indicated quite dramatically the political importance of such a development in moving the PRC down the road toward acceptance of Taiwan's international legitimacy. Approval of the ROC's request to rejoin GATT as the "Taiwan, Pescadores, Kinmen, and Matsu Tariff Area" would be an obvious and important step in this direction. This also tracks very well with the present policies of the Lee Teng-hui government on liberalizing contacts with China, permitting travel, investment, and sport and cultural exchanges — all of which have the effect of creating a reassuring (to the PRC) web of relationships at the same time as the ROC pursues autonomous policies internationally.

- Least likely of all would be a return to the stonewalling policy of "No contact, no negotiations, no compromise," a tactic endorsed only by the Neanderthal wing of the Kuomintang and without popular support on Taiwan.

Taiwan's separation and its de facto independence is something successive PRC leaderships have had to live with since 1949. Since Taiwan today has an economy that outperforms even certain West European countries (for example, Greece), and given the more skillful handling of mainland policies by the present ROC government, there seems every indication that although its propaganda organs doubtless would continue to agitate and denounce, in more practical ways the PRC would continue to have to accommodate to this reality.

Washington and Beijing

Beijing, of course, sees the situation differently. Far from regarding the contrast between their political and economic situations as the major determinant of Taiwan's continued separation, for forty years it has emphasized that the United States' actions have interfered with and prevented reunification — forcibly in the days when the United States had a military presence on the island; through cunning use of trade and investment, arms supply, and political advice after transferring recognition to the PRC.[7] It is a theme emphasized in PRC media when relations with the United States go sour (as in the days following the Tiananmen massacres), or when the Beijing leadership is disturbed by events in Taiwan (such as the rise of the Democratic Progressive party); it is muted at other times. In the decade following normalization, the PRC several times has signaled, and at least once has said outright, that it hoped the United States would use its influence to nudge the ROC into negotiations.[8] The United States has not done so, and thus the Taiwan issue continues to be a factor in the Washington-Beijing relationship.

But in the past Taiwan has not been the most important factor. The "opening to China" in the Nixon administration was based upon a common Sino-American view of the global strategic situation, particularly with regard to the threat perceived at the time from the Soviet Union.[9] This was even more clear after the Soviet invasion of Afghanistan, with Washington and Beijing working together to assist the Afghan resistance. American policymakers also appreciated Chinese assistance to the Sihanouk-led coalition opposing the Vietnamese-installed government in Cambodia despite reservations about the Khmer Rouge component in that coalition. A pattern of cooperation was established in which jointly manned electronic listening posts were established on Chinese territory and the CIA briefed Chinese leaders on the results of satellite intelligence as it pertained to the PRC's border areas.

The world situation now has changed quite considerably. NATO has proclaimed the cold war ended; Bush and Gorbachev speak by telephone, the Soviet Union cooperates with the United States in the Kuwait crisis; Soviet troops are out of Afghanistan, and the war there is drawing to an end; and the United States is negotiating with Vietnam and has withdrawn recognition from the anti–Hun Sen Cambodian coalition. The Bush administration still refers to China as an emerging superpower.[10] It is also prepared to argue with Congress about the importance of maintaining bridges to the Beijing regime. China still holds a seat and a veto in the UN Security Council, but it clearly is regarded as much less important to the United States in present world circumstances.

In terms of economics, too, the "China fever" of the late 1970s and early 1980s has dissipated. Few American firms investing in joint ventures in China have made a profit. As waves of reform have advanced and receded, the inability to predict what PRC policy will be in any time frame has caused confusion and loss. China has been a good source for low-value manufactures but a poor market for American goods — which means a United States trade deficit with the PRC and ongoing American arguments about unfair Chinese trade practices.

Meanwhile, although it wants and needs American markets and technology, and American investment, the PRC leadership regards the United States as the major source of infection of that insidious disease, "spiritual pollution," and as the inventor of the strategy of "peaceful evolution." Such Chinese apprehensions have been graphically represented in the Chinese press. The following passage is illustrative:

> The United States uses democracy, freedom and human rights as weapons to force the West's value system onto socialist countries. . . . It propagandizes that socialism has no future, at least not within the next 100 years; it spread the notion that the third and fourth generation of the communist party is decadent, losing power, unqualified to represent the people, and even less qualified to lead; and it seeks to create trouble between the socialist populace and their leaders, and among ethnic groups by spreading rumors and sensational exaggerations to weaken people's wills and sow discord domestically and abroad.[11]

Even without the suspicions and tensions engendered by the rise of the democracy movement in China and its brutal suppression, it was likely that the evolving world situation and the persistence of irritating trade issues would lead to some distancing in the Sino-American relationship. In the aftermath of the Tiananmen demonstration and the wave of repression that followed, unless and until a liberal reform group returns to power in China, the Washington-Beijing relationship is unlikely to regain anything resembling its former warmth and closeness. Japan is once again the foremost Asian power in Washington's calculations, a position to which Tokyo is entitled by its growing worldwide political influence as well as its economic muscle.

Hong Kong, too, has become a factor in Sino-American relations. The Sino-British Joint Declaration of September 1984, under which the British colony was to be returned to Chinese sovereignty on July 1, 1997, came at a time of special closeness in relations between Washington and Beijing. Ronald Reagan had given the PRC leadership his imprimatur during a visit the previous May, and China seemed well embarked on the road to something resembling a market economy. As a result, the United States took the most bullish view possible of the Joint Declaration and of Hong Kong's future prosperity as part of China.

That too is no longer the case. Following the events in Tiananmen Square, Beijing canceled its earlier pledge to accept a consensus on the speed of democratic development in the colony's proposed Basic Law and insisted on a formula that would allow direct election of only 50 percent of the legislature, and that not before the year 2003.[12] It also insisted on inserting into the final draft of the Basic Law language banning "subversion" in terms vague enough to be defined in any way Beijing chooses.[13] It has warned the Hong Kong government against allowing adoption of a Bill of Rights which would have supremacy over other Hong Kong laws.[14] And China has insisted on stationing troops in the colony after its 1997 takeover date.

Hong Kong was supposed to be the one place where the PRC would place economics rather than politics in command. But given the most recent pattern of behavior, there is little reason to hold to the earlier belief that Beijing will rule Hong Kong with a light, even deft hand. Unless the reformers come back to power in China, we can expect continuing interference before 1997 and serious mismanagement after that date. If that is the case, substantial American economic interests in Hong Kong will be damaged, and this too will become a cause of tension in Sino-American relations.

All in all, it appears the 1990s will not be a decade of particular closeness between the United States and China. Arguments on trade matters will persist, and the divergence in policy on Southeast Asian issues will continue. And as has happened in the past each time relations between the United States and the PRC become strained, the Taiwan issue is likely once again to come to the fore.

Harvey J. Feldman

Washington and Taipei

It has been argued throughout this chapter that except in the realm of economic and trade matters, the United States has never really had a Taiwan policy; instead, policy with respect to the island was governed primarily by Washington's relationship to Beijing and the view of China as being either a threat or a potential ally. It seems likely that with the ending of the cold war, the PRC will be seen as neither one nor the other, that the United States will come to see China for what it is: a large, overpopulated, very poor, politically unstable country in need of infusions of foreign investment and technology and access to the American marketplace. If that change of view indeed comes to pass, perhaps the United States will also see Taiwan as what it is: a dynamic, democratizing country which (with early help and encouragement from the United States) successfully made the transition from poverty to economic resilience, complete with a broad and satisfied middle class. Under these circumstances, how might future American policy toward Taiwan take shape?

That will largely depend upon how the Republic of China on Taiwan defines itself. While, legalistically speaking, President Lee Teng-hui's decision to end the "Period of Mobilization for Suppression of the Communist Rebellion," announced in his inauguration speech on May 20, 1990, does not in itself alter the ROC claim to be the sole legitimate government of all China, it is another in the series of practical steps which he has taken to distance his government from that claim. The end of the forty-one-year-old "Temporary Provisions" for the period of "Communist rebellion," which is to occur in 1991, is a further step. New elections for Taiwan's three parliamentary bodies, the Legislative Yuan, the Control Yuan, and the National Assembly, will have to take place; and those members of the "Class of 1947" who have been frozen in office finally will have to retire. Add to this the principal recommendations of the July 1990 National Affairs Conference on direct election of the mayors of Taipei and Kaohsiung, the governor of Taiwan, and ultimately the president of the Republic.[15]

When this series of steps concludes, a new political, constitutional, and juridical system will have been created on Taiwan. This certainly will bolster Taiwan's attempts to reenter the mainstream of international life through the "flexible diplomacy" policies of the Lee Teng-hui government. Until now, the United States has neither encouraged nor actively discouraged the "flexible diplomacy policy," but it has been more than a little uneasy and has quietly cautioned against steps to institutionalize Taiwan's separation in ways that might provoke an intemperate reaction from Beijing. With the PRC "looming smaller," however, this American concern is likely to recede.[16]

Reflections and Conclusion

In the December 15, 1978, communiqué stipulating the United States' formal recognition of the People's Republic of China, the American side noted that it "acknowledges the Chinese position that there is but one China and Taiwan is a part of China." This could be interpreted as a polite way of saying, "We hear you," without taking a firm position. Perhaps because of this, in the joint communiqué of August 17, 1982, in which the Reagan administration pledged to reduce arms sales to Taiwan, the Chinese side insisted upon language stating that the United States would follow neither a "two Chinas" nor a "one China, one Taiwan" policy. But the essence of Washington's successive positions going back to the Shanghai Communiqué is that the question of Taiwan is one to be settled by the parties themselves, and by peaceful means. These several statements have been interpreted by successive American administrations as meaning neither party could impose a solution on the other — neither forcible incorporation nor a unilateral declaration of formal independence.

But there is nothing in these several formulae that would necessarily inhibit a future American administration from openly supporting an ROC application to rejoin GATT as soon as possible, or the World Health Organization (whose rules permit membership by entities other than recognized states), or the World Bank and other international financial institutions.[17] What has prevented American support in the past is fear of damaging relations with Beijing.

We can expect that this concern will diminish as more accurate appreciations take hold of the actual comparative positions and strengths of the PRC and Taiwan. Beyond that, we have the example of Soviet attitudes on the issue of German reunification as an example of how national policy can shift. If the Soviet Union can drop its insistence that there must always be two separate German states, and that one of them must be communist, and agree to one noncommunist Germany within NATO, is it too far-fetched to believe that the United States could drop its continuing "acknowledgment" that there can only be one China, including Taiwan?

Given a continuation of present trends, it is entirely possible that by the end of the 1990s a continued refusal to treat Taiwan as a full member of the world family of nations will have become so completely anomalous as to be no longer supportable on any ground. At that point, it will be up to the Republic of China to decide just what it intends to be.

NOTES

1. For a summary treatment of events in this period see Harvey J. Feldman, "The Development of U.S.–Taiwan Relations, 1948–87," in Harvey J. Feldman and Ilpyong J. Kim, eds., *Taiwan in a Time of Transition* (New York: Paragon House, 1988), pp. 129–75. There are many works, of course, which treat this period at greater length. One of the best of them is Ralph J. Clough, *Island China* (Cambridge, MA: Harvard University Press, 1978).
2. For a full-scale analysis of the Taiwan Relations Act and its functioning, see William B. Bader and Jeffrey T. Bergner, eds., *The Taiwan Relations Act, A Decade of Implementation* (Indianapolis: The Hudson Institute, 1989).
3. For examples, see Don Oberdorfer, "Two Top Reagan Advisors Are on Taiwan's Payroll," *Washington Post,* 6 June 1980, p. A-8, and Katherine Macdonald, "Reagan Acts to Reassure Peking on Ties," *Washington Post,* 17 August 1980, p. A-4.
4. The Taiwan Relations Act, Section 2(a)(5).
5. Data taken from table 1, "Key Economic Indicators," *Economic Trends Report for Taiwan,* prepared semi-annually by the American Institute in Taiwan and published by the International Trade Administration, U.S. Department of Commerce. The latest report was released in December 1990.
6. Ungrudging concurrence is hardly to be expected.
7. The PRC-controlled Hong Kong magazine *Liaowang* (Outlook), No. 45, 7 November 1988, published an article by Zhang Jingxu ("U.S.-Taiwan Relations and Peaceful Reunification across the Strait") which bitterly attacked the United States for blocking reunification. The tenor of the article can be inferred from some of the subheads: "On the question of reunification across the Strait, the deeds of the U.S. do not match its words"; "The U.S. is still strengthening infiltration into and control over Taiwan"; "The U.S. supports Taiwan's policy of 'being content to retain sovereignty over a part of the country and refusing peace talks.'" The New China News Agency announced on November 9, 1988, that the article had been published in error and was being withdrawn. Nevertheless, it was understood by most analysts to reflect the views of senior PRC officials.
8. There is no open source I can give for the explicit PRC request. However, I was a senior State Department official on active duty at the time and vouch for the statement's authenticity.
9. See Richard M. Nixon, *The Memoirs of Richard Nixon,* Vol. 2 (New York: Warner Books, 1979), p. 8. See also Henry A. Kissinger, *White House Years* (Boston: Little, Brown & Company, 1979), pp. 169–82.

10. It has been described as an emerging superpower for some thirty years now — an interesting example of Plato's distinction between *being* and *becoming*.
11. Yu Zimu, "Resistance to Peaceful Evolution," in *Xuexi yu yanjiu,* No. 10 (October 1989), as translated and reprinted in Foreign Broadcast Information Service, *China,* 28 December 1989, pp. 5–8.
12. See "China Cancels Pledge to Accept Consensus on Democracy," *Financial Times,* 15 September 1989, p. 4, and John Elliot, "Democracy Squeezed Out in Basic Law Debate," *Financial Times,* 15 February 1990, p. 4.
13. *Hong Kong Standard,* 12 December 1989, p. 1.
14. Lincoln Kaye, "The Old and the Restless," *Far Eastern Economic Review* 147, No. 13 (29 March 1990), pp. 10–11.
15. For a report on Lee's inaugural speech, see David Sanger, "Taiwan's President Signals Major Softening in Relations with China," *New York Times,* 21 May 1990, p. A-3. For the end of the Period of Mobilization, etc., see "Ending Mobilization Poses Major Problems," *Free China Journal* 7, No. 39 (28 May 1990), p. 1. For recommendations of the National Advisory Conference, see Julian Baum, "Taiwan's Negotiators Reach Consensus on Democratic Reforms," *Washington Post,* 5 July 1990, p. A-22 and "NAC Ends, Work Begins," *Free China Journal* No. 51 (9 July 1990), p. 1.
16. "Looming smaller" is a felicitous phrase coined by Harry Harding in "China's Changing Roles in the Contemporary World," Harry Harding, ed., *China's Foreign Policy in the 1980s* (New Haven: Yale University Press, 1984), p. 218.
17. In fact, Section 4(d) of the Taiwan Relations Act states that derecognition of Taiwan is not a "basis for supporting exclusion or expulsion of Taiwan from continued membership in any international financial institution or any other international organization."

ELEVEN

The Strategic Triangle Revisited: Virtuous Geometry

Gerald Segal

SINCE THE REVOLUTIONARY EVENTS OF 1989, it seems as if every aspect of the balance of the great powers needs to be reassessed. In the lexicography of pre-1989 geopolitics, the "great power triangle" describing Sino-Soviet-American relations ranked just after "superpower balance" as the most important relationship to be described. But even before 1989, it was clear that perhaps a more important great power triangle was that of the European Community (EC), East Asia, and North America. The importance of this economic/political geometry became clearer as the Sino-Soviet-American triangle appeared oversold.

In the analysis that follows, the central theme will concern the impact of the Sino-Soviet and Soviet-American relations on the Sino-American relationship. While some time will be spent on the period before the Sino-Soviet detente of the 1980s, the bulk of the analysis will focus on more recent periods. But in all phases, it is remarkable just how much the Sino-Soviet-American triangle was misunderstood — an error that is still all too prevalent.

The Soviet Factor to 1971

As historians now explore the documents from the late 1940s and early 1950s, it becomes increasingly clear that the early signs of a great power triangle were misread.[1] This is not the place to evaluate the new literature, but simply to recap some of its more important conclusions. First, it seems that at least before the outbreak of the Korean War in June 1950, there was an opportunity for the United States to establish decent working relations with the communists that had just come to power in China. But the view of the Soviet Union was so hostile and the suspicions about Chinese communists were so intense that the true extent of the differences between the members of the so-called Sino-Soviet alliance could not be fully appreciated.

With hindsight these "lost opportunities" always seem clearer than they really were. Moscow and Beijing did sign a thirty-year treaty of friendship and alliance in February 1950, and there was little to distinguish between the Chinese and Soviet rhetoric on international relations. Both communist powers did see the United States and Japan in East Asia as adversaries, and both had good reason to be suspicious of American protestations, especially because they were so feeble, that no anticommunist coalition was intended.

Second, China was certainly clear that, despite the problems in relations with the Soviet Union, their comrades in Moscow were far more favorably disposed to communism in China than was the United States, which had supported the opposing side in a civil war. It would have taken a major, and unimaginable, demonstration of change of heart by the United States to convince the Chinese communists that the United States genuinely wanted friendship. It was not just that the Americans supported Chiang Kai-shek but that they supported every anticommunist force in East Asia, when China was on the opposite side of the conflict in every instance. Why should Beijing not believe that the Soviet Union, for all its faults, was likely to be more friendly than the hostile United States? It is one thing to suggest there were problems in Sino-Soviet relations even during the honeymoon of the early 1950s, but it is quite another thing to suggest relations with a strongly anticommunist United States could have been better.[2]

Thus if the Sino-Soviet alliance in the early 1950s was "inevitable," then so were many of the tensions in the great power triangle. This was a time when only China and the Soviet Union had decent relations, and all sides of the triangle were far more hostile. It was sensible for China to seek Soviet support in settling international disputes in East Asia, and in many cases the Soviet Union could be considered a generally reliable ally. In the Korean War, Soviet aid was crucial to the prosecution of the war. Soviet airpower was used in a defensive role, and Soviet advisers were killed in combat. Of course, there was more that the Soviet Union might have done, but it too was in a poor state after the Second World War. Should it be so surprising that Moscow insisted that Beijing pay back many of the loans for a war on whose basic character both communist powers apparently agreed? In the ensuing Offshore Islands crisis in 1954–55, China also received the kind of support from the Soviet Union that it might have reasonably expected.[3]

By the time of the second Offshore Islands crisis in 1958 there were increasing signs of Chinese dissatisfaction with Soviet policy. There were also problems in Sino-Soviet relations about the nature of China's domestic politics and the extent to which the Soviet Union should assist China's ambitions to have nuclear weapons. But in all cases, any sensible Western observer would have taken the Soviet side of the arguments. Did it make any sense to give nuclear weapons to a country that could launch the Great Leap Forward and kill some 25 million of its citizens as a result?

In fact, what was happening was a simultaneous maturing of Soviet-American relations and a radicalization of Chinese foreign policy. Thus by the late 1950s the triangle had shifted to a form where the Soviet Union could be seen as the pivotal power — that is, the power with decent relations with the other two members of the triangle. Of course, the more the Soviet Union improved relations with the United States (such as the discussions between President Eisenhower and Soviet leaders leading to the "spirit of Camp David" during the mid-1950s) the more China's radical inclinations and suspicions of Soviet perfidy were fed. It is probably fair to say that because of its internal policies, China would have radicalized its policies even without superpower detente, but the process was certainly accelerated by Soviet actions.[4]

As these shifts were under way in the late 1950s, the United States grew more aware of their existence. There is good evidence that American policymakers knew what was going on, but they were undeniably slow in reacting with new policies. The discussions, especially in the Kennedy administration, were remarkably sophisticated about the causes of the Sino-Soviet rift. But taking advantage of the widening split was quite another matter. There is no substantial evidence of a change in American policy to take advantage of the split. Most observers have looked at Sino-American relations in this period in search of American signals to Beijing about the possibility of detente. But this was always the least likely of the outcomes given the geopolitical alignments of the time.[5]

What was far more likely, and indeed far more important, were American overtures to the Soviet Union. After all, it was Moscow that had indicated a desire to improve relations with Washington, and it was China that was radicalizing its foreign policy. There was every reason for the United States to first try isolating China by making use of Soviet influence. There was even an American expectation that the United States could take a tougher line in East Asia because the Soviet Union would not support China and its friends. Hence American escalation in the Vietnam War was accompanied by regular signals to the Soviet Union that this was not a threat to Soviet interests as much as to China and a radical Vietnam.[6] After the public declaration of the Sino-Soviet split in 1963 and the severance of inter-party ties in March 1966, there was no excuse for the United States not to understand that it was a player in a great-power triangle. Indeed, the United States played the game as well as it thought it could, by trying to widen the Sino-Soviet split.

Needless to say, no American assistance was needed in widening the Sino-Soviet split. As China lurched into another phase of radicalism, the Cultural Revolution, there was all the more reason for the Soviet Union to treat China as much as a rival as an asset. There were attempts to patch up the split after the political demise of Khrushchev in October 1964, and the Soviet Union was serious about wanting "united action" with China as the Vietnam War escalated, but China was in no mood for anything quite so sensible. This was also not a time when Sino-American relations were ever likely to improve, despite the intermittent contacts at the time.

By the mid-1960s the triangle had merely settled more deeply into a pattern it had established earlier in the decade. The Soviet Union remained the most pivotal of the powers, and the Sino-American axis was easily the most strained. The only change, with longer-term implications, was the widening of the Sino-Soviet rift. So long as the Soviet Union tried to hold onto its pivotal position, it found itself in much pain trying not to worsen superpower relations while keeping open contacts with China. In the end, the Soviet Union had to choose between good relations with China and those with the United States, not because it wanted to make a choice but because China forced it.[7]

The choice was obvious. Superpower relations were far too important to be left hostage to what was an increasingly radical China.[8] There were enough problems in superpower relations, especially in the vital European theater (the Soviet invasion of Czechoslovakia took place in 1968), and there were far more important opportunities (SALT) still pending on the agenda. But even in the late 1960s the Soviet Union was not yet ready to abandon its search for a more comfortable pivotal position in the great power triangle. The final step would be forced upon the Soviet Union by a radical China.

The 1969 border clashes between the Soviet Union and China constituted the turning point in triangular relations.[9] China, responding to what it perceived to be an implicit threat from the Soviet Union in the declaration of the Brezhnev Doctrine and the Soviet invasion of Czechoslovakia, attacked Soviet forces along the Ussuri River in an effort to teach the Soviet Union that China was not Czechoslovakia. Of course, there is no evidence that leaders in the Kremlin ever thought anything quite so daft. But the Chinese ambush certainly ensured that the Soviet Union would retaliate. The ensuing border skirmishes were all won by Soviet forces, and China was bullied to the negotiating table by the autumn of 1969. Moscow had enough of the uncertainty along this vulnerable frontier and was fed up with the problems caused in its relations with the West every time it tried to compromise with the Chinese. The Soviet Union chose detente with the United States and abandoned its pivotal position. In 1969 only the Soviet-American axis was positive and the other two were overwhelmingly hostile. For a brief few years, there was no pivotal power in the triangle.

The Soviet Factor: 1971–1989

By the time China and the Soviet Union were actually killing each other's troops, the United States began to think there might be a way to improve relations with both communist states at the same time. After having played the triangle for close to a decade in the obvious way of improving relations with the more amenable power, it was a far more ambitious idea to try to seize the pivotal position. A close observer of the Soviet experience in this painful place might have warned against trying to be so ambitious, but this was not a time for pessimism. The United States had a new administration in 1969 with an ambitious national security adviser in Henry Kissinger and a nasty war in Vietnam which needed to be wound up. What better way to get out of the war than to play one communist power against the other?[10]

The strategy was sophisticated. If the Soviet Union was so sure that it could not get on with China and wanted to get on with the United States, then Washington could scare the Soviet Union with Sino-American detente, while trading superpower detente for pressure on Vietnam to let the United States get out of the Vietnam War with honor. An even trickier part of the strategy was persuading China that, because it was so fearful of the Soviet Union, it could seek assistance in deterring the threat by cooperating with the United States, despite superpower detente. If China would accept that strategic logic, then the United States might even be able to get China to help pressure Vietnam so there could be a decent American exit from Indochina.

One of the most important flaws in the strategy was not that China might fail to see the benefits of improved relations with the United States, but the erroneous American belief that both communist powers would feel they had to pressure Vietnam in order to obtain a deal with Washington. Sure enough, the Soviet Union improved relations with the United States, culminating in the SALT deals of 1972. Despite much crowing at the time, there is no significant evidence that the Soviet Union agreed to anything in the SALT accords that was harmful to Soviet interests.[11] Nor is there evidence that the Soviet Union browbeat Vietnam into a deal that allowed American withdrawal from the war. The outcome in 1975 is powerful evidence that Vietnam got just the outcome it wanted, even if it might have wanted more active support from the Soviet Union earlier in the decade.

China's deal with the United States was harder to arrange, if only because the basic machinery of negotiations had to be established.[12] But China obtained recognition from the United States and the prospect of wider international acceptance. The United States obtained tentative friendship with the one power apart from itself that could pose a basic threat to Soviet security. But the

United States clearly did not obtain Chinese assistance in pressing Vietnam to accept a settlement in Indochina that was favorable to the Americans.

The changes in the great power triangle in the early 1970s were the most important since the Sino-Soviet split. The communist rift had been the single greatest strategic loss suffered by the Soviet Union since the end of the Second World War.[13] But the movement of China from an ally to an enemy of the Soviet Union was not nearly as damaging as the movement of China from ally to ally of an enemy — the United States. By 1972, had it not been for superpower detente, the Soviet Union would have been in a worse strategic position than at any point since the 1940s. Superpower detente also meant that the triangle had taken on a new form, with the Soviet-American relationship the warmest of any, followed by Sino-American relations and then the cool Sino-Soviet axis. The United States had become the pivotal power, but in a difficult way because of the special warmth in the superpower relationship. The challenge would be whether Sino-American relations could be improved to the level of superpower relations.

But as with most plans in the triangular game, the unknown factor was how the other axes would be manipulated. As it happens, Sino-Soviet relations in the 1970s remained cool, providing the United States with the opportunity to improve relations with China on the basis of mutual concern with the Soviet Union. Superpower relations in the latter 1970s could never quite reach the height of 1972, and so the attractions of "the China card" were seen to grow. By 1979, with the Soviet invasion of Afghanistan (a Chinese neighbor) and the Soviet-backed Vietnamese invasion of Cambodia (a Chinese ally), superpower relations cooled and Sino-American relations warmed.[14]

For the first time, and only briefly, the United States became the pivotal power in the triangle. Indeed, Sino-American relations may not have been as important as superpower relations, but they were more positive. Sino-Soviet relations remained the least cooperative of the three, but they were not quite as bad as a decade earlier. Thus China and the United States both obtained reinforcement for their concern with the Soviet threat, and neither was being asked to pay an excessive price. Sino-American trade relations improved and diplomatic relations were fully normalized in

January 1979. The course looked set for a long run with the United States as the pivotal power, masterfully manipulating its great power rivals.

But the love affair with the triangle was about to die. From the American point of view it was seen that there were distinct limits to the assistance China could give in taking on the Soviet Union. China was unable to provide real aid in such third world conflicts as the war in Afghanistan, and it could not even force Vietnam to retreat from Cambodia. Further afield, China could not deploy forces in aid of American causes, although it was long on rhetorical flourishes.[15]

The United States also accepted, even in the darkest days of the Reagan administration, the idea that contacts had to be maintained with the Soviet Union because the nuclear relationship was far too important. What is more, Sino-American relations suffered because of continuing disputes over Taiwan, trade rows, and even Chinese criticism of American policy in Central America, Africa, and the Middle East. In the Iran-Iraq war it was China that provided the arms that sank Western-flagged tankers. It was China that sold IRBMs to Saudi Arabia and fueled an arms race in the Middle East. President Reagan was eventually to visit China, but he remained an anticommunist who saw Chinese rulers as communists, even while many of his fellow Americans thought China was going capitalist. The limits to Sino-American relations were found.[16]

Sino-Soviet relations had also begun to warm in the 1980s.[17] The first steps were taken by China when it realized that the Soviet Union was not as much of a threat as first thought. The invasion of Afghanistan seemed to bog down Soviet troops, not presage a spread of Russian power. The Soviet economy also ground to a halt, and the United States under President Reagan was already making life as difficult for the Soviet Union as anyone might want. In addition, when the Chinese looked at their policies around the world to see where their strong anti-Sovietism had got them, they found they had leaned so much to the American side of the triangle that they had become nearly horizontal. China had lost its independence when it had assumed knee-jerk anti-Soviet positions in the developing world. As a supporter of the regimes in Chile or Zaire, China was losing its reputation as an independent third world leader. As Alexander Haig spoke of China as NATO's sixteenth member, the message went out that China was a card to be played by American geopoliticians.

The obvious solution was to improve relations with the Soviet Union. Matters were made easier by the fact that the Soviet Union also thought the post-Mao Chinese leadership might be in the mood for some detente. As superpower relations cooled in the Reagan administration, the attractions of improving relations with China grew accordingly. Thus the Soviet Union responded to China's initial overtures. Beijing had declared in 1980 that the Soviet Union was, after all, a socialist state and therefore not quite as irredeemably hostile as once thought. In 1982, Brezhnev agreed that China was also a socialist state and therefore there was a basis for cooperation not present when China was guided by Maoism.

While superpower relations drifted down to the depths of a new cold war, Sino-Soviet relations warmed.[18] Trade and cultural ties were the first to see the benefits, and inter-state contacts gradually moved to a higher level. The Soviet Union thinned out its troops along the border with China, and the Chinese reciprocated with cuts of a similar size as part of their major troop reductions. But the process was confused and hampered by the death of Brezhnev, Andropov, and then Chernenko in 1982–1985. While Andropov had seemed seriously intent on improving relations with China, Chernenko was less interested in making, or less able to make, important concessions. It was not until the Gorbachev administration began to take charge in early 1985 that Sino-Soviet detente was given a shove forward.[19]

In a speech at Vladivostok in July 1986, Gorbachev accepted the Chinese definition of the river frontier, announced that troops would be cut in Afghanistan and Mongolia, and offered better trade relations. In subsequent initiatives, the Soviet Union promised more troop cuts, pulled out of Afghanistan and promised to do the same in Mongolia. Pressure was exerted on Vietnam to withdraw from Cambodia. The communist states of Eastern Europe were even allowed to restore party-to-party relations with the Chinese before the Soviet Union was able to do the same. Gorbachev seemed to be serious about reasonable sufficiency in defense and tolerating pluralism in the socialist world, and anxious to open up to wider contact with the capitalist world in East Asia and around the globe.

For its part, China was prepared to accept a Sino-Soviet summit meeting in May 1989 without a full Vietnamese withdrawal from Cambodia and a proper demarcation of the frontier. Soviet troops had been thinned out but were not yet gone. Thus Sino-Soviet detente was a mutual process, with the Soviet Union making more of the concessions to sanity. The entire process took less time than the normalization of Sino-American relations between 1971 and 1979. The strategic balance was shifting again. Just as the Sino-Soviet split was the single greatest loss suffered by the Soviet Union between 1945 and 1989, so the healing of the rift was the single greatest gain since the consolidation of communist rule in various states in the late 1940s.[20]

In the 1980s the strategic triangle achieved a more balanced shape. Sino-Soviet detente raised that axis to more or less the significance of Sino-American relations. The superpower axis for a time seemed to slip into line with the stalled talks on an INF accord and the series of failures at summit meetings to agree to any new arms control measures. For a time around 1986–87, the triangle was almost equilateral. The United States had lost its pivotal position for a number of reasons, most of which had to do with deliberate American actions. The cooled, or more properly, the boring and stable state of Sino-American relations was part of a general sense that the China market had been oversold and that China's more independent policy (officially since 1982) was leading to more numerous squabbles over developments in the developing world. Superpower relations were cool because of the Reagan administration's determination to take on the challenge they saw coming from the Soviet Union and the refusal to compromise on SDI and arms control in general.

By the late 1980s, both superpower and Sino-Soviet relations were moving forward in tandem. The initiative had passed to the Soviet Union, although it could not yet be termed the pivotal power. Since the era of strategic collaboration in Sino-American relations had passed with the advent of the new superpower detente, it was inevitable that the only power that could take the initiative would be the Soviet Union. China might have chosen to react to superpower detente as it had earlier and cause a breakdown in Sino-Soviet relations, but Beijing had learned the lesson of the past and allowed itself to be wooed by Moscow. Thus by 1989 the triangle had reached an admirable state with all powers more or less satisfied with basically warm relations, and with the recognition that each axis also contained elements of competition as well as coexistence. Detente was breaking out all over. The question whether the triangle could last in this blissful state was soon overtaken by the question whether the triangle was still important when no one was seeking to play one power off against the other.

The Triangle in 1989–90

1989 began with the triangle in its most balanced state yet. President Bush visited China in February, President Gorbachev was due in May, and the leaders of the superpowers had already met in New York before President Bush took office. And yet none of these high-level meetings focused on the major revolution that would jolt the strategic balance from Europe later in the year. Nor could any of the leaders envision any of the smaller changes that in quieter times might have had a major impact on the pattern of international relations.

In May 1989, Mikhail Gorbachev managed what no Soviet leader had done since 1959, a summit meeting with the Chinese. But on the very days of the summit in May and later in June 1989, protests occurred in China that eventually led to the use of troops against demonstrators, and several hundred people were killed. The price of continued communist rule was the use of force to defend the party. Gorbachev, whose own political reforms were part of the inspiration for the Chinese demonstrators, recognized the limits of a system that had to be defended with tanks. Although Khrushchev had also recognized that "you cannot herd people into paradise and post sentries at the gate," he was still prepared to do just that in Hungary in 1956. Gorbachev was not prepared to defend his outer empire with such force, and thus on a day that Chinese troops were still killing people on the streets of Beijing, Poles were allowed to vote for the first noncommunist government in Eastern Europe. In ensuing months, five other Warsaw Pact states deposed their communist rulers, and the Soviet Union wished the reformers well. The cold war ended on November 9, 1989, when the Berlin Wall was breached, and by July 1990 the two Germanys were well on their way to full union.[21] After all these momentous events, what had become of the great power triangle?

From the American perspective, the most obvious change in the strategic triangle was the rapid warming of superpower relations. Indeed, as far as Europeans were concerned, by the end of the year it was hard to find any threat except the collapse of the Soviet Union itself. At its summit in July, NATO agreed to invite President Gorbachev to address a NATO meeting, and arms controllers could not keep up with the pace of unilateral cuts. Superpower relations had never been better since the two had cooperated in the war against Germany in the early 1940s. To be sure, these two once-super superpowers still maintained the world's most powerful nuclear arsenals, but it was difficult to envisage any sensible scenario in which they would be used against each other. An agreement on a START accord was initialed, and more deals were expected.

In such a world it was difficult to imagine either the Soviet Union or the United States allowing itself to be played off in any possible great power triangle. Americans grew far more worried about economic relations with Japan and the European Community—yet another triangle. It was certainly true that the United States was unlikely to allow China, of all countries, to interfere in the superpower relationship. President Bush had done his best to ensure that the Beijing massacre did not lead to a serious reversal of Sino-American relations, but the lineup of "good communists" in the USSR and the "bad communists" in China was in sharp contrast to that of earlier years, when the labels were reversed.

To be fair, China did not try to worsen superpower relations. But China was far more skeptical about the importance of the changes in Europe.[22] In a country still ruled by communists, it was less easy to accept that Communist parties had lost power elsewhere so convincingly. Neither could China believe that the Communist Party of the Soviet Union (CPSU) was also a fading force. The visit by Premier Li Peng to Moscow in April 1990 resulted in restatements of support for socialism from both sides, but it was clear that political and economic reform in the two countries were of very different sorts. In effect, ideology virtually ceased to be a factor in the Sino-Soviet relationship because the Soviet Union was no longer a Communist party-dominated state. To be sure, there was still an element of transition in this process, for despite the declaration in February that the CPSU had abandoned its "leading role," communists still retained control of the KGB and the Soviet armed forces. It would take some time for reality to catch up with rhetoric.

Sino-Soviet relations were kept firmly on the rails of detente set out before everything exploded in April 1989. The normalization of inter-party relations was obviously less important than it once was, as inter-state relations took on the leading role. Agreements were announced at the May 1990 summit on a range of subjects, including the promise to complete a confidence-building pact regarding the once-disputed frontier. China kept a resolutely positive line about Sino-Soviet relations, even though it was clearly displeased with political trends in Europe. China correctly established relations with the new regimes with commendable promptness and promised to keep relations normal.

Of course, what else could China do? If it had been in a truly bad mood it could have begun a Cultural Revolution–like radical policy denouncing both superpowers. With sharp American criticism and unspoken Soviet disapproval of the events of June 1989, the basis for such xenophobia was present. But as months elapsed after the first emotional reactions to the events of June, it became clear just how little of the real economic reform had been undone in China. Most of the changes were the result of austerity policies adopted in late 1988, and even those were being lifted in 1990.[23] Economic reform was still on the agenda, even if political reform was not. But in order to have serious economic reform the open door policy had to be maintained, which in turn required doors open to both the Europeans and the Americans. The Soviet Union and its former friends in Eastern Europe were increasingly seen as part of the European option for China as a Eurasian power. Trade with the East Europeans was coming to be conducted on a hard currency basis, and all but border trade with the Soviet Union was set to follow.[24]

China was now able to put into practice its often-declared desire for a genuinely independent policy. Neither superpower demanded much of China, and China wanted much from both. There was every reason to continue to have good relations with both superpowers and to try to improve relations with the emerging great powers of Japan and the European Community. The superpowers were clearly less interested in China than ever before, but largely because they had so much else on their plates. It is not that China was intrinsically less important, only that it was relatively less valuable as other states and issues rose in importance. Certainly if China were to have suddenly turned more hostile in its relationship with either the United States or the Soviet Union, then the superpower concerned would have had major problems. Would Moscow have been so tolerant of the loss of its empire in Europe if it had had a major threat in the east?

Thus by the autumn of 1990, the great power triangle seemed to be less important because other issues were more important. Triangular relations also seemed less vital because they were still basically blissful and positive all around. The mix of competition and coexistence in the detentes was different, with far more coexistence in the superpower relationship. But the central point was that good relations all around made people less worried about the triangle, though geometry was still present.

Where To from Here?

With the great power triangle less prominent, the tendency is to dismiss it as a once-important consideration now virtually obsolete.[25] But as we have already seen, there is a long tradition of misunderstanding the triangle, sometimes by way of exaggeration and sometimes by way of neglect. In the post-1989 world, the great power triangle remains important, for who can deny that the role of the Soviet Union is crucial to a consideration of Sino-American relations? Consider a number of key issues in Sino-American relations that are affected by Soviet policies.

Conflict on the Korean peninsula has become much less likely in recent years and much of the credit can be given to Soviet policies and the interaction in the triangle.[26] China took the first steps in opening trade contacts with South Korea as part of its open door strategy in foreign economic relations. The result was pressure on Pyongyang to take a more moderate position on Korean issues. But it was only when the Soviet Union joined in the regional detente that North Korea was really left without options. Under President Gorbachev's new policies of joining the emerging Pacific prosperity, it was decided that trade relations could be opened with South Korea. The East Europeans, even before the revolutions of 1989, were allowed to establish formal diplomatic relations with Seoul. In June 1990 a Soviet–South Korean summit ended with an agreement to establish full diplomatic relations, even though China remains reluctant to do the same.

Clearly the improvement in Sino-Soviet relations made it harder for North Korea to play one patron off against the other. The United States could applaud the process and even open a dialogue of its own with North Korea. The mutually reinforcing detentes on the great power triangle level encouraged a more complex regional detente. Should there be a change in Soviet policy (most unlikely), then Sino-American relations in this vital area of East Asia will also be harmed.

Second, there is the impact of Sino-Soviet detente on the conflict in the South China Sea. China was only able to defeat Vietnamese forces in the March 1988 clash in the Spratly Islands because the Soviet Union was anxious not to harm its detente with China by supporting Vietnam. In the Chinese operation in the Paracels in 1974, it was the unwillingness of the United States to damage its detente with China that allowed Beijing to poach islands from the failing regime of South Vietnam. China knows that the great power triangle can be manipulated to allow it to satisfy its regional aspirations.

Of course, the South China Sea operations are far from over; China continues to covet territory held by Vietnam, Malaysia, the Philippines, and Taiwan. So long as the great power triangle continues in its all-round detente form, it seems likely that neither superpower will stop China from taking what it wants. It is vital to China's calculations that good relations are maintained with both superpowers. Should Sino-Soviet relations deteriorate, the Soviet navy might try to stop the Chinese from extending their reach. The United States, still holding onto selected bases in the region, seems reluctant to support its friends. Yet is it possible that concerted Soviet-American action might dissuade China from taking islands in Malaysia? Clearly the policies to be adopted in the triangle in the future are crucial to how local conflicts are worked out.

Third, consider the impact of a possible Soviet-Japanese detente on Sino-American relations in East Asia. It looks increasingly likely that there will be a Soviet-Japanese accommodation on the Northern Territories before the planned Soviet-Japanese summit in 1991. Might Japan seriously consider major investment in the

Soviet Far East, and might this also be part of a Japanese attempt to lessen its dependence on the United States?

If so, neither the United States nor China is likely to be pleased. The risks of a resurgent and more independent Japan are inherent in the new multipolarity developing in East Asia. Prospects of a Japanese strategic resurgence would upset both the United States (the predominant power) and China (which has its own great-power aspirations). The involvement of a fourth power (at least in Asia) might well drive the United States and China closer together. Of course it might also be merely part of the growing complexity of regional interdependence. The Soviet-Japanese relationship is the last missing piece of regional detente, and its insertion into the geopolitical map might merely make the virtuous triangle of detente even stronger, thereby serving Chinese and American interests. Whatever the case, the policies of the Soviet Union are vital (as are those of Japan) to predicting the future course of Sino-American relations.

Fourth, consider the impact on Sino-American relations of a major superpower arms control deal. The first START accord promises only a 30-some percent cut in the size of superpower arsenals, but a second or third START accord could begin to turn up the heat on such middle-rank nuclear powers as China, who would then have to accede to the arms control process. Sino-American relations have so far not had to face the tough kind of talks that concern such touchy issues as transparency, on-site inspections, and provision of basic data on arms procurement and defense budgets. Could the Sino-American relationship take the strain? Could China accept a role in a complex multi-party arms control? What would China say to proposals for limits on its conventional forces?

It is not inconceivable that future progress in the superpower axis of the triangle will put pressure on the Sino-American side. Of course, any serious, sweeping arms control in East Asia must involve China and the United States as active participants. China's attitude towards arms control so far gives little ground for optimism. But the triangle in its detente mode might well entice China to join the detente process and eventually widen it out to include other regional actors. China is already used to dealing with Western firms in the marketplace; perhaps it will acknowledge the need for transparency, so vital to modern arms control.[27]

Of course there are a number of other issues that can be outlined in which the Soviet factor will have an impact on Sino-American relations. Consider the impact of a collapse of Soviet power in Central Asia and the problems that would cause for China, Pakistan, and India. Consider the prospects of sweeping reforms in the Soviet Union leading to a closer integration with the European Community (EC). Will that harm the United States' relations with the European Community, or will they grow closer and therefore distract the United States from the supposed benefits of the Pacific Century? And what if the Soviet Union collapses in a failed attempt at reform? Will China pick off the pieces it wants, or will it work with other powers anxious to reduce the risks of fallout from the disintegrating USSR? The list of questions is seemingly endless at this time of great shifts in the strategic balance.

Thus we return to the central point. We risk minimizing the importance of the strategic triangle, just because it is harder to see in the maze of other important issues. The relative importance of the Sino-Soviet-American triangle has undoubtably declined, but it still remains a key component of the strategic calculations of the future. We are looking at an age where Soviet and even American power are in relative decline. China, and especially Japan and the EC, are clearly on the rise, creating a multipolar world that varies depending on the nature of the issue. If the matter at hand concerns economic issues, then China and the USSR are far less important compared to the elements of the great economic triangle of EC-East Asia-North America. If the issue is one of territorial disputes in East Asian waters, the EC is less important, and so might be the United States. Who will be major actors if China and Taiwan fall out?

The Soviet Union remains important to China as a means of containing Japan and the United States. The Soviet Union is also another door to the international economy and perhaps even a source of knowledge about how to marketize a planned economy. The United States needs the Soviet Union as a partner in arms control, as the two superpowers look set to dominate the nuclear arms business for some time to come. The Soviet Union is also still a vital power in Europe and to some extent in East Asia — both regions whose stability is important to the prosperity of the United States. Some cynics might also argue that the continued treatment of the Soviet Union as a superpower to some extent validates the continued American belief in their superpower status.

In sum, the Chinese-Soviet-American triangle remains important. Although in its mutual detente version the triangle seems less interesting, such a dismissive attitude would soon pass if something went wrong in the mutually reinforcing virtuous tendencies in the triangle. Just as it took a crisis in Sino-American relations in 1989 to show how important the relationship still was, so a virtuous triangle lulls people into a tendency to dismiss the strategic geometry.

NOTES

1. John Garver, *Chinese-Soviet Relations* (Oxford: Oxford University Press, 1988); James Reardon Anderson, *Yenan and the Great Powers* (New York: Columbia University Press, 1980); Marc Gallicho, *The Cold War Begins in Asia* (New York: Columbia University Press, 1988).
2. Roger Dingman, "Atomic Diplomacy during the Korean War," and Rosemary Foot, "Nuclear Coercion and the Ending of the Korean Conflict," both in *International Security* 13, No. 3 (Winter 1988–89); and Hao Yufan and Zhai Zhihai, "China's Decision to Enter the Korean War: History Revisited," *China Quarterly*, No. 121 (March 1990), pp. 94–115.
3. Gerald Segal, *Defending China* (Oxford: Oxford University Press, 1985).
4. Michael Yahuda, *China's Role in World Affairs* (London: Croom Helm, 1978).
5. Gerald Segal, *The Great Power Triangle* (London: Macmillan, 1982), and Timothy Maga, *John F. Kennedy and the New Pacific Community* (London: Macmillan, 1990).
6. Allen Whiting, *The Chinese Calculus of Deterrence* (Ann Arbor: University of Michigan Press, 1975), see especially pp. 170–95.
7. Segal, *Great Power Triangle*, especially chapter 3.
8. Raymond Garthoff, *Detente and Confrontation* (Washington, DC: Brookings Institution, 1985), pp. 201–02, 212–13, and 240–43.
9. Background is provided by Richard Wich, *Sino-Soviet Crisis Politics* (Cambridge, MA: Harvard University Press, 1980).
10. Henry Kissinger, *White House Years* (London: Weidenfeld, 1979), and Seymour Hersh, *Kissinger* (London: Faber and Faber, 1983).
11. Michael McGwire, *Perestroika and Soviet National Security* (Washington, DC: Brookings Institution, 1991), chapter 3.
12. Jonathan Pollack, *The Lessons of Coalition Politics* (Santa Monica: The RAND Corporation, February 1984), pp. 9–23; and David Shambaugh, "China's America Watchers," *Problems of Communism* 37, Nos. 3–4 (May 1988), pp. 71–94.
13. Gerald Segal, *The Soviet Union and the Pacific* (Boston: Unwin/Hyman for the Royal Institute of International Affairs, 1990), Chapter 5.
14. Gerald Segal, *Sino-Soviet Relations after Mao*, Adelphi Paper no. 202 (London: International Institute for Strategic Studies, 1985), part one.
15. Segal, *Rethinking the Pacific* (Oxford: Oxford University Press, 1990), section three.
16. Michael Yahuda, "Sino-American Relations," in Gerald Segal, ed., *Chinese Politics and Foreign Policy Reform* (London: Kegan Paul Interna-

tional for the Royal Institute of International Affairs, 1990), and Bernard K. Gordon, *New Directions for American Policy in Asia* (London: Routledge, 1990), chapter 4.

17. See details in Segal, *Sino-Soviet Relations,* and Gerald Segal, "Taking Sino-Soviet Relations Seriously," *Washington Quarterly* 12, No. 3 (Summer 1989), pp. 53–63.
18. Mike Bowker and Phil Williams, *Superpower Detente* (London: Sage for the Royal Institute of International Affairs, 1988), chapter 10.
19. Segal, *Soviet Union and the Pacific,* chapter 5.
20. Segal, *Soviet Union and the Pacific,* chapter 5, and Gerald Segal, "The Asian Road to Conventional Reductions," *Arms Control Today* 19, No. 4 (May 1989), pp. 16–20.
21. Gerald Segal and John Phipps, "Why Communist Armies Fight for Their Parties," *Asian Survey* 30, No. 10 (October 1990), pp. 959–76.
22. Alyson Bailes, "China and Eastern Europe," *The Pacific Review* 3, No. 3 (1990), pp. 222–42.
23. See generally, Segal, ed., *Chinese Politics.*
24. Bailes, "China and Eastern Europe," pp. 236–38.
25. For example, see Yahuda, "Sino-American Relations."
26. Gerald Segal, "East Asia: New Balances of Power," *World Policy Journal* 6, No. 4 (Fall 1989), pp. 731–57.
27. Gerald Segal, "For China, A Test of Sincerity," *International Herald Tribune,* 30 June 1990.

TWELVE

Determinants of PRC Arms Control: Policies in the 1990s

Douglas T. Stuart

THIS CHAPTER WILL SPECULATE on the future direction of Chinese arms control policies in the 1990s. "Arms control" will be defined broadly to include policies aimed at the limitation, eschewal, or reduction of the instruments of war as well as policies aimed at confidence building and risk reduction.[1] My arguments will be based upon two propositions:

1. That Chinese arms control policies are developed in support of and by reference to Chinese strategy
2. That Chinese strategy has been developed to conform to determinate circumstances, capabilities, and perceived vulnerabilities

The first proposition is uncontroversial. It is tantamount to asserting that China acts rationally in the formulation of its arms control policies. The early (September 1966) assessment by the Hoover Institution that "Communist China regards arms control essentially as an instrument of political warfare which she can use to enhance her influence or consolidate her strategic position" remains true today.[2] China is not alone in treating arms control as the handmaiden of strategy, of course. In fact, it can be argued that the United States is the only nation with an arms control policy which has occasionally changed in isolation from, or in conflict with, its overall strategy.[3]

The second proposition is more controversial and requires more elucidation. To assert that Chinese strategy has been shaped primarily by circumstances, capabilities, and perceived vulnerabilities is to depict Chinese decisionmaking as reactive and ad hoc. This interpretation assumes that Chinese strategy is largely determined by structural and situational factors which would be interpreted and responded to in a similar fashion by most decisionmakers, regardless of nationality.[4] It places greater emphasis on what China does and where China is in the global and regional power balance at a particular point in time and downplays what Chinese leaders say. It stresses present conditions rather than aspirations.

The "Nature/Nurture" Dispute

During the last decade specialists in Chinese defense affairs have been engaged in a political variant of the "nature-nurture" debate in the field of psychology. Spokespersons for the "nature" school, including Chong-pin Lin and Harlan Jencks, have looked within the PRC for the sources of Chinese strategy. They have stressed the unique characteristics of Chinese thought and argued that the PRC leadership has developed a distinct approach to strategy.[5] This is an important and fruitful area of inquiry, but it can also be misleading. It tends to rely too much upon the statements of Chinese spokesmen, in spite of the fact that most of the proponents of this approach agree that deception and ambiguity are central elements of Chinese strategy. More importantly, by focusing on internal debates among representatives of the People's Liberation Army (PLA) about the theory of war or about goals for the future, the "nature" argument can lead scholars away from the analysis of current threats and capabilities which must necessarily occupy the bulk of the attention of Chinese leaders.

By contrast, the "nurture" school stresses the logic of the situation. These writers assume that if one is interested in making broad generalizations about China's strategic options and policies at a certain point in time, it is far more cost-effective to focus upon the objective realities which confront Chinese defense planners and to assume that, regardless of what "intellectual baggage" Chinese planners bring to their work, they cannot overlook these objective realities.

John Lewis and Xue Litai provide us with an informative example of a scholarly attempt to grapple with the "nature/nurture" distinction. In the early portions of their comprehensive history of the development of China's nuclear weapons program they engage in a close exegesis of the writings and speeches of Mao Zedong. This predisposes them toward a "nature" perspective regarding the sources of Chinese strategy. Thus the reader is advised that "Mao Zedong seems never to have entertained the notion that nuclear weapons had changed the basic military and political realities or undermined his preconceptions about war."[6] As their narrative progresses, however, they move steadily in the direction of the "nurture" camp. They observe that in spite of the unique world views of the PRC leaders, China developed a *de facto minimum deterrence posture* which in its broad outlines was not dissimilar to the minimum deterrence posture of other middle nuclear powers. Lewis and Xue conclude that

> in China, as elsewhere, the possession of nuclear weapons exposed the country to the nuclear paradox: such power imposed unprecedented risks. Over time, the acquisition of nuclear weapons undermines familiar modes of nationalism and drives nuclear states to a tacit reciprocal tolerance in order to survive. . . . Nuclear weapons did impose their implacable logic of caution on Beijing's war preparations.[7]

My arguments also favor nurture over nature explanations as a general rule. My analysis does diverge from the nurture school in one important respect, however. I assume that as a nation gains greater control over its political environment it finds more opportunities to develop its strategy in accordance with its unique world view. As I will discuss below, this exception to the rule of environmental determinance has only become relevant to the study of Chinese strategy during the last decade.

Three Sources of Chinese Strategy

The strategy of the People's Republic of China evolved in the context of three realities. First, China is large, poor, and geostrategically vulnerable. It shares 14, 000 kilometers of border with ten neighbors, and its leaders have not been able to assume that the People's Liberation Army could defend these borders against all likely threats. The PLA has been even less capable of projecting force beyond China's borders. In 1982, John Sloan of the U.S. Defense Intelligence Agency offered this assessment:

> They [Chinese forces] probably cannot capture Hanoi without large losses. They cannot move against India, Japan or into noncontiguous Southeast Asian nations. They cannot project significant power outside China's border with the exception of Indochina and Korea. Practically speaking, they cannot successfully invade Taiwan.[8]

China has taken some significant steps since the 1979 Sino-Vietnamese war to improve its force projection capabilities, under the rubric of "People's War under Modern Conditions." Sloan's assessment is still valid, however, as a benchmark for making predictions about PLA capabilities in the 1990s.

The fact that more than 70 percent of China's population are peasants — about 20 percent of the world's population on 7 percent of the world's arable land — imposes strict limits on Beijing's ability to make qualitative improvements in its armed forces. Defense modernization has been accorded lowest priority in China's Four Modernizations program since Deng Xiaoping came to power in 1977. Since the Tiananmen Square incident there has been some increase in the PLA's share of the overall national budget (11.5 percent for 1990), but much of this adjustment has been eaten up by inflation, and it cannot compensate for the monotonic decline in military spending during the 1980s. Under these circumstances, the traditional doctrine of people's war, which is designed to make a virtue of China's very considerable military weaknesses, continues to reflect current realities more accurately than the theme of "People's War under Modern Conditions."

The second reality which has shaped Chinese strategy is that the PRC cannot rely upon any other nations to guarantee its security. During the formative period of the cold war many Chinese planners encouraged and applauded Soviet friendship. But Moscow's actions during the 1950s and 1960s confirmed Mao's doubts about the costs and benefits of close ties to the USSR. And when Mao felt compelled to "lean to the other side" in the early 1970s by courting the United States, he understood that American support was conditional and fundamentally unreliable. Sino-

American disputes during the Reagan years and conflicts with the Bush administration over issues of human rights and domestic sovereignty have reinforced this lesson for Deng Xiaoping.

The bipolar structure of the post–World War II international system is the third reality which has shaped Chinese strategy for nearly four decades. Bipolarity meant that China could not be fully sovereign if it accepted the direct hegemonic control of either superpower. But in a situation in which Beijing was not willing to submit to hegemonic control, China could not be confident of the backing of either superpower in the face of threat from the other. Bipolarity also presented the PRC leadership with the specter of a dual hegemony should the superpowers come to resolve their differences.

Bipolarity was not entirely disadvantageous for China, however. It presented Beijing with a field of maneuver between the United States and the Soviet Union and offered the possibility to manipulate cold war tensions in ways which might enhance Chinese influence and bolster Chinese security. To achieve these goals, however, China would have to acquire enough political, economic, and military strength to be taken seriously by the superpowers. Furthermore, the benefits of bipolarity could only be obtained if Soviet-American animosity remained high — a situation which was largely beyond China's control.

Background: The Evolution of Chinese Strategy in the Era of Hegemonic Threat

In view of China's problems — poverty, vulnerability, and the unreliability of allies in a world dominated by the two superpowers — Mao's decision to develop a nuclear strike capability seems highly rational. Nuclear weapons were a cost-efficient way to redress a number of vulnerabilities in a relatively short time. In China's case, both the cost and the time required were further reduced by the active assistance of the Soviet Union during the early years of research and development of nuclear weapons. By 1958 Mao had convinced the PRC leadership, including Defense Minister Peng Dehuai, that nuclear deterrence represented the most reliable quick fix to China's major security problems and that nuclear weapons would permit China to reduce overall defense spending in order to fuel economic growth.[9]

Nuclear weapons also offered China two collateral benefits: enhanced prestige among many of the developed and underdeveloped nations of the world and greater independence from Moscow. Chong-pin Lin illustrates the first point by a quote from Zhou Enlai shortly after the detonation of China's first nuclear device: "Have we not exploded an atom bomb? Has not the label 'sick man of the East,' fastened on us by Westerners, been flung off?"[10] The second collateral benefit is perhaps best illustrated by China's actions. Following the 1964 test, the PRC became bolder in its anti-Soviet rhetoric and policies, attempting to organize third world revolutionary movements against Moscow's interests.[11]

France and China: Words and Deeds

A brief comparison to the evolution of strategic doctrine in France is useful in explaining Chinese strategy. The same three considerations which drove the Chinese to develop nuclear weapons — cost-effective compensation for relative military weakness, prestige, and independence — guided French defense planners in their decision to go nuclear. Even before he came to power in 1958, Charles de Gaulle had developed plans for cutting much of the French expeditionary force in order to finance the development of "five atomic divisions." He viewed the nuclear weapon as an essential prerequisite for great-power status in the postwar world and believed that France would never be able to ensure its own security, or regain its influence in European affairs, without a *force de frappe*.[12]

China's nuclear program was also similar to the French program in terms of its strategic rationales. Rhetorical differences notwithstanding, both middle nuclear powers were wedded to a doctrine of minimum deterrence throughout most of the cold war era. In France's case, minimum deterrence was presented as a complex and theoretically refined concept. In China's case, neither the term nor the strategic logic associated with it were present in public pronouncements, but China was nevertheless committed by necessity to the policy.

The basic premises of this minimum deterrence posture,

which were shared by France and China, included the following elements:

1. **The concept of proportionality, which assumes that any potential enemy will make a cost-benefit calculation before engaging in aggression.** It further assumes that the benefits to a superpower of conquering a middle power are limited. The doctrine of proportionality assumes, ipso facto, that a middle power does not have to match a superpower in military might in order to deter that superpower from invading. The middle power only needs to be able to threaten costs which exceed perceived benefits. This requires the development of a secure countervalue retaliatory capability.
2. **Reliance upon contextual power to compensate for defects in indigenous power and to enhance deterrence.** For France, this has meant remaining comfortably ensconced within the Atlantic Community and under the American nuclear umbrella while preaching national independence and opposition to domination by either superpower. China's situation has been less secure, since geography and politics conjoin to make it more exposed and vulnerable than France. Indeed, while the theory of middle power independence and self-reliance has been most fully developed by French strategists, it has been Beijing rather than Paris which has had to live with the risks and responsibilities inherent in such a theory. China has nonetheless been able to derive marginal increments of security from association (however tenuous) with the Soviet Union and, subsequently, the United States.

   Both France and China have also recognized the benefits of threatening to play a wild-card role in any evolving superpower dispute. Thus, Andre Beufre has discussed France's ability to "restrict to some extent the freedom of action of the two principals." Beufre avoided explicit references to a nuclear "trip wire" role for France, but his arguments nonetheless assume that the superpowers recognize that they no longer have exclusive control over the decision to escalate to nuclear war.[13]
3. **Emphasis upon psychological rather than technological deterrence, which further liberates middle powers from the need to match the superpowers one-for-one in terms of nuclear**

capability. Both France and China have relied upon the *communication of resolve* to compensate for relative deficiencies in the quality and quantity of their nuclear stockpiles. But because China has had to take more seriously than France the risks inherent in a situation of minimum deterrence vis-à-vis both superpowers, the demands on Beijing for the maintenance and periodic resuscitation of an image of resolve have been much greater than for Paris.[14] What Allen Whiting has referred to as the "controlled use of force" for demonstrative and educative purposes was best illustrated by China's policies during the 1979 border war with Vietnam.[15] Beijing's incursion into Vietnam was justified as a campaign to "teach Vietnam a lesson." But the principal message was directed at Moscow — a deterrent warning in a situation of increasing Soviet military pressure on China's borders. Just prior to delivering the message, however, Deng Xiaoping took out as much insurance as the situation permitted by visiting the United States and bolstering the image of Sino-American friendship.

A comparison of the French and Chinese strategic doctrines must balance the above-listed similarities against one important difference, which relates to the ultimate rationale for use of nuclear weapons. For de Gaulle, the nuclear weapon was the first weapon in history which gave a nation the option of committing suicide. Because of France's size, population concentration, and location in the center of any East-West European conflagration, de Gaulle believed that his nation could be completely destroyed in a nuclear exchange. Under these circumstances, he felt that it was essential that the national leader, rather than an ally, have the authority over the final decision to invite nuclear destruction upon France. If France must die, it had to be by its own choice, rather than by inadvertence.

By contrast, China's geostrategic circumstances — its vast size and population — mitigated the risks of deterrence failure. Chinese leaders viewed nuclear war as a catastrophe, but they also believed that China would be able to survive as a nation. As a consequence of this distinction, France placed almost exclusive emphasis upon survival through deterrence in the face of a Soviet threat. While Mao and his successors have pursued programs designed to enhance China's warfighting and damage limitation capabilities, at the same time they were improving the PRC's ability to deter an attack by either or both superpowers.[16] This distinction comes out most clearly in the ways in which the two nations have integrated tactical nuclear weapons (TNWs) into their strategic doctrines. France avoids reference to the battlefield uses of TNWs and treats them instead as a device for communicating resolve *in extremis* — a "shot across the bow" of an advancing aggressor. China also recognizes the utility of tactical nuclear weapons as a device for enhancing deterrence and controlling escalation. But the People's Liberation Army also treats TNWs as just another item in its stockpile of warfighting instruments and regularly (and publicly) trains its forces for mixed conventional/nuclear contingencies.

The priority that China has accorded to post-attack survival in a nuclear age is perhaps best illustrated by Mao's "third front" program. Recent Chinese and Western scholarship has discussed this previously secret campaign to develop a vast, self-sufficient industrial infrastructure in southwestern and western China between the years 1964 and 1971. According to Barry Naughton, "The basic purpose of the Third Front was to provide an alternative industrial base that would allow China to continue to produce — and thus to fight — in the event of an attack on its primary urban centers."[17]

Fueled by the Cultural Revolution and fear of confrontation with American forces in Vietnam, the PRC committed more than 40 percent of its national investment to the Third Front program. Naughton also asserts that "in the short run, the Third Front undoubtedly enhanced China's ability to deter a major attack."[18] This is debatable, but for our purposes it is worth emphasizing that neither the Third Front nor any other Chinese efforts to enhance China's ability to survive a major war ever came close to reassuring the PRC leadership that they could move beyond the constraints of a minimum deterrence posture during the cold war era.

To conclude this discussion, although Chinese policymakers have thought about and planned for post-attack survival since 1949, their overriding interest in nuclear weapons has been as a means of minimum deterrence of one or both of the superpowers. China, rather than France, has actually had to develop a *tous asimuts* deterrent capability. China, rather than France, has had to take seriously the dangers inherent in a situation of true national independence from both superpowers. Beijing, much more than Paris, has felt compelled to rely upon the implicit threat of a nuclear wild card to keep both superpowers at bay. And China, to a much greater extent than France, has felt the need periodically to bolster its image of resolve by means of educative military actions along or beyond its borders. On the other hand, as I will discuss further on in this paper, China's more "authentic" situation of independence has made it possible for the PRC to manipulate Soviet-American competition in ways that France was never able to do.

Strategy and Arms Control in the Era of Hegemonic Threat

China's sense of vulnerability, and the priority that Chinese policymakers accorded to both national independence and nuclear deterrence, foreclosed any Chinese participation in strategic arms control or nuclear nonproliferation talks during the first three decades of the PRC's existence. The superpower-sponsored Nuclear Nonproliferation Treaty (NPT) was not only disdained, it was ridiculed by the Chinese as a ploy for preserving hegemonic dominance. PRC spokesmen treated China's acquisition of nuclear weapons as a contribution to world peace because these weapons helped to deter superpower adventurism anywhere in the world and discouraged both superpowers from nuclear saber-rattling.

In the other field of arms control, confidence building and risk reduction, China offered two unilateral commitments:

1. No first use of nuclear weapons (the PRC periodically invited the other nuclear powers to join her in this commitment)
2. No nuclear use against non-nuclear nations

These unilateral concessions were not very reassuring to China's enemies, however, since there was no way other than the threat of retaliation to hold China to either commitment. Furthermore, at least from the point of view of the West during the cold war era, any Chinese confidence building initiatives were more than offset by China's destabilizing activities as the leader of the forces of third world revolution.

Chinese Strategy in the Era of Diminished Threat

The Hoover Institution demonstrated uncommon prescience in the late 1960s when it offered the following prediction:

> We believe that when Communist China has attained what she conceives to be an actual and credible deterrent capability vis-a-vis the United States and the USSR, she may be willing to discuss nuclear arms control measures in more concrete terms, if her military capability in other respects would remain unaffected or be enhanced.[19]

It took more than twenty years for the PRC to reach the point where, through a combination of self-help and external circumstance, it could begin to feel reasonably confident about its national security. As has usually been the case with the PRC, the official doctrinal reassessment was preceded by a long period of hints and self-references. These indications were finally elevated to the status of doctrine in 1985, when the Military Commission of the Central Committee of the Chinese Communist party issued its statement that the risk of major war (that is, war with the Soviet Union or the United States) was "minimal."[20]

The most important change which reduced China's sense of vulnerability in the early and mid-1980s was external, and beyond China's control. This was the relative decline of both superpowers in an international system which had been predominantly bipolar in structure.[21] The persistence of superpower competition had provided Beijing with opportunities for manipulating the system to its advantage, while the preoccupation of both Washington and Moscow with their own internal problems had reduced the likelihood that either nation would be inclined to undertake global initiatives which would directly or indirectly threaten China's interests.

Concurrent with this important change in the global balance of power, China's efforts to develop a survivable second-strike retaliatory force came to fruition. By the mid-1980s, China's nuclear arsenal consisted of six ICBMs, over a hundred IRBMs and MRBMs, and China's first *Xia*-class nuclear-fueled ballistic-missile submarine (SSBN).[22] More significant than these numbers, however, was China's success during the 1970s and early 1980s in dispersing and protecting its nuclear assets to enhance their survivability in the event of a preemptive attack.

These changes in China's indigenous military capability, in conjunction with the changes taking place in the global balance of power, encouraged the Chinese leadership to believe that for the first time in the PRC's history China had some control over its international environment. Consequently, Beijing began to play a more active role in foreign affairs in general and arms control in particular.

The clearest indication that China was prepared to play a new role in the field of arms control was the offer by Huang Hua, during an United Nations speech in 1982, to stop the production and development of nuclear weapons and enter into negotiations to eliminate existing systems if the superpowers would freeze their own nuclear programs and reduce their nuclear stockpiles by 50 percent. Harking back to China's traditional stance on nuclear disarmament, however, Huang noted that real progress in arms reduction had to be preceded by changes in the superpowers' policies regarding the actual or threatened use of nuclear weapons. Huang Hua argued that to pursue nuclear reductions in a situation in which the superpowers still reserved the right to use nuclear weapons against states that did not possess them and reserved the right to be the first to use nuclear weapons in a confrontation, was as "absurd as putting the cart before the horse."[23]

One year later China began to take positions regarding the evolving Soviet-American INF negotiations, and a year after that began to speak out on issues relating to the control of ballistic missile defense systems. The PRC also became much more supportive of, and active in, the UN Conference on Disarmament after Huang Hua's important speech in that forum. All of these actions reflected a new Chinese view of strategic arms talks per se — that such talks were not necessarily a superpower ploy to deceive and manipulate the other nations of the international system and that contributions from and even participation by other nations were useful and necessary.[24]

American policymakers were particularly encouraged by China's more flexible posture regarding nuclear proliferation. While still refusing to sign the NPT, Beijing stated categorically in 1984 that it was opposed to nuclear proliferation and would not help other nations to obtain nuclear weapons. Beijing backed up its rhetoric by agreeing to join the International Atomic Energy Agency (IAEA), thereby opening itself up to IAEA monitoring of its nuclear sales to non-nuclear nations. This action, coupled with informal assurances from Chinese policymakers, paved the way for the 1985 Sino-American Agreement on Nuclear Cooperation, which made it possible for American firms to participate in the development of China's civilian nuclear energy program.[25]

Finally, China developed a foreign policy of "friends with (almost) everybody" in the 1980s, which can be considered its most important contribution to confidence building and risk reduction in Asia. Encouraged by its reassessment of the global balance of power, China embarked on an ambitious foreign policy campaign designed to enhance its influence in the region while reducing the danger of a replay of the 1979 Sino-Vietnamese confrontation. This campaign had its most direct impact along the Sino-Soviet border, on the Korean peninsula, and in Indochina.

Mikhail Gorbachev came to power in the Soviet Union at the time that Deng Xiaoping was establishing the theory of diminished threat as official Chinese doctrine. Both leaders soon recognized a coincidence of interest in a more cooperative relationship. Economic problems were accorded the status of national security threats by both Gorbachev and Deng, and the two leaders recognized that their large standing forces were an obvious place to effect dramatic savings. China took the first important step in 1985, when it announced plans to reduce the overall size of the PLA by about 25 percent (one million men). This commitment was fulfilled by the end of 1987. Moscow reciprocated in 1988 with an offer to cut 500,000 troops from the Soviet armed forces, with 200,000 coming from the Far East. Bilateral discussions aimed at further cuts along the Sino-Soviet border are ongoing, and in April of 1990 the two governments pledged to reduce their troops "to a minimum corresponding to normal good neighborly relations."[26] Moscow and Beijing are now engaging in "military economy" talks which may result in new agreements for co-production of weapons and barter-based arms purchases by the PLA. The Soviet Union is interested in such cooperation not only for its political and economic benefits but also for what the USSR can learn about managing the transition from military to civilian production. About 80 percent of China's defense plants already turn out some consumer goods, and the 1991–95 PLA defense program calls for further civilianization of the defense sector.[27] Gorbachev has made it clear that he intends to move in the same direction.

China and the Soviet Union have also worked in parallel, and sometimes in tandem, since the mid-1980s to encourage North Korea to moderate its policies toward the South. Many Western analysts believe that Kim Il Sung was under strong and growing pressure during the 1980s to take precipitous action against the South Korean governments of Chun Doo Hwan (until 1987) and Roh Tae Woo (since 1987).[28] During this period the economic gap between North and South widened, and South Korea made a concerted effort to build up its armed forces to the point where it could safely assume that it could rebuff any attack from the North, even without the assistance of the United States. Seoul also hosted the 1988 Olympic games, which added insult to injury from the point of view of Pyongyang, since it highlighted the relative success of South Korea in establishing itself as an influential actor in world affairs. It is impossible to judge whether these circumstances were in fact driving Kim to take a dangerous gamble in the 1980s, but it would seem to be beyond doubt that China and the Soviet Union made clear to Pyongyang that they opposed any such action.[29]

It is also worth noting that China and Japan engaged in mutually supportive policies toward the Korean peninsula during the 1980s, with Beijing periodically serving as interlocutor between Tokyo and Pyongyang, while Japan performed the same service for China in dealings with South Korea. Finally, the United States helped to contain the level of tension on the peninsula by preserving its troop presence in the South while taking care not to exacerbate North Korean fears. Thus, for example, the annual Team Spirit exercises came to be carried out on an east-west rather than north-south axis.

These and other initiatives by the PRC during the 1980s are best understood as "informal" arms control (Gerald Segal's fortuitous term).[30] "Informal" does not mean "ineffective," of course. In fact, it can be argued that some of these policies (most notably the concerted efforts of China, the Soviet Union, Japan, and the United States on the Korean peninsula) have been more significant and useful than China's more "formal" arms control activities, such as its participation in UN disarmament fora and its membership in IAEA.

The limits of China's commitment to these more formal arms control activities have become apparent in recent years. China backed away from its commitment to participate in strategic arms reductions once it became clear that the two superpowers might actually fulfill China's precondition of a 50 percent reduction in their nuclear stockpiles through the START process. The revised Chinese formula requires much more than a 50 percent cut by the United States and the Soviet Union — according to one Chinese spokesmen, a 90 percent reduction of the American and Soviet stockpiles — before China will enter actively into the strategic arms reduction game.[31]

Beijing has also frustrated Washington by its policies relating to nuclear nonproliferation. The United States' decision to suspend nuclear assistance to the PRC (an estimated $50 million in export licenses) was influenced primarily by the Tiananmen crackdown. But congressional accusations that Beijing has circumvented aspects of ongoing Sino-American nonproliferation understandings also contributed to this decision.[32]

Congressional critics have taken special note of China's exports of ballistic missile technology to the Middle East. China's refusal to participate in the Missile Technology Control Regime (MTCR) has been described as "a major setback for the constraint of ballistic missile proliferation in the Third World."[33] During the nine-year-long Iran-Iraq war, Beijing is suspected of having sold Iran (directly or through third parties) Silkworm short-range missiles.[34] More recently, China has been accused of negotiating with Syria for the sale of its 600 kilometer-range M-9 missile and with Libya for the sale of both M-9 missiles and materials for the production of chemical weapons.[35] The issue of Chinese arms sales in the Middle East took on a new salience after the Iraqi invasion of Kuwait. At the time of the invasion China was the third-largest arms supplier to Baghdad (behind the Soviet Union and France).[36] Xiaochuan Zhang placed the issue of Chinese arms transfers in the broader context of changing Sino-American relations:

> On the one hand, Beijing sees that the bilateral relations are well grounded and able to stand occasional problems. . . . On the other hand, it seems evident that China does not have overexpectations concerning the further development of the bilateral relationship, particularly in strategic terms. . . . Had there not been the issue of arms sales, other issues, such as that of Tibet, would be noisier. Without the Tibet issue, the Taiwan issue still exists. The bottom line is that, given Chinese emphasis on an independent foreign policy, there is hardly any significant development of the bilateral relationship that either side could achieve at this point in time.[37]

The Future: Strategy and Arms Control in a Situation of Diversified Threat

The People's Republic of China had very little control over its geopolitical environment during the first three decades of its existence. It was either the victim or the beneficiary of events which were largely beyond its control. Consequently, its strategy was ad hoc, reactive, and defensive. By the mid-1980s, however, the opportunities afforded by the international system had come to outweigh the risks, and the PRC leadership was able for the first time in its history to experiment with an ambitious, positive foreign policy. Arms control was one element of this new foreign policy.

China's new-found optimism in the mid-1980s was partly attributable to its own efforts. By this time the PRC had developed a modest second-strike nuclear retaliatory capability against the principal superpower threat and was on its way to establishing a true *tous asimuts* minimum deterrence capability based upon ICBMs and IRBMs. But the most important factor determining China's security in the 1980s was still external, and still largely beyond China's influence. This was the situation of "late bipolarity," in which the two superpowers, while still overwhelmingly stronger than other actors in the international system, were becoming preoccupied with their own internal problems and were no longer actively expanding their spheres of influence. To the extent that the United States and the Soviet Union were still fundamentally at odds, China was able to manipulate their antagonism at relatively low risk. At the same time, residual bipolarity constrained the actions of other Asian states so that China could concentrate the bulk of its political and military attention on the superpowers.

Unfortunately for China, the situation did not last very long. By the start of the 1990s, late bipolarity was giving way to early multipolarity and presenting China with new strategic problems.[38] As the PRC leadership looks ahead, it must accord greater priority to those middle powers which can challenge it for the position of regional hegemon. Thus, India's diplomatic and military efforts to dominate the Indian Ocean region will have to be continually monitored for their implications for China. Likewise, Japan's ongoing program of defense modernization will be a continuing source of interest, if not insecurity, for the PRC. Chen Yun, chairman of the CCP Central Advisory Committee, put the matter this way: "No world war will break out fifteen years hence, but fifteen years hence Japan will come to acquire capability to wage war. China must complete preparations for war with Japan during the fifteen years left for China."[39]

This means that China's campaign to improve its ability to fight "local wars" with conventional and battlefield nuclear weapons will have to be accelerated. The PLA will have to downplay its training for "an early war, a major war, and a nuclear war," in order to "win a small war, and check a medium war."[40] At the same time, however, China will have to continue to develop its IRBM and MRBM capabilities so that these weapons can perform double duty as anti-Soviet deterrents and instruments for regional escalation control. These "actual and potential threats from some of the peripheral countries" were cited as the main justification for a proposed 250 percent increase in the PLA defense budget over the next decade in a recent article in the Chinese journal *Military Economic Research*.[41]

China will also have to take more seriously the possibility of Soviet-American condominium in the new situation of multipolarity. At the very least, Beijing's opportunities for manipulating the situation of superpower antagonism will be undermined by the politics of East-West reconciliation. The first signs of this are already surfacing in United States government statements and American media treatment of China. To the great consternation of PRC leaders, Washington has effectively demoted Beijing, at least rhetorically, since the Tiananmen crisis. China is no longer accorded pride of place in United States discussions about Asia's future, in large part because American policymakers no longer feel the need to assure themselves of China's strategic cooperation to balance Soviet power in the Far East. Ironically, some PRC representatives have sought to bolster China's importance in American strategic calculations by warning members of the American policy community that the United States will soon need the PRC to cope with a rising *Japanese* challenge in Asia.

Strategic demotion is only one aspect of the problem from Beijing's point of view. Chinese planners will also have to consider the more threatening scenario of Washington and Moscow's joining forces to impose their rule upon the rest of the international system. Under these circumstances, China's commitment to foreign policy independence, and its relatively exposed geostrategic position, would make it an ideal candidate for an object lesson to the rest of the international community. This assumes, of course, that the superpowers will continue to develop a condominium approach to world security in the wake of the ongoing Persian Gulf crisis. Chinese policymakers will also continue to be sensitive to signs of closer United States–Soviet cooperation in strategic arms talks, out of concern that the superpowers will try to press their new standards of strategic sufficiency on the nuclear middle powers.

Finally, China will have to cope with these new challenges to its security and its foreign policy independence while at the same time allocating a larger share of its assets and its attention to matters of internal security. The PRC leadership is presently engaged in a massive campaign of political indoctrination of both students and PLA cadres. With reference to the PLA, General Secretary Jiang Zemin recently spoke in terms that could have been torn from the pages of Mao's "little red book": "Only under the party's leadership can the army maintain its proletarian character, serve the people, and preserve a correct political orientation during the current complicated struggles."[42] This program of indoctrination will seriously degrade the professionalism and effectiveness of the PLA if it is permitted to remain in place for much longer.

China's "friends with (almost) everybody" foreign policy will also be harder to manage in a multipolar system. Having attained a position where it is finally able to engage in active diplomacy, China is not likely to turn inward in the 1980s. Indeed, the continuing commitment of the PRC leadership to economic modernization would not permit such a policy. But the PRC's demotion within the superpower triangle and the increased international reliance upon economic power to achieve national goals do not augur well for Beijing.[43] On the other hand, China is better equipped than many other states to play multipolar balance-of-power politics in one respect. Because the PRC is still an authoritarian regime, it will be comparatively easier for it to engage in secret diplomacy, make and break commitments, and change sides in accordance with the demands of multipolar balancing.

With reference to future Chinese arms control policies, the PRC's limited interest in strategic arms control is likely to decline even further as the international system moves toward multipolarity. But other forms of arms control can play an important part in China's new diplomacy. It is not inconceivable, for example, that China will conclude that it is in its interest to use confidence building measures to ameliorate some of the more threatening aspects of the new Asian system in order to enhance its own security. If so, four areas of opportunity seem open to Beijing.

First, China can continue to reduce tensions along its northern border. This is potentially the most useful area of Chinese arms control for the next few years, since it will permit the PRC to continue to acquire status by its direct negotiations with one of the two superpowers and may provide modest opportunities for manipulating the other. Moscow and Beijing will need to engage in a series of troop reduction talks in order to reach the established goal of "a minimum corresponding to normal good neighborly relations," and both sides will be able to extract some public relations benefits from these ongoing talks. Sino-Soviet relations can be further enhanced if a portion of the savings which China achieves from reductions in its border forces are applied to the purchase of Soviet military hardware such as the MiG-29.[44] An active arms trade with Moscow will be much cheaper than reliance upon Western sources, and the PRC can afford to make several such major purchases without confronting the problem of excessive dependency on Soviet goodwill. Furthermore, cross-border arms trade will inevitably serve to drive down the prices of Western competitors while making it easier for China to disdain those potential suppliers who seek to interject a human rights element into arms sales discussions.

Second, China can attempt to reduce the threat of war on its eastern flank. Because of the risk of spillover from a North-South Korean conflict, Chinese commentators view Korea as one of the "two hot spot areas in northeast and southeast Asia" (the second being Cambodia).[45] In light of the progress which has been made in North-South Korean relations over the past year, this situation may soon be conducive to a collaborative initiative by China, the United States, Japan, and the Soviet Union. An Asian "four plus two" forum might facilitate North-South reconciliation by providing a multilateral security guarantee for the peninsula and putting coordinated international pressure on both Pyongyang and Seoul. From the point of view of *realpolitik,* however, one might inquire whether it is really in China's interest to encourage North-South Korean union in an era of evolving multipolarity. Does China want to deal with a nation of 66 million people on its northeastern border which presently has more than a million and a half men under arms and would continue to have an impressive industrial base after unification?

The PRC leadership may also recognize a greater stake in controlling the pace and scope of Japanese militarization in the 1990s. But Beijing will discover that its influence over Tokyo is fairly limited. Japan's decisions about the nature and size of its armed forces will continue to be determined largely by internal Japanese developments and by the actions of the two superpowers. The PRC may be able to fuel Japanese militarization, or provide Tokyo with a pretext for such militarization, if it engages in actions at home and abroad which can be interpreted as threats by Japan. But Beijing can do little directly to encourage restraint and moderation in Japanese military programs.

China could also choose to reduce the dangers of war along its western border. Here, Beijing must weigh the risks of a nuclear and conventional arms race against the costs of contributing to an atmosphere of restraint. The PRC recognizes a stake in convincing India not to develop its armed forces in general and its nuclear ballistic missile delivery capability in particular. But the triangular nature of the regional balance means that Pakistan and China must jointly offer inducements to India if this trend is to be slowed or reversed. If, for example, the PRC wishes to see more progress toward a South Asian nuclear-free zone, it will not be sufficient for Beijing to press Islamabad to be more forthcoming in its offers to New Dehli. China itself will have to become directly engaged in the talks. And the PRC will have to offer India more than a commitment not to deploy its nuclear systems south or west of an agreed-upon line, in light of the fact that China is working to enhance the mobility of its shorter-range systems.[46] Under these circumstances, Beijing is likely to conclude that the costs of moving its South Asian neighbors toward arms restraint are simply too high.

China can also contribute to regional cooperation by working with the United Nations, the governments of ASEAN, and the United States to reach a peaceful solution to the Cambodian situation. Considerable progress has already been made in this regard, and it could not have been achieved without China's active cooperation. But the real test of China's goals in Southeast Asia will come as the date for a UN-administered election in Cambodia approaches. Will the PRC try to manipulate the situation in order to ensure the return of the Khmer Rouge as the dominant political force in Cambodia, thereby providing itself with a *point d' appui* for Chinese political influence in the region? Or will China, under pressure from other governments concerned about the future of Cambodia, distance itself from the Khmer Rouge and permit the process of national reconciliation to go forward? China's record to date would seem to favor the first option.[47]

Finally, China can make its greatest contribution to regional and global security by continuing to integrate itself into the international economic system and by accepting the inevitable linkage between economic liberalization and political reform. Until the PRC leadership resolves the contradictions inherent in this situation China's future cannot be predicted. And as Deng Xiaoping recently observed, China in chaos means instability for the whole world.[48]

Conclusion

The PRC has had to live with a relatively high degree of insecurity since its founding in 1949. During the first thirty-five years of its existence, preoccupation with security severely restricted the foreign policy and strategic options of the Chinese leadership. Under these circumstances, China's interest in arms control, broadly or narrowly defined, was almost non-existent. By the mid-1980s, however, the situation had begun to improve, and the PRC leadership began to feel that it could exercise some control over its external environment. Arms control proposals reflected this new sense of strategic confidence and served as one element of a new, ambitious, and proactive foreign policy. But China's new sense of security and control was based upon the following two somewhat contradictory contextual factors: (1) the relative decline of the superpowers vis-à-vis the international community in general and China in particular, and (2) the persistence of bipolarity in spite of the relative decline of the superpowers.

Since the end of the decade, however, the situation has been changing in ways which do not bode well for China. As the world moves from late bipolarity to early multipolarity, China's ability to manipulate superpower competition to its advantage will continue to decline. New challenges to China will arise, and PRC leaders will no longer enjoy the luxury of being able to concentrate most of their attention on the superpowers. Concurrently, China's leaders will have to allocate more of their time and energy to domestic political and economic problems arising out of a commitment to modernization which cannot be reversed. The situation may not be as immediately threatening as it was in the 1950s. But it is more complex than ever before, and by no means satisfying from the point of view of Beijing.

For the next few years, then, China's behavior in the field of arms control is likely to be more cautious and reactive. Even in those circumstances where the PRC recognizes that it has a stake in encouraging arms reductions, nonproliferation, or confidence building, it will be very reticent to take the necessary steps if they will constrain China's indigenous defense modernization program or further restrict its foreign policy options.

Under these circumstances, the one step forward which China took in the field of arms control in the mid-1980s is likely to be followed in the next few years by at least a half step back.

NOTES

1. See the discussion of these two types of arms control in Douglas T. Stuart, "The International Context of Asian Arms Control," in Gerald Segal, ed., *Arms Control in Asia* (New York: St. Martin's Press, 1987), pp. 161–75.
2. Quoted in *Communist China and Arms Control* (Stanford: Hoover Institution Press, 1966), p. 2.
3. See Thomas Schelling, "What Went Wrong with Arms Control?" *Foreign Affairs* 65, No. 1 (Winter 1985–86), pp. 219–33. It will be left to the next generation of experts to judge whether Mikhail Gorbachev's arms control policies have evolved in isolation from, or in conflict with, Soviet strategy.
4. This article uses the term "strategy" to refer to very general political-military precepts regarding the rationale for one's armed forces, circumstances under which these forces should be employed, and the nature of the threat. It is worth noting, however, that the Chinese tend to reserve the term "doctrine" for this highest level of military thought, and to use "strategy" to refer to operational and tactical issues. See Georges Tan Eng Bok, "Strategic Doctrine," in Gerald Segal and William Tow, eds., *Chinese Defense Policy* (London: Macmillan, 1984), pp. 8–9.
5. See, for example, Chong-pin Lin, *China's Nuclear Weapons Strategy* (Lexington, MA: Lexington Books, 1988), and Harlan Jencks, "PRC Nuclear and Space Programs," *SCPS Yearbook on PLA Affairs,* 1987 (Kaohsiung, Taiwan, R.O.C.: Sun Yat-sen Center for Policy Studies, 1988), pp. 105–23.
6. John Lewis and Xue Litai, *China Builds the Bomb* (Stanford: Stanford University Press, 1988), p. 190.
7. Ibid., pp. 225–26.
8. Sloan testimony before the Senate Foreign Relations Committee, published as *The Implications of U.S.-China Military Cooperation,* 97th Cong., 1st Sess., January 1982, p. 28.
9. See Roderick MacFarquhar, *The Origins of the Cultural Revolution,* Vol. 2, *The Great Leap Forward 1958–1960* (Oxford: Oxford University Press, 1983), p. 63.
10. Chong-pin Lin, *China's Nuclear Weapons Strategy,* p. 106.
11. See Richard Lowenthal, "The Degeneration of an Ideological Dispute," in Douglas T. Stuart and William T. Tow, eds., *China, the Soviet Union and the West: Strategic and Political Dimensions in the 1980s* (Boulder: Westview Press, 1982), pp. 65–68.
12. See the author's discussion of the theoretical underpinnings of

French strategic doctrine in "France," a chapter in Douglas T. Stuart, ed., *Politics and Security in the Southern Region of the Atlantic Alliance* (Baltimore: Johns Hopkins University Press, 1988), pp. 46–68.

13. Discussed in Stuart, "France," p. 57.
14. The implications of minimum deterrence for China's crisis behavior since 1949 are developed by the author in "Quest for Security," in Harish Kapur, ed., *The End of Isolation: China after Mao* (The Hague: Martinus Nijhoff, 1985), pp. 112–63. Also see William T. Tow, *Encountering the Dominant Player* (New York: Columbia University Press, 1991), pp. 216–18.
15. Allen Whiting, *The Chinese Calculus of Deterrence* (Ann Arbor: University of Michigan Press, 1975), pp. 233–43.
16. In recent years, France's pure deterrence posture has become more confused and more vulnerable to public criticism. Thus, for example, Paris's commitment to the development of an enhanced radiation weapon is hard to justify according to the logic of pure deterrence.
17. Barry Naughton, "The Third Front: Defense Industrialization in the Chinese Interior," *China Quarterly,* No. 115 (September 1988), p. 370.
18. Ibid.
19. *Communist China and Arms Control,* p. 3.
20. The significance of this statement is discussed by Paul Godwin, "China's Perceptions of NATO's Role in Beijing's Post-INF Security Environment," Unpublished paper in author's possession, International Studies Association, London, England, March 1989, pp. 5–7.
21. Some Chinese experts continue to differentiate between the superpowers, even though they perceive both as being less threatening to China than in the past. See the article by Pang Tongwen in the Chinese journal *Guoji Wenti Yanjiu* (International studies) No. 1 (13 January 1990), pp. 10–18; translated and reprinted as "Initial Analysis of the Beyond Containment Strategy," *Joint Publications Research Service, China 90-025* (hereafter cited as JPRS, CAR-), 30 March 1990, pp. 5–11.
22. *The Military Balance: 1984–1985* (London: The International Institute for Strategic Studies), pp. 91–92.
23. "Huang Hua Speaks at the UN Disarmament Session," a Xinhua dispatch reprinted in Foreign Broadcast Information Service, China (Daily Report) [hereafter cited as FBIS-CHI) 14 June 1982, pp. A1-A4.
24. For an incisive analysis of Chinese arms control policy during this period, see Alastair Johnston, "China Enters the Arms Control Arena," *Arms Control Today* 17, No. 6 (July/August 1987), pp. 11–17.

See also, John Prados, "China's 'New Thinking' on Nuclear Arms," *Bulletin of the Atomic Scientists* 45, No. 5 (June 1989), pp. 32–35.

25. For background on the Agreement of Nuclear Cooperation, see Qingshan Tan, "U.S.-China Nuclear Cooperation Agreement," *Asian Survey* 29, No. 9 (September 1989), pp. 870–82.
26. For background, see Gerald Segal, "Informal Arms Control: The Asian Road to Conventional Reductions," *Arms Control Today* 19, No. 4 (May 1989), pp. 16–20. Regarding the recent statement of intent, see "Chinese, Soviets Sign Troop Cutback Pact," *Washington Post,* 25 April 1990, p. 29.
27. James Tyson, "China and Soviet Union Improve Military Ties," *Christian Science Monitor,* 12 June 1990, p. 1.
28. See, for example, Edward Luttwak, "Korean Security: An Outsider's View," in Douglas T. Stuart, ed., *Security within the Pacific Rim* (London: Gower/The International Institute for Strategic Studies, 1987), pp. 97–106.
29. Sheldon Simon has speculated that increased Soviet arms transfers to Pyongyang in the mid-1980s may have been Moscow's payment for North Korean good behavior during the 1988 Olympics. See "Some PRC Perspectives on the Sino-Soviet Future: An Asian *Tour d'Horizon,*" Unpublished paper in author's hands, International Studies Association, London, England, March 1990, p. 17.
30. Segal, "Introduction," in Gerald Segal, ed., *Arms Control in Asia* (New York: St. Martin's Press, 1987), p. 16.
31. Statement by Pan Zhenguang, a senior military analyst, quoted by Arthur Ding, "PLA in the Year 2000: Nuclear Force and Space Program," *SCPS PLA Yearbook: 1988–89* (Kaohsiung, Taiwan, R.O.C.: Sun Yat-sen Center for Policy Studies, 1989), p. 128. Regarding nuclear proliferation, see statements by Hou Zhitong, PRC ambassador for disarmament affairs, *Xinhua* (in English) 21 June 1990; reprinted as "Diplomat on Nuclear Proliferation Responsibility," in FBIS-CHI, 25 June 1990, p. 2.
32. "One Crackdown Leads to Another," *Bulletin of the Atomic Scientists* 46, No. 1 (January/February 1990), p. 3.
33. Martin Navias, *Ballistic Missile Proliferation in the Third World,* Adelphi Papers No. 252 (London: The International Institute for Strategic Studies, Summer 1990), p. 56.
34. See Dennis Van Vranken Hickey, "New Directions in China's Arms Export Policy: An Analysis of China's Military Ties with Iran," *Asian Affairs* 17, No. 1 (Spring 1990), p. 19.
35. See *SIPRI Yearbook, 1990* (New York: Oxford University Press, 1990), pp. 48–49. The Stockholm International Peace Research Institute

contends that Syria turned to Beijing because the Soviet Union could no longer offer its SS-23 systems for sale after the INF Treaty was signed. Regarding China's assurances that it is not talking with Libya about chemical weapons and assertions that it has "consistently stood for a comprehensive and complete destruction of chemical weapons," see FBIS-CHI, 11 June 1990, p. 1.

36. "China Ranks Third in Arms Sales to Iraq," *Journal of Commerce,* 13 August 1990, p. 5.
37. Xiaochuan Zhang, "Chinese Nuclear Strategy," in Yufan Hao and Guocang Huan, eds., *The Chinese View of the World* (New York: Pantheon Books, 1989), p. 95.
38. For a representative Chinese assessment, see Wu Yikang, "The European Situation and the International Strategic Picture," *Guoji zhanwang* (World outlook) No. 2, 23 January 1990, pp. 3–5; as translated and reprinted in JPRS-CAR-90-025, 30 March 1990, pp.1–2.
39. See dispatch submitted by the correspondent Tamura from Beijing, "Japan and U.S. Are Hypothetical Enemies. . . ." *Asahi Shimbun,* 18 September 1990, p. 6; as translated and reprinted in *Daily Summary of Japanese Press,* 28 September 1990, p. 3.
40. Quoted and analyzed by Georges Tan Eng Bok, "How Does the PLA Cope with 'Regional Conflict' and 'Local War'?" Unpublished paper, Third Annual Workshop on PLA Affairs, Sun Yat-sen Center for Policy Studies, Taiwan, ROC, 14–16 April 1990, p. 23. In author's possession.
41. Article by Li Yuansheng in the May 1990 issue of *Military Economic Research,* as cited in "Chinese Army Urges Big Buildup," *Atlanta Journal and Constitution,* 13 December 1990, p. D-4.
42. Quoted by Robert Delfs, "Back to the Future," *Far Eastern Economic Review* 149, No. 34 (23 August 1990), p. 31.
43. For a Chinese assessment, see Sa Benwang, "The Sharpening Competition for Overall National Superiority among All Countries throughout the World" *Liaowang* (Outlook), No. 4, 22 January 1990, pp. 38–39; as translated and reprinted in JPRS-CAR-90-023, 29 March 1990, p. 1.
44. See Tai Ming Cheung, "Comrades in Arms," *Far Eastern Economic Review* 149, No. 29 (19 July 1990), p. 30.
45. See, for example, the editorial, "A New Balance in Asia-Pacific Region Is Brewing," *Hsin wan pao* (New talk), 11 June 1990, p. 1; translated and reprinted in FBIS-CHI, 11 June 1990, p. 1.
46. Joseph Yager offers an insightful analysis of the Chinese-Indian-Pakistani triangle, with a proposal for moving India and Pakistan toward a commitment to nonproliferation. See Center for National Security

Negotiations, "Nuclear Nonproliferation Strategy in Asia," CNSN Paper, Vol. 1, No. 3 (McLean, VA: Center for National Security Negotiations, July 1989).

47. For a critique of China's role in the development of the UN plan for Cambodia, see Michael Horowitz, "The 'China Hand' in the Cambodia Plan," *New York Times,* 12 September 1990, p. A-31.
48. Quoted in Delfs, "Back to the Future," p. 31.

Contributors

THOMAS P. BERNSTEIN is professor of political science, Columbia University.

JUNE TEUFEL DREYER is professor of politics, University of Miami.

HARVEY FELDMAN is a thirty-year veteran of service with the U.S. State Department and is currently an independent consultant.

JOHN FRANKENSTEIN is senior lecturer in the Department of Management Studies and the Hong Kong Business School, University of Hong Kong.

ROBERT ROSS is assistant professor of political science, Boston College.

STANLEY ROSEN is an associate professor of political science, University of Southern California.

GERALD SEGAL is a reader at Bristol University, research fellow at the Royal Institute for International Affairs (London), and editor of *The Pacific Review.*

DOROTHY J. SOLINGER is associate professor of political science, University of California, Irvine.

DOUGLAS T. STUART is associate professor of political science and director of international studies, Dickinson College.

ROBERT G. SUTTER is senior specialist in international politics, Congressional Research Service, Library of Congress.

RICHARD P. SUTTMEIER is professor of political science and director of the Center for Asian and Pacific Studies, University of Oregon.

WILLIAM T. TOW is senior lecturer of international relations,

Department of Government, University of Queensland, Brisbane, Australia.

DAVID ZWEIG is associate professor of international relations, Fletcher School of Law and Diplomacy, Tufts University.

Index

Index

Index

Index

Index

Index

Index

Index

Index